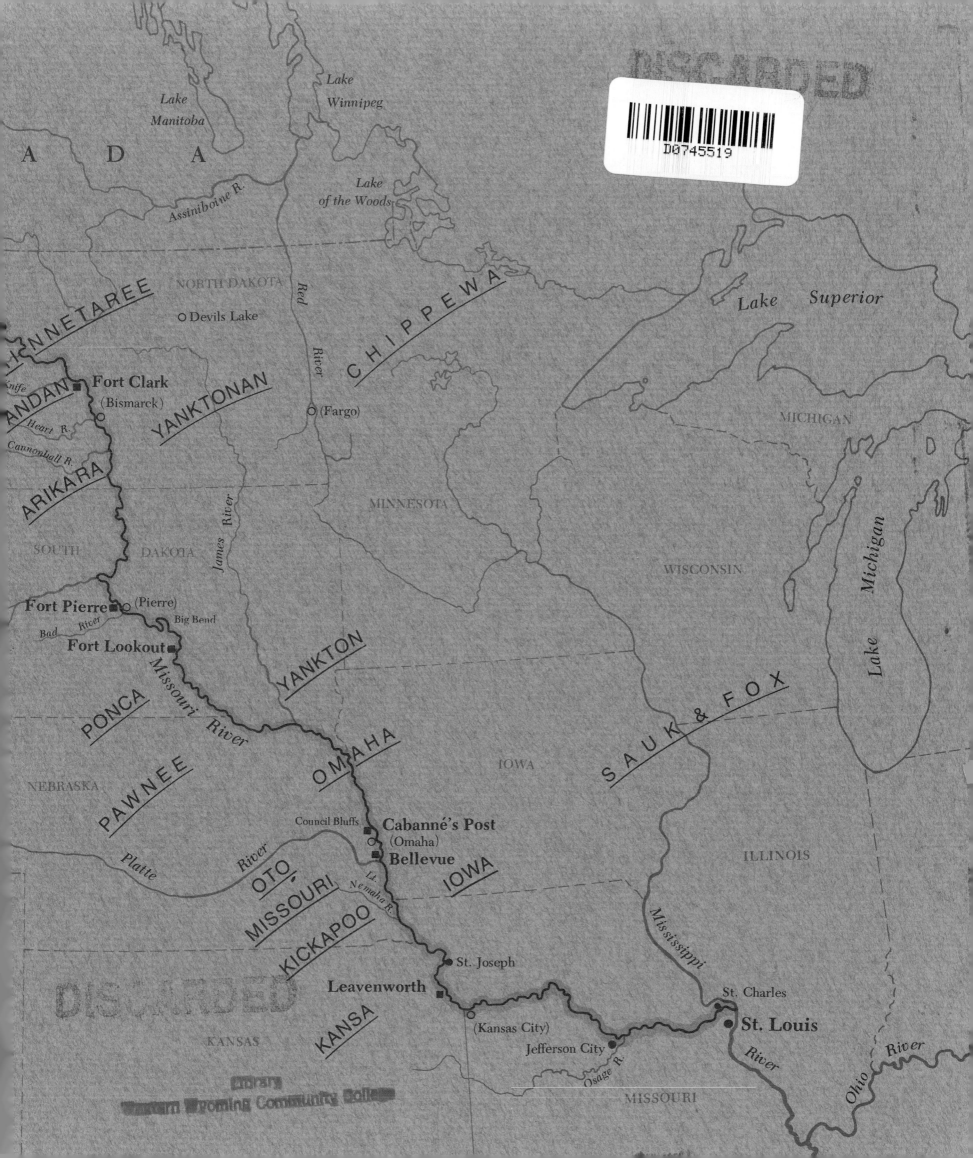

A   D   A

Lake
Manitoba

Lake
Winnipeg

Lake
of the Woods

Assiniboine R.

NORTH DAKOTA

O Devils Lake

Red

River

MINNETAREE

Knife

MANDAN   **Fort Clark**
(Bismarck)

Heart R.

Cannonball R.

YANKTONAN

O (Fargo)

CHIPPEWA

Lake   Superior

MICHIGAN

ARIKARA

James River

SOUTH   DAKOTA

MINNESOTA

WISCONSIN

Lake   Michigan

**Fort Pierre**   O (Pierre)

Bad   River   Big Bend

**Fort Lookout**

Missouri   River

PONCA

YANKTON

NEBRASKA

PAWNEE

OMAHA

SAUK & FOX

IOWA

ILLINOIS

Platte   River

Council Bluffs   **Cabanné's Post**
(Omaha)
**Bellevue**

OTO

MISSOURI

Lt.
Nemaha R.

IOWA

KICKAPOO

St. Joseph

**Leavenworth**

Mississippi

St. Charles

**St. Louis**

KANSA

KANSAS

(Kansas City)

Jefferson City

Osage R.

Ohio   River

River

MISSOURI

# People of the First Man

The First Man was once on the banks of the Missouri, when a dead buffalo cow, in the side of which the wolves had eaten a hole, floated down the stream. A woman was on the bank, who called to her daughter, "Make haste, pull off your clothes, and bring the cow on shore." The First Man heard this and brought the cow to the spot. The girl ate some of the flesh, which the First Man gave her, and became pregnant. She was ashamed and said to her mother, that "she could not tell how she came into this state, as she had had no intercourse with any man," and her mother was ashamed with her. The daughter was afterwards delivered of a son, who grew with extraordinary rapidity and soon became a robust young man. He was immediately the first chief of his people—a great leader among men. The new chief was of the nation of the Numangkake—the Mandans.

From the *Mandan Legend of Creation*
as transcribed by Prince Maximilian
Fort Clark, December, 1833

Deep in Indian territory, Maximilian is introduced to Minnetaree chiefs at Fort Clark. Bodmer is to his left, Dreidoppel behind.

2

# People of the First Man

## Life Among the Plains Indians in Their Final Days of Glory

THE FIRSTHAND ACCOUNT OF PRINCE MAXIMILIAN'S
EXPEDITION UP THE MISSOURI RIVER, 1833-34

## Watercolors by Karl Bodmer

EDITED AND DESIGNED BY DAVIS THOMAS AND KARIN RONNEFELDT

E. P. DUTTON & CO., INC. NEW YORK

Illustrations from the Maximilian-Bodmer Collection owned by and used with special permission of the Northern Natural Gas Company, Omaha, Nebraska.

Published, 1976, in the United States by E. P. Dutton & Co., Inc., New York, and simultaneously in Canada by Clarke, Irwin & Co., Ltd., Toronto and Vancouver.

Printed and bound by Dai Nippon Printing Co., Ltd., Tokyo, Japan.

Library of Congress Catalog Card Number: 76-16577
ISBN: 0-525-17732-9

# Contents

# Editors' Preface

The surpassing importance of Maximilian's published account of the year he spent among the Plains Indian tribes along the Missouri has long been acknowledged by scholars. Bodmer's handcolored aquatint engravings were hailed as masterpieces of ethnographic reporting from the moment of their first publication in 1839. Together, the text and engravings constitute an unmatched record of early trans-Mississippian exploration that is generally considered to be second in importance only to the journals of Lewis and Clark, written some twenty years earlier.

This present edition differs from Maximilian's original book in two major aspects. First, although we have edited Maximilian's lengthy and often repetitive text into a shorter version, we have also incorporated a considerable amount of previously unpublished material from the prince's longhand field journal. Second, Maximilian's text is here supplemented for the first time with Bodmer's original watercolors, rather than the aquatint engravings that accompanied the nineteenth-century editions. Of the seventy-six watercolors that are reproduced in color, fewer than half have been published before in any form (most generally in museum catalogues or specialized publications). The other paintings are published here for the first time. Of the seventy-five black and white illustrations included in the book, forty-eight are watercolors that have been converted to black and white half-tone plates, the remainder being either sketches or engravings. Almost all of these watercolors and sketches are previously unpublished. Thus, through the courtesy of the Northern Natural Gas Company, of Omaha, owners of both the field journal and the watercolors, we are able to combine a revised text of Maximilian's expedition with a comprehensive selection of Bodmer's best watercolors.

That these watercolors are not only far superior to the aquatints in ethnographic detail but far excel them as works of art can easily be seen through a comparison of any of the watercolors with the aquatints that comprise the frontispiece and the introductions to the six sections of the book. Although the aquatints, which were made in Paris under Bodmer's supervision, contribute drama and action, the watercolors exceed them in every other respect.

The editing of the narrative presented a number of problems: one of the principal ones being its extreme length. Maximilian's published text in the original German edition of his work runs to nearly 300,000 words. The English edition, which was published in 1843 with a translation by H. Evans Lloyd, is somewhat shorter due to the omission of scientific tables and Indian vocabularies. The prince's meticulously kept field journal, on which he based his published text, contains some 500,000 words of handwritten narrative, notes, and tables, and includes a number of pertinent observations that Maximilian omitted from his published text for reasons of taste or diplomacy. It is rife with descriptions of the alcohol trade and the sorry bacchanals it produced among the Indians. These and some unflattering observations of a few of the whites encountered during the trip went unpublished, doubtless out of deference to Maximilian's hosts, the American Fur Company. We have seen fit to include a number of these field journal entries, in the interest of producing a more comprehensive, if less tactful, narrative.

For the main body of our text, we have used the Lloyd translation. We gave serious consideration to making a modern English translation from the original German narrative, or even from the unpublished field journal. But in the end, it seemed best to use a translation made by a contemporary of Maximilian so that the style and flavor of his nineteenth-century text could be preserved. For the same reason we have retained the over-punctuated style, the Briticisms and the occasional archaic spellings. Finally, because of the heavy editing involved in bringing Maximilian's unwieldly text down to manageable size, we have put the narrative into journal form. This procedure not only obviated the excessive use of ellipses and editors' notes but, it is hoped, has made the narrative easier to follow. We have taken frequent recourse to the field journal in dating the entries. We found it necessary to take other liberties with Lloyd's translation, from time to time, most generally for purposes of clarity. We have also altered the spelling of proper names, including those of Indian tribes, to conform with modern usage.

In Maximilian's published narrative, covering the entire two years that he spent in America, approximately two-thirds of the text is devoted to his Missouri River expedition. Of these 190,000 words, we have excerpted somewhat less than half and have used introductions and bridges to summarize those portions of the text that we deemed expendable. Although we have been at pains to omit no significant event or incident of more than passing interest, the text in this book obviously cannot be used for purposes of serious scholarship. Specialists will want to work with the original editions or the 1906 reprint of the English text, published in volumes XXII through XXIV of Reuben Gold Thwaites' *Early American Travels*.

A number of persons have provided invaluable help and encouragement on this project. We would like to thank the officers of the Northern Natural Gas Company, of Omaha, for their generosity in granting us permission to publish the watercolors and other materials from the Maximilian-Bodmer Collection that constitute so major a portion of this book. In particular, we owe a great debt to Earle A. Clark, vice president of the company, for his unfailing encouragement and patience during what has proved to be a protracted gestation period. We want, also, to express our admiration for the dedicated labors of Dr. Emery C. Szmrecsanyi of Omaha, whose German transcript and English translation of Maximilian's voluminous, handwritten field journal proved indispensable to our editing of the text and the preparation of captions for the illustrations. The color and black and white photographs from which the plates were engraved were made specially for this volume and are the work of Geoffrey Clements of New York. Finally, we want to acknowledge the unflagging and extremely valuable assistance of Mildred Goosman, Curator of Western Collections at the Joslyn Art Museum. Her encyclopedic knowledge of the Maximilian expedition, so generously shared with us, has saved much time and effort. Not only did she cheerfully supervise the complete dismantling of an extensive and complicated museum exhibit so that the watercolors could be photographed, but she graciously consented to provide the Introduction for this book. For this she has our special gratitude.

Maximilian's interest in the various personalities he encountered during his thirteen months on the Missouri was largely restricted to leading men among the Indians. After all, his was a scientific expedition and the biographies of the white men in whose company he traveled were of secondary importance. Consequently, his references to many of the whites with whom he dealt are often so cursory as to be enigmatic. As an aid to readers unfamiliar with the literature of the fur trade, we think it useful to include a few words about the leading whites encountered in the narrative.

**General William Clark,** who with **Meriwether Lewis** led the great 1804–06 expedition from St. Louis to the Pacific and back, was the greatest name on the frontier in 1833. As Superintendent of Indian Affairs, his permission was required for anyone wishing to enter Indian country. He entertained Maximilian in St. Louis and advised him on his undertaking. **Pierre Chouteau, Jr.,** was the head of a leading St. Louis family and chief of the American Fur Company's Western Division. With **Bernard Pratte,** a St. Louis banker who also held an interest in the Company, he was to buy the Western Division in 1834, when John Jacob Astor, detecting a decline in the demand for beaver, sold out his controlling interest in the trust. **Kenneth McKenzie,** Scots-born like many of the fur traders, had joined the Company in 1827 when the trust bought out a rival firm. Although only thirty-two years of age when Maximilian met him, his forceful personality and ruthless methods had gained him the principal partnership in the Upper Missouri Outfit, the Company's most important subdivision. Because of his far-reaching power, McKenzie was known as "King of the Missouri." From his headquarters at Fort Union, deep in the interior, he held sway over a domain substantially larger than many European kingdoms of the day. Two other Scots, the terrible-tempered **William Laidlaw** (director of Fort Pierre during Maximilian's visit) and **Daniel Lamont,** were likewise partners in the Upper Missouri Outfit. Laidlaw was to succeed McKenzie as director at Fort Union. **David Mitchell,** director at Fort McKenzie in 1833, had a long and illustrious career in the West. He left the fur trade in the mid-1830s and was lured back only by the offer of a partnership in the Company. Later, he became an Indian agent and a celebrated cavalry officer in the Mexican War. He closed out his career by serving for more than ten years as Superintendent of Indian Affairs in St. Louis. **John P. Cabanné,** at whose post Maximilian witnessed his first Indian dances in early May, 1833, held a partnership in the Company. Although Maximilian doesn't say so, his replacement by **Joshua Pilcher** (which the prince mentions) was occasioned by an incident known as the Leclerc affair. The year before, Congress had prohibited the import of alcohol into Indian country and a Company shipment of 1,400 gallons had been confiscated. An Opposition trader named Leclerc, however, somehow succeeded in smuggling 250 gallons of alcohol past the army at Leavenworth. To blunt this dangerous competition, Cabanné had taken it upon himself to arrest Leclerc and expropriate his whiskey. Leclerc complained to the authorities in St. Louis and sued the Company. In the uproar that followed, a settlement was made that cost the Astor interests nearly $10,000, and Cabanné was recalled. **Francis A. Chardon,** who took Maximilian buffalo hunting at Fort Union in the fall of 1833, had become director at Fort Clark by 1837 when the smallpox epidemic wiped out the Mandans. He subsequently took command at Fort McKenzie, replacing **Alexander Culbertson** (who had succeeded David Mitchell at that post and then moved on to take command at Fort Union). At Fort McKenzie, Chardon and **Alexander Harvey,** a Company desperado whom Maximilian encountered on the upriver voyage of the *Assiniboin,* massacred a number of Blackfeet from ambush, in retaliation for the murder of Chardon's Negro slave. This act aroused such hostility among the Blackfeet that the fort was abandoned and subsequently burned to the ground by the Indians. **James Archdale Hamilton,** McKenzie's second in command at **Fort** Union, was a cultivated English gentleman who had changed his name and come to the West apparently because of difficulties of some sort in England. An extremely capable man, he was fastidious in his dress, wearing the latest in European fashions. He astonished the rough *engagés* with his regimen of daily baths and change of linen. Hamilton ended his career with the Company as cashier in St. Louis. **Honoré Picotte,** who as the Company agent among the Yanktonan Sioux during the severe winter of 1833–34 kept Fort Clark alive with occasional shipments of buffalo meat, had a long career with the Company, ending at Fort Pierre. **William Sublette** and **Robert Campbell** were old hands in the fur trade. Their partnership served as bankers and carriers for the Rocky Mountain Fur Company, the chief Opposition outfit. **William Drummond Stewart,** the Scots aristocrat whom Maximilian met in St. Louis, accompanied Campbell, who led the annual supply caravan to the mountain fur rendezvous held on the Green River that year. In 1833 Sublette and Campbell were establishing trading posts along the Missouri in opposition to the Company, as retaliation for the trust's

invasion of the Rockies via Fort McKenzie. When Maximilian broke his downstream journey at Fort Union in October, he paid a number of visits to Campbell, who had come down the Missouri from the rendezvous to direct the completion of the partners' new post on the Missouri several miles below Fort Union. McKenzie's tactics of buying pelts at any cost from the Indians forced Sublette and Campbell to sell out in 1834. **John F. A. Sanford, John Dougherty,** and **Jonathan L. Bean** were all government agents to various Indian tribes on the Missouri entrusted with attending to the welfare of their charges and delivering the annual government subsidy. The Opposition had tried for years to force the removal of Sanford, who was married to a daughter of Pierre Chouteau and was accused of favoring the interests of the Company. This pressure finally succeeded in 1834 and Sanford was officially transferred to the Company payroll, eventually moving to New York as its representative. There, he gained himself a footnote in history by becoming the technical owner of Dred Scott when that slave's landmark case was appealed to the U.S. Supreme Court. Of a remarkable group of hardy men, perhaps the hardiest was wily old **Toussaint Charbonneau,** who was well into his seventies when Maximilian encountered him at Fort Clark. Charbonneau had been working as guide, interpreter, and trader along the Missouri for anyone who would hire him since the 1790s. He had served as interpreter on the Lewis and Clark expedition. Sacajawea, the Shoshone Indian woman who played a crucial role in the success of that expedition, was one of his many wives. As Maximilian sourly noted, he was forever chasing after women, and five years after the prince's visit he was still at it. Francis Chardon, then in command at Fort Clark, reported in his journal that, having bought a fourteen-year-old Assiniboin girl who had been captured by the Arikaras, he sold her to Charbonneau, whose "marriage" was solemnized thusly:

> . . . the young Men of the Fort and two *rees* [*Arikaras*] gave to the Old Man a splendid Chàrivèree, the Drums, pans, Kittles &c Beating; guns fireing &c. The old gentleman gave a feast to the Men, and a glass of grog—and went to bed with his young wife with the intention of doing his best.

The spelling and usage of Indian names have been a special problem. We have altered Maximilian's spelling of Indian tribal names to conform with modern spellings. But we have *not* modernized his tribal designations (*e.g.* by substituting Hidatsa for Minnetaree, Atsina for Gros Ventres des Prairies) since these classifications were unknown to him at the time. In the matter of individual Indian names, we have done the best we could. We have attempted to arrive at a "consensus" spelling based on a comparison of Maximilian's published work and his original field journal. Spellings from these and other sources vary wildly. Since these proper names were transliterated by the prince from oral interviews, there can be no definitive source, but we have tried to be consistent. Maximilian uses the designations Sioux and Dakota interchangeably. Of the modern classification listing seven Sioux councils, Maximilian encountered three: the Tetons, Yanktons, and Yanktonans. (For complicated reasons, we retain Maximilian's spelling of Yanktonan, in preference to the modern Yanktonai.) His classification of the three branches of the Blackfeet—Piegan, Blood, and Siksika—conforms to modern usage. There has always been some confusion about Bodmer's Christian name. He became a French citizen in later life and thereafter generally used "Charles." Bodmer spoke both French and German and even on the Missouri he sometimes signed his paintings "C. Bodmer" rather than "K. Bodmer." But as he was born into a German-speaking Swiss family, we have decided to follow the school of thought that holds to "Karl" in preference to "Charles."

The map that forms the end papers was drawn specially for this volume. It is based on the facsimile map of the Lewis and Clark expedition that was given to Maximilian by General Clark in St. Louis, as annotated by Maximilian. The approximate territorial ranges of the various tribes encountered by the adventurers are shown, as of 1833. In addition to landmarks existing at the time, half a dozen modern cities are spotted on the map (with names enclosed in parentheses), as an aid to orientation. The borders of present-day states are also shown for the same reason, although at the time of Maximilian's journey only Missouri and Illinois of the states shown had been admitted to the Union and, with the exception of Michigan, none of the others had even been organized as territories.

The typography of the book is as straightforward as we could make it. Our editorial introductions and bridges are set in large type, Maximilian's narrative in somewhat smaller type. Bracketed and italicized entries are editors' inserts. Entries headed with the bracketed slug, [FIELD JOURNAL], contain previously unpublished text from Maximilian's field journal. As explained above, the spellings, punctuation, and usage of the original nineteenth-century translation by H. Evans Lloyd have been retained with minor modifications. When a specific date is used in the picture captions, this is meant to indicate that text material supplementing the caption is to be found in Maximilian's entry for that date.

Bodmer's watercolors were executed on heavy sketching paper. Most of them range in size between roughly 9″ by 11″ and 12″ by 18″, although a few are smaller. As we took special pains to select a page size that would accommodate double-page reproduction of landscapes with an absolute minimum of cropping, all of the watercolors are presented essentially uncropped, with two major exceptions. These are the paintings of the steamboat *Yellowstone* on pages 42–43 and the view of the Bear Paw Mountains on pages 142–143. As for the black and white illustrations, the great majority are watercolors that have been converted to black and white half-tone plates. All of the Indian portraits fall into this category. The remaining black and white illustrations are either woodcuts, engravings or pencil sketches. In some cases we have specified the type of technique employed in the caption. In others, the technique is self-evident. Seven of the color illustrations—the frontispiece and the action scenes that introduce the six sections of the book—are handcolored, copper plate engravings reproduced from Maximilian's personal copy of the German edition of his work. Several of these have been slightly cropped in order to fit the design of the pages.

Because of the great number of easily available works—both popular and scholarly—on this period of western history, we have decided to dispense with a bibliography. There are scores of good ones. Anyone interested in further reading in the period could not do better than to begin with Bernard DeVoto's classic, *Across the Wide Missouri,* which deals with the same period, but on a larger scale. This book contains a comprehensive and discriminating bibliography upon which we could hardly hope to improve.

Davis Thomas, Karin Ronnefeldt
New York City  July, 1976

# Introduction

Maximilian and Bodmer were privileged to see the West in all its pristine glory, before the successive waves of settlers irrevocably altered the face of the land and, sadly, the way of life of its original inhabitants forever. At the time of Maximilian's expedition, the vast herds of buffalo and other game still roamed the prairies, great flocks of fowl filled the skies during migratory seasons, and the Missouri itself flowed wild and unchecked by dams from the Rockies to the Mississippi. Although by the 1830s the Indians on the Upper Missouri had already been in contact with fur trappers and traders since Lewis and Clark first opened the country to the white man in the first decade of the century, the intrusion of European culture had not yet effected dramatic changes in the social customs or religious beliefs of the Plains Indians. Dependence on trade goods had only just begun to modify their traditional creativity and craftsmanship. Thus, the report compiled by Maximilian and Bodmer is invaluable, not only to ethnologists and historians, but to anyone interested in the history of the American West.

The narrative and pictorial material that forms the content of this book are drawn from a unique record of early Western exploration, the Maximilian-Bodmer Collection, which has been in the custody of the Joslyn Art Museum since 1962. The word "unique" has at least two applications to this splendid collection. Maximilian's text and Bodmer's paintings are incontestably unique in terms of their level of excellence. Maximilian was a highly educated man for his time, indeed for any time, and he was by far the best trained scientific observer to explore the West in the early period. Bodmer was easily the most accomplished artist to paint the Plains tribes. To praise his superb draftsmanship and meticulous ethnographic detail is not to belittle the work of other early painters such as Alfred Jacob Miller and George Catlin. Catlin's accomplishments, in particular, were extraordinary. During six summers, from 1830 through 1836, he ranged the West

from the headwaters of the Mississippi and the Upper Missouri south to Texas and the Southwest. He painted portraits, landscapes, and Indian activities at a furious pace and before he was through he had chronicled nearly fifty tribes. Catlin had not had the advantage of Bodmer's European art training and his work was uneven. Bodmer often spent two or three days on a single watercolor, whereas Catlin often painted half a dozen oils in a single day.

The Maximilian-Bodmer Collection is unique not only in terms of its quality, but also because all of its documentation—the paintings, journals, reference works, correspondence, account books, and maps—have remained intact as a single body rather than being dispersed among a number of museums and libraries, as is the case with documents from most nineteenth-century Western expeditions. This fact is due to a series of fortunate circumstances.

When Maximilian and Bodmer returned to Europe in August, 1834, they separated. Maximilian went back to Neuwied to edit his field journals into a coherent narrative for his book. Bodmer took up residence in Paris where he was to spend a good part of the next four years supervising the execution of the aquatint copper plate engravings that were to accompany the German, French, and English editions of the book. After publication of the book and its accompanying atlas of prints, all of Bodmer's watercolors and pencil sketches, along with the copper plates themselves, found their way to the Wied estate on the Rhine. Maximilian died in 1867, rich with honors. After his death, little attention was paid to his library and the collection of material that underlay his book, although the book itself became a collector's item and a standard reference for scholars. The fact that there might be surviving field notes and original watercolors of even greater beauty and ethnological interest than Bodmer's published aquatints was either discounted or ignored.

It was not until after World War II, in the early 1950s, that serious inquiries uncovered the existence of the watercolors, field journals, and other items. Dr. Stanley Pargellis of the Newberry Library in Chicago and a German scholar, Dr. Joseph Roeder, in cooperation with Prince Karl Viktor, Maximilian's great, great grandnephew, played major roles in the rediscovery of the collection. In 1953 a group of 118 Bodmer watercolors was brought to the United States for a traveling exhibition, under the auspices of the Smithsonian Institution. The exhibit opened at the Newberry Library in November,

1953, and traveled across the country on a constantly expanding exhibition schedule, finally concluding in 1959 at Cody, Wyoming.

Meanwhile, as the late William F. Davidson of the New York art firm of M. Knoedler & Co., Inc., was making arrangements to sell the entire Maximilian-Bodmer Collection, archivists assiduously searched for additional material in the Wied family library, archives, and even the small estate house where Prince Maximilian spent his last years. Because of the significance of the material to the Missouri Valley region, interest in acquisition of the Collection ran high in Omaha. In 1962 the Northern Natural Gas Company, of Omaha, under the leadership of John F. Merriam, chairman of the board (now retired), and W. A. Strauss, president (and now chairman as well), purchased the Collection as a public service. The company then assigned the Collection to the Joslyn Art Museum for study and display. In addition to a major permanent display of Bodmer watercolors designed by the late Eugene Kingman, then the museum's director, the company has underwritten a program of traveling exhibits to bring Bodmer's work to schools, museums, and other institutions throughout the Plains area.

For a number of years it was hoped that it would be possible to publish a definitive scholarly work incorporating all the significant elements of the Collection, or at least those pertaining to the Missouri River expedition. Because of the enormity of the task and the mounting expense of color reproduction, this project has been shelved. The decision of the owners to permit publication of this volume is therefore to be welcomed as a means of bringing the work of Maximilian and Bodmer to a much wider audience than has heretofore been possible. It should serve to whet the appetites of scholars as well.

One of the most remarkable aspects of this remarkable expedition was the personality of the man who led it. Alexander Philipp Maximilian of the Prussian principality of Wied, located at Neuwied just below Coblenz on the east bank of the Rhine, was born in 1782. As the eighth child in a large family, it was not anticipated that he would be called upon to assume leadership of the house. He was encouraged, therefore, to pursue a career in the natural sciences for which he had shown an early aptitude. He studied with private tutors and at leading German universities. The eminent naturalist Alexander von Humboldt became a friend and advisor.

During the Napoleonic Wars, he served as an officer in the Prussian army, participating in the Battle of Jena. Soon after that disaster, he was captured and eventually exchanged. When the tide finally turned against Napoleon, Maximilian returned to the field, was decorated with the Iron Cross, and entered Paris with the victorious coalition armies in 1814. Released from military service, he hastened to embark on a long-planned journey to South America. He joined two other German scientists and together they spent two years exploring the coastal forests of Brazil. Maximilian made detailed notes and sketches on the aborigines and their customs. Returning home, he published his *Reise nach Brasilien in den Jahren 1815 bis 1817*. This book was translated into Dutch, Spanish, French, and English and established Maximilian's reputation as an explorer, naturalist, and ethnologist.

Following publication of his account of the Brazilian expedition in 1820–21, Maximilian traveled extensively in Europe and continued his studies and correspondence. This led, by 1831, to intensive planning for his second great expedition, the trip to North America. The illustrations for the Brazilian book were prepared from the prince's own field sketches, with the assistance of a sister and a brother. They encouraged him to engage a professional artist for his new expedition and Maximilian finally found a thoroughly schooled young Swiss who seemed to suit his purposes perfectly.

Karl Bodmer was born near Zurich in 1809. He and his older brother Rudolf studied with their maternal uncle, Johann Jakob Meyer, a competent artist who trained the young men in drawing, painting, and engraving. After further studies in Paris, Karl joined his brother for a sketching trip through Germany in 1832. While at Coblenz, arrangements were made for Karl to accompany Maximilian on the North American expedition. A contract was signed providing that all drawings and watercolors would be the property of Maximilian except for scenes executed at Bodmer's leisure—aboard ship, for example. The prince was to furnish round-trip passage money and cover travel expenses in America. It was specified that no food supplies would be taken, making it necessary for the travelers to accommodate themselves to local American culinary tastes as they moved. Bodmer would be expected to assist in collecting natural history specimens and to share in the hunt. He would receive a cash stipend for each month of the trip, but would have to supply his own art materials, excluding paper, and furnish his own clothing and personal necessities. Accompanied by David Dreidoppel, the retainer who had participated in the Brazilian expedition, Maximilian and Bodmer took ship down the Rhine and on May 17, 1832, set sail for the New World from Rotterdam. Thus, Bodmer's future career was launched. The next ten years were dedicated to the North American adventure and the subsequent preparation of illustrations for Maximilian's book.

Stimulated by the responsibility of depicting a strange new environment and guided by the erudition and enthusiasm of a highly perfectionist employer, Bodmer completed what we now can assess as the most significant body of his life's work. As we view this rich collection of landscapes, portraits, and scenes of Indian life, we risk today the charge of ingratitude in wishing that the artist's patron had set a less exacting schedule of required subjects and that Bodmer had devoted more time to picturing the everyday life of the expedition. What did the visitors' quarters look like at the fur posts or on the river steamers and keelboats? We have Maximilian's description of the party's visit at Cabanné's post just north of the present site of Omaha. If only Bodmer had sketched that establishment as he did Major Dougherty's agency. How useful it would be to have likenesses of McKenzie, Hamilton, Mitchell, and other principal men of the fur companies. Alas, these subjects held little pictorial interest for Maximilian. He was interested only in Indian ethnology, and we should be grateful enough for that.

After completing his work on the plates for the book, Bodmer stayed on in Paris, marrying and becoming a French citizen. In 1849 he moved his family to Barbizon in the forest of Fontainebleau where other artists of the plein-air school had settled. His paintings were accepted regularly by the French Salon exhibits and received medals of honor. His later years were devoted chiefly to magazine and book illustration. Blindness marred his final years. He died October 30, 1893, and was buried at the village of Barbizon. His studio home there is now an inn.

Because there was no means of reproducing colored paintings on a printing press in the 1830s, a number of Bodmer's Indian portraits are unfinished. Colored illustrations for book publication were made by printing black and white engravings that were then individually colored by hand. Thus, Bodmer's watercolors were intended primarily as "notes" for the eventual process of engraving the copper plates that were used to make aquatint prints, a number of which were then handcolored for the most expensive of the various editions. Many of the Indians shown in the unfinished watercolors turn up time and again in the aquatint action scenes. Others were worked up into completed portraits for the engravings.

The trials and tribulations involved in publication of the book are a story in themselves—a case history of delay and frustration. The number of aquatints was finally reduced to eighty-one, thirty-three of which were small "vignettes" that were designed to be bound into the book. The remaining forty-eight were of much larger size and were intended to be bound together into a separate atlas volume. The German and French editions were sold by subscription. Text chapters and aquatints were delivered as they came off the presses, twenty shipments in all. Subscribers had to make their own arrangements for binding. The English edition was delivered in a single volume. The German edition, entitled *Reise in das Innere Nord-America in den Jahren 1832 bis 1834*, gives a publication date of 1839–41; the final delivery, however, was not made until 1843. Delays in delivery obviously hampered sales and the project was not a financial success. The total number of sets published in all editions has not been determined but undoubtedly the number is well under one thousand.

Financial success or not, the book stands as the crowning achievement of Maximilian's career. The North American adventure was his last expedition. A lifelong bachelor, he shared a small stone house with his brother Charles on the family estate. He busied himself with his collections and correspondence until death removed him in his eighty-fifth year.

Maximilian was typical of the early nineteenth-century European man of science. He was abreast of contemporary knowledge in geology, zoology, and botany; he was also what we today would call an ethnologist. He observed and recorded all aspects of natural phenomena. His book supplied reliable information on what was to most of the world an unknown territory. He refuted the misconception that the interior of North America was a desert wasteland and concluded correctly that only rich soil could create the grasslands that supported such vast herds of bison and antelope. His prediction that farms and towns would soon appear across the prairies proved true. Only twenty years after his visit, in 1854, Nebraska Territory was opened for settlement. Within ten years, a transcontinental railroad was being surveyed.

Maximilian lived during a decisive period in history, at the beginning of the industrial revolution and the rise of republicanism. His voyage to the United States was made by sailing vessel, yet steam-powered ships were in service on inland waterways. Six years later, a full steamship crossed the Atlantic. In 1832, in New Jersey, he saw a railroad being built, and two years later rode on it. He required an artist-illustrator to make visual records of his expedition, yet within three years of his return to Europe, Daguerre perfected a process that opened the door to photography. He was born before the Constitution of the United States was ratified, and he lived to see the conclusion of the War between the States. He traveled in the interior of the North American continent when it was still a wilderness, but in the year he died, Omaha was a flourishing young city and Nebraska had become a state. Only thirty-four years earlier, he had spent the evening at Cabanné's trading post on the frontier of civilization, entertained by Indian dancers in a clearing of the primeval forest. The timing of his trip was fortunate in the extreme. Three years after he returned to Europe, a smallpox epidemic did its deadly work along the Missouri. The relentless tide of emigration did the rest and only the work of Maximilian and Bodmer and others like them remains to remind us of the pristine grandeur of our continent and the Indians who were its first inhabitants.

Mildred Goosman, Curator of Western Collections
Joslyn Art Museum, Omaha, Nebraska

Aground on a sandbar, the *Yellowstone* is offloaded by crew members during an early stage of the upstream voyage.

# PART I

# St. Louis to Fort Union

April 10-June 24, 1833

The tenth of April, 1833, was an important day in the social and commercial life of St. Louis, then—as now —gateway to the Far West and the chief port on the Mississippi above New Orleans. The considerable prosperity of many of the town's 7,000 inhabitants depended upon the operations of the American Fur Company, the powerful trust put together by John Jacob Astor to monopolize the rich traffic in beaver pelts from the western rivers. On this mild spring morning, the Company's steamboat *Yellowstone* was due to depart for the fur company's posts along the Missouri River, carrying provisions and the year's supply of trade goods for barter with the Indians. Alerted by the firing of cannon salutes, many hundreds of the local citizenry trooped down the dusty streets to the riverbank to give the little steamer a hearty send-off. This was to be the *Yellowstone*'s third annual trip on the Missouri. Built specially for Missouri River navigation, she had proved so successful in transporting trade goods upstream and beaver pelts and buffalo hides downstream that a somewhat larger sister ship, the *Assiniboin*, had been added to the Company's fleet this spring and had already departed for the interior.

On board the *Yellowstone* as she prepared to depart was a mixed company numbering about a hundred in all. In addition to a motley array of free trappers, deckhands, and Company employees known as *engagés* (rough, illiterate men, mostly French-Canadians and half-breeds, who had signed up to work for the Company on terms that amounted to indenture), there were a few personages of higher rank. Pierre Chouteau, Jr., managing partner of the Astor trust in St. Louis, had brought his daughters and several of their friends along for a taste of river travel. An experienced Company brigade leader, Joshua Pilcher, was bound upstream, as were John F. A. Sanford and Jonathan L. Bean, government Indian agents. But the most remarked-upon members of the party were three Europeans who were setting out on a year-long adventure of exploration among the Plains Indians of the Upper Missouri. The leader of the trio was a squat, splenetic German aristocrat with the resounding name of Alexander Philipp Maximilian, Prince of Wied-Neuwied. His companions were a strapping twenty-four-year-old Swiss artist named Karl Bodmer, who was later to win fame as a landscapist of the Barbizon school, and a family retainer with the improbable name of David Dreidoppel, who served as general factotum and specimen hunter to the prince. A contemporary account by Alexander Culbertson, a young Company clerk whom the travelers encountered farther upstream, gives an indication of the impression that they made:

> In this year an interesting character in the person of Prince Maximilian from Coblenz on the Rhine made his first appearance on the upper Missouri. The prince was at that time nearly seventy years of age [*actually, he was fifty*], but well-preserved, and able to endure considerable fatigue. He was a man of medium-height, rather slender, sans teeth, passionately fond of his pipe, unostentatious, and speaking very broken English. His favorite dress was a white slouch hat, a black velvet coat, rather rusty from long service, and probably the greasiest pair of trousers that ever encased princely legs. The Prince was a bachelor and a man of science, and it was in this latter capacity that he had roamed so far from his ancestral home on the Rhine. He was accompanied by an artist named Boadman [*Bodmer*] and a servant whose name was, as near as the author has been able to ascertain its spelling, Tritripel [*Dreidoppel*]. . . .

Ever since establishing his reputation as a naturalist and ethnologist with the publication of a book describing his Brazilian explorations in 1815–17, Maximilian had been planning an expedition into the Far West of North America to study the Plains Indian tribes. After years of correspondence and study, he had landed in Boston on July 4, 1832. Proceeding methodically westward, he wintered at New Harmony, Indiana, Robert Owen's failed commune on the Wabash, where he availed himself of the library

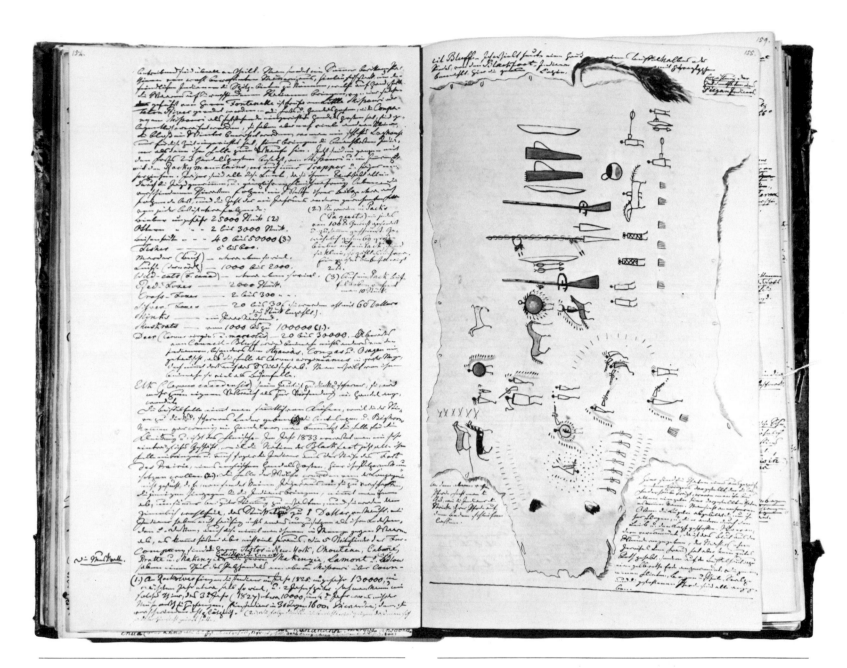

During the thirteen months of his 5,000-mile Missouri River expedition from St. Louis to the Rockies and back, Prince Maximilian meticulously set down his experiences and observations in a series of field journals. He not only described the day-to-day happenings of the trip, but filled page after page with botanical, zoological, and geological observations. He recorded tribal histories, religious beliefs, and social customs. He compiled twenty-three linguistic vocabularies, wrote a dissertation on sign language, noted daily temperature readings, and even kept a bird calendar. In all, his journals covering the two years spent in America ran to more than 500,000 words. Occasionally Maximilian made drawings to supplement his text, as in the entry for June 30, 1833 (*above*). While waiting at Fort Union for the keelboat that was to take him on the last leg of his upstream journey, the prince purchased a painted Blackfoot buffalo hide, which he copied into his journal and described in the margins: "Illustrated here are the deeds of an outstanding warrior whom we may recognize in each exploit by his long feather cap. In several places we may discern bullets flying around him. . . . Captured rifles, bows and arrows, scalps taken, and stolen horses are all represented."

and counsel of Thomas Say and Charles Lesueur, two eminent naturalists. By late March, Maximilian and his companions had descended the Ohio by steamboat and, arriving at St. Louis, spent two weeks making final arrangements for their expedition.

On the advice of General William Clark, Superintendent of Indian Affairs and the partner of Meriwether Lewis on the epic 1804–06 expedition, Maximilian had decided to accept the offer of Pierre Chouteau and Kenneth McKenzie of the American Fur Company to convey him and his party into the interior on their steamers and keelboats. While buying tomahawks, beads, and other trade goods and provisions for his journey, the prince had struck up an acquaintance with another European aristocrat who was bound for adventure in the Far West. Captain William Drummond Stewart, next in succession to the Scottish barony of Murthly and Grandtully, was like Maximilian a veteran of the Napoleonic wars. He was preparing for the first of his half-dozen annual journeys to the Rockies, and, for a time, there was talk of the two joining forces, but the plan was abandoned since their objectives differed so widely. Maximilian was mounting a scientific expedition. River travel and the Company's system of established posts promised certain contact with large numbers of Indians, plus a relatively easy means of transporting the extensive collections that the prince hoped to amass. The thirty-seven-year-old Stewart, a restless adventurer and sportsman, was primarily interested in hunting and the romance of life in the wild. He would travel overland along what was to become the Oregon Trail, accompanying the supply caravan for the annual fur rendezvous held by the mountain men in the heart of the Rockies.

In 1833 the three-cornered battle between the American Fur Company (the Company), the Opposition (the Rocky Mountain Fur Company and a number of smaller outfits), and the Hudson's Bay Company had reached its zenith. The Astor interests were invading the mountains, the traditional battleground of the RMF Company and the Canadian-based Hudson's Bay Company, by way of the Missouri, using steamboats and swarms of *engagés*. The Opposition outfits continued to transport their goods and furs by horse and mule train. The Astor trust was soon to win out, and Maximilian was to witness the tactics it employed to do so. But the deadly rivalries of the fur trade were undoubtedly far from the minds of him and his companions on this spring morning. They had behind them months of travel and preparation. Ahead stretched a vast wilderness brimming with Indians and a wealth of uncatalogued phenomena— animal, vegetable, and mineral—calculated to excite Maximilian's scientific curiosity and to offer employment for Bodmer the artist and Dreidoppel the specimen hunter.

Cannons boomed as the *Yellowstone*, flags flying, backed from her slip into the Mississippi current. The salutes from shore were answered from the foredeck by the muskets of the *engagés* (most of them the worse for drink, according to Maximilian). The side-wheeler turned her bows upstream and ran swiftly along the levee accompanied by the cheers of the assembled populace and several bands of Indians dressed in their finest attire. Pushing against the current, the *Yellowstone* ran along under limestone bluffs. Maximilian began to make notes on the burgeoning countryside: extensive stands of timber in early leaf and everywhere the crimson of blossoming redbud. Soon the proximity of the Missouri could be detected in the widening stream of muddy water flowing along the western bank of the Mississippi. By the time the *Yellowstone* turned into the broad mouth of the Missouri itself, to the accompaniment of another round of musket fire from the *engagés*, a high wind had sprung up and the muddy ribbon had grown to a vast flood. At sunset ("blood red . . . stupenduously beautiful," noted Maximilian) the *Yellowstone* passed a *memento mori* of western river travel: the hulk of a steamboat, sunk by snags. Toward dusk, the steamer eased into the bank and tied up for the night. No

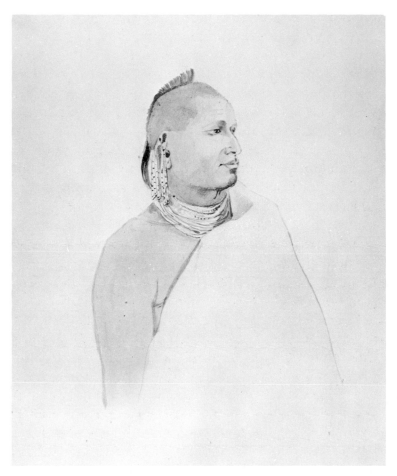

steamboat ever attempted to navigate the Missouri after dark.

The next day, at St. Charles, some twenty-five miles above the river mouth, the *Yellowstone* put in to take on cordwood for its boilers and to disembark Chouteau and the ladies for their return by coach to St. Louis, twenty miles due east. The party was joined by Kenneth McKenzie, boss of the Company's Upper Missouri Outfit, and Major John Dougherty, an Indian agent. Both had arrived overland that morning from St. Louis. The expedition now settled down to the serious business of the voyage. Steamboat navigation on the Missouri, even on its lower stretches, was no easy task. The longest river in the country, the Missouri drains a vast area of the West now occupied by ten states. Its wild waters are largely tamed today

by a system of dams on its upper reaches, but in 1833 the Missouri was considered by far the most treacherous of all western rivers. It was subject to violent storms and sudden flooding in the spring. Its channels and sandbars shifted constantly. And there were the snags—uprooted trees precipitated into the flood by the continually eroding banks of the great river. Steamboats were in constant danger of being holed below the waterline by this driftwood as they were tossed about the river by whirlpools and current. Ships would become stranded on sandbars, sometimes for days, waiting for a rise in the river to set them free. At other times the entire ship's company would have to drag the steamer upstream by huge hawsers called cordelles. Accompanying keelboats were used to lighter part of the cargo ahead so that

Men from two Missouri tribes: a Missouri (*left*) and an Omaha.

Indian artifacts from the Middle Missouri. Top to bottom: an Omaha war club, three Dakota pipes, a Ponca war club. Pipes played an important role in Plains Indian ritual and everyday life. Every man of substance had his medicine pipe, as well as the one that he used daily. The medicine pipe was brought out only on ceremonial occasions; otherwise it was kept in a special wrapping. The best pipe bowls were made by the Dakota Sioux from a soft red stone that was cut from a secret quarry located deep in their territory. These pipes were highly prized and served as a major article of trade throughout the entire Missouri River basin.

the ship's draft could be reduced for shallow sections of the twisting river. As the *Yellowstone* laboriously thrashed its way upstream, Maximilian, Bodmer, and Dreidoppel had plenty of opportunity to go ashore for botanizing, sketching, and collecting specimens. All in all, the *Yellowstone*'s 1,200-mile voyage from St. Louis to Fort Pierre, on the site of present-day Pierre, South Dakota, would require fifty days of unremitting toil.

For the first eleven days of the journey the *Yellowstone* followed the course of the river due west across the state of Missouri. After the state's admission to the Union in 1821, colonists flocked to the rich agricultural lands along the river and the Indians were soon driven out. Thus, on the early stages of the voyage, instead of investigating Indian life firsthand, Maximilian had to content himself with Indian yarns from the lips of McKenzie, Dougherty, Bean, and Sanford. Finally, on the morning of April 21, the *Yellowstone* reached the mouth of the Kansas River and passed from Missouri into the Indian territories. There, a bit upstream from where Kansas City is now located, Maximilian glimpsed his first wilderness Indian:

APRIL 21, 1833

We were now in the free Indian territory, and felt much more interested in looking at the forests, because we might expect to meet with some of their savage inhabitants. We examined the country with a telescope, and had the satisfaction of seeing the first Indian, on a sand bank, wrapped in his blanket; but our attention was soon called to the obstacles on the river: we avoided one dangerous place, where the Missouri was so full of trunks of trees that we were forced to put back; but at noon, when the thermometer was at 75°, we got among drift wood, which broke some of the paddles of our wheels, so that it was necessary to stop the engine. Forty-two of our men, most of whom had been out with their fowling-pieces, came on board. Among them was Dr. Fellowes, a young physician, going to the cantonment of Leavenworth. We halted, for the night, near Diamond

Island; our people cut down some trees, and kindled a large fire, which illumined the tall forests.

About six o'clock in the morning, we passed several islands, separated by narrow channels, where our pilot steered so close to the left bank that the hens which we had on board flew to the land. We soon came to a place where most of the trees were cut down, and we were not a little surprised at the sight of a sentinel. It was the landing-place of Cantonment Leavenworth, a military post, where four companies of the sixth regiment of infantry of the line, about 120 men, under Major [*Bennett*] Riley, were stationed to protect the Indian boundary. There were also 100 rangers, who are mounted and armed militia, well acquainted with Indian warfare. We were stopped at this place, and our vessel searched for brandy, the importation of which, into the Indian territory, is prohibited; they would scarcely permit us to take a small portion to preserve our specimens of natural history. Major Dougherty rejoined us here, and brought with him several Kickapoo Indians who had come from St. Louis to receive land in these parts. The Kickapoos, and Delawares, and some other Indians, are settled at no great distance from this place; the officers of the garrison were on board the whole day, and our hunters rambled about the surrounding country.

Maximilian's field journal gives a fuller account of this incident, which he discreetly glosses over in his book. A thorough search of the steamer was made and "a number of barrels" of whiskey were confiscated, to the great distress of Kenneth McKenzie. From the earliest days of the fur trade, alcohol had always proved an indispensable item of barter for trading with the Indians. The Indians' fatal weakness for the white man's firewater made it impossible for any trading company to do without it; the customers would simply take their pelts to the competition. In the United States and its territories it had been illegal for some years to give or sell alcohol to the Indians. But the law was nearly impossible to enforce, particularly in the Far West where many of the Indian agents and military officers were related by blood or financial interest to principal men in the fur companies. Vast quantities of whiskey were taken into Indian country every year, ostensibly for "medicinal purposes" or simply by payment of a bribe. As competition between the Company and the various outfits that made up the Opposition became fiercer, the alcohol trade had gotten completely out of hand. As a result, in July, 1832, Congress had enacted a law prohibiting the importation of alcohol for whatever purpose into Indian country.

News of the new law precipitated a thunderclap of consternation among the traders on the frontier. Big and small, they had ignored the existing prohibition against the alcohol trade for years. Now all subterfuges were denied them. If they couldn't get whiskey into Indian country, they couldn't break the law by trading it to their customers. A scramble ensued, everyone trying to get as much alcohol upstream as possible before the army clamped down. Indian superintendent Clark, a fast friend of the Astor interests, granted the Company permission to take in 1,400 gallons of alcohol for "medicinal" purposes. Chouteau hastened to turn the *Yellowstone* around after its downstream trip in the late summer and sent it off upriver crammed with whiskey barrels. But he was too late. The army had confiscated the entire stock at Leavenworth.

Thus, in 1833 McKenzie faced a crisis. The smaller outfits that made up the Opposition would have a relatively easy task in smuggling in the small amounts of alcohol they needed. The Company, on the other hand, needed substantial stores in order to maintain its dominance. The 1832 confiscation and the Leclerc affair (see Editors' Preface, pp. 7–8) had aroused a great outcry against the trust, and its activities were being closely scrutinized. To make matters worse, the Company faced a serious challenge this year from Sublette and Campbell, who were setting up Opposition posts all along the river.

Ever resourceful, McKenzie devised a dual strategy.

He not only secreted whiskey aboard the *Yellowstone*, but also took along a dismantled still, most probably sending it on ahead aboard the *Assiniboin*. The still got through, but not the whiskey. A disgruntled McKenzie wrote Chouteau from St. Joseph:

> We have been robbed of all our liquors, say seven barrels of shrub, one of rum, one of wine and all the fine men and sailor's whiskey which was in the two barrels. They kicked and knocked about everything they could find and even cut through our bales of blankets which had never been undone since they were put up in England.

Farther upstream, McKenzie set some *engagés* with agricultural implements ashore to plant corn for use in his still. (Characteristically, Maximilian passes this off by noting that "probably he wants to establish here a settlement and plantations.") McKenzie also purchased corn from the Mandans and it was undoubtedly alcohol from this still, set up at Fort Union, that fueled the trade at Company posts that year.

Late in the summer the still was discovered by an Opposition entrepreneur who denounced McKenzie to the military authorities when he got back downriver. The reverberations reached all the way to Washington and McKenzie's effectiveness on the Upper Missouri was ended. Recalled from the field, he made a trip to Europe in late 1834, paying a visit to Maximilian at Neuwied during the winter. He returned briefly to Fort Union but then retired to private business in St. Louis.

Regardless of intermittent attempts by the government to enforce the law, the trade in alcohol was never effectively controlled. For one thing, there was little the U.S. government could do about the Hudson's Bay Company, which was happy to supply the Indians with as much alcohol as they could afford from their posts in Canada. This deadly traffic played a role secondary only to that of smallpox in the demoralization of the Plains tribes.

In the English edition of Maximilian's book, trade alcohol is generally translated "brandy," although the Americans referred to it as "whiskey." Strictly speaking, it was neither, of course. It was crudely distilled grain alcohol, marked up by as much as a thousand percent over St. Louis prices and then diluted with river water before being purveyed to the Indians.

### April 23, 1833

The next morning brought us a storm, with thunder, but without lightning. Early in the morning a large branch of a tree, lying in the water, forced its way into the cabin, carried away part of the door case, and then broke off, and was left on the floor. After this accident, when one might have been crushed in bed, we came to Cow Island.

### April 24, 1833

We saw the chain of the Blacksnake Hills, but we met with so many obstacles in the river that we did not reach them till towards the evening. Near to the steep bank a trading house had been built, which was occupied by a man named Roubedoux, an agent of the Fur Company. [*Joseph Robidoux's post is now the site of the city of St. Joseph.*] When the steam-boat lay to, between 500 or 600 paces from the trading house, some of the *engagés* of the company came on board, and reported that the Iowa Indians, whose village was about five or six miles distant, had made an incursion into the neighbouring territory of the Omahas, and killed six of these Indians, and brought in a woman and child as prisoners, whom they offered for sale. Major Dougherty, to whose agency the Iowas belong, immediately landed to rescue the prisoners, accompanied by Major Bean and Mr. Bodmer, but they returned at eleven o'clock at night, without having accomplished their object, because the Iowas, fearing his reproaches, had completely intoxicated both themselves and their prisoners.

### April 25, 1833

On the forenoon we passed the mouth of the Nadaway River, and met with many difficulties, so that we were even obliged to back for some distance, and landed our wood-cutters in

Nadaway Island. [*For a watercolor made on this date, see page 41.*] A Captain Martin wintered on this island for two seasons, 1818 and 1819, with three companies of riflemen. At that time there was so much game that they entirely subsisted on it. We were told that in one year they killed 1,600, in the other 1,800 head of game (Virginia deer), besides elks and bears; and wounded, perhaps, as many more.

APRIL 26, 1833

We saw great numbers of water fowl, and many wild geese with their woolly young; the parents never abandoned them, even when our people shot at them. The care and anxiety which these birds shewed for their young interested us much. Picturesque forests alternate with the verdant alluvial banks of the river, and Indian hunting huts were everywhere seen, but no inhabitants. From the mouth of the Nishnebottoneh to Council Bluffs, there is a narrow green prairie before the chain of hills; the mouth itself is between lofty trees on the east bank. In the wood below, Major Dougherty once killed twenty elks, all belonging to one troop. They had divided, and part broke into the ice in the river, where they fell a prey to the Otos who pursued them. Beavers formerly abounded in this river, but they are now extirpated. When the evening sun, gradually sinking behind the tall forest, illumined the whole country, we had a lovely view of the chain of hills, variously tinged with brilliant hues of violet, pink, and purple, while the broad mirror of the river and adjacent forest shone as if on fire. Silence reigned in these solitudes, the wind was hushed, and only the dashing and foaming of our steam-boat interrupted the awful repose.

APRIL 27, 1833

At the mouth of the Little Nemahaw River, the Missouri was very shallow. Our vessel having received several violent shocks by striking, and a storm, accompanied by heavy rain, arising, we ran aground, about noon, on a sand bank, and were obliged to put out a boat to take soundings, but the wind, which blew with increasing violence from the open prairie on the south-west, drove us further into the sand bank. Every moment it became more furious; our vessel lay almost on her side, which the people endeavoured to counteract by fastening her with strong cables to the trees lying in the

Unfinished watercolor sketch of an Omaha Indian, made on **May 4.**

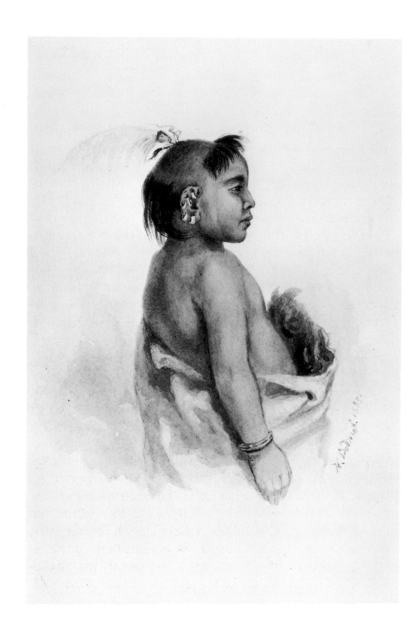

water. After dinner several of our hunters went on shore, but the boat had scarcely returned, when the storm suddenly increased to such a degree that the vessel appeared to be in imminent peril. One of our chimneys was thrown down, and the foredeck was considered in danger; the large coops, which contained a number of fowls, were blown overboard, and nearly all of them drowned. As they got upon the sand banks they were afterwards taken up, with other things which we had been obliged to throw overboard; our cables had, happily, held fast, and, as the wind abated a little, Captain Bennett hoped to lay the vessel close to the bank, which was twenty feet high, where it would be safe, but the storm again arose, and we got deeper and deeper into the sands. Some of our hunters and Mr. Bodmer appeared on the bank, and wanted to be taken on board, but the boat could not be sent, and they were obliged to seek shelter from the storm in the neighbouring forests. Mr. Mc Kenzie, and other persons acquainted with the Missouri, assured us they had never encountered so violent a storm in these parts.

The next five days were spent in negotiating the sixty-odd miles of river to Major Dougherty's Indian agency at Bellevue, a few miles above the mouth of the Platte River where the city of Omaha was later to rise. The *Yellowstone* was unloaded and heaved off a bar. She became stuck again and was once more unloaded, backed down to another channel, and poled and cordelled upstream by cursing *engagés*. Maximilian made notes on birds, including a large flock of pelicans headed north, and examined three large catfish that were caught by the crew. The largest weighed 100 pounds and measured more than fifty inches in length. At dusk on the fifth day the steamer was met by Lucien Fontenelle, one of the Company's most experienced traders, who had come down from his post at Bellevue in a dugout.

MAY 3, 1833

We were now near the mouth of the Platte River. After passing the sand bank at its mouth, we reached, in twenty minutes, Papilion Creek, and saw before us the green-wooded chain

Watercolor sketch of an Omaha boy, made at Cabanné's trading post on May 4. A portrait of his father is on the preceding page.

of hills with the buildings of Bellevue, the agency of Major Dougherty. [*For a view of this post, see page 44.*] There were many sand banks in the river, on which there were numbers of wild geese, and some quite white birds, with black quill feathers—perhaps cranes or pelicans. At two in the afternoon we reached M. Fontenelle's dwelling, consisting of some buildings, with fine plantations of maize, and verdant wooded hills behind it. A part of the plantations belongs to the government. The prairie extends beyond the hills. The land is extremely fertile; even when negligently cultivated, it yields 100 bushels of maize per acre, but is said to produce much more when proper care is bestowed on it. The cattle thrive very well, and the cows give much milk, but some salt must now and then be given them. M. Fontenelle expected to possess, in a few years, 5,000 swine, if the Indians did not steal too many of them.

Bellevue, Mr. Dougherty's post, is agreeably situated. The direction of the river is north-west. Below, on the bank, there are some huts, and on the top the buildings of the agents, where a sub-agent, Major Beauchamp, a blacksmith, and some servants of the company, all lived with their families, who attend to the plantations and affairs of the company. These men were mostly married to women of the tribes of the Otos and Omahas; all, on our landing, immediately came on board. Their dress was of red or blue cloth, with a white border, and cut in the Indian fashion. Their faces were broad and coarse, their heads large and round, their breasts pendent, their teeth beautiful and white, their hands and feet small and delicate. Their children had agreeable features.

It was near this place that a marauding party of twelve Iowas lately crossed the river, and pursued a defenceless company of Omahas, who had just left Bellevue; and, having overtaken them three miles off, killed and plundered all of them, except some who were desperately wounded, and whom they believed to be dead. The victors returned by another way. A woman and a child recovered. [*This was the same incident first reported on April 24.*] Major Dougherty took leave of us at Bellevue, intending to go to the Omahas, and appease the vengeance of that tribe. About five in the afternoon we also left, and were proceeding along the west bank, when we met two Mackinaw boats, which had been obtained for our vessel by a boat which we had sent before. On the bank we suddenly saw three Omaha Indians, who crept slowly along. They were clothed in buffalo robes, and had bows, with quivers made of skin, on their backs. About the nose and eyes they were painted white.

## MAY 4, 1833

The noise and smoke of our steamer frightened all living creatures; geese and ducks flew off in all directions. We soon saw the white buildings of Mr. Cabanné's trading post, which we saluted with some guns, and then landed. We were very glad to see, at the landing-place, a number of Omaha and Oto Indians, and some few Iowas, who, in different groups, looked at us with much curiosity; all these people were wrapped in buffalo skins, with the hairy side outwards; some of them wore blankets, which they sometimes paint with coloured stripes. In their features they did not materially differ from those Indians we had already seen, but they were not so well formed as the Sauks. Many of them were much marked with the small pox. Several had only one eye; their faces were marked with red stripes: some had painted their foreheads and chins red; others, only stripes down the cheeks.

This trading post consists of a row of buildings of various sizes, stores, and the houses of the *engagés*, married to Indian women, among which was that of Mr. Cabanné, which is two stories high. He is a proprietor of the American Fur Company, and director of this station. He received us very kindly, and conducted us over his premises. From the balcony of his house was a fine view over the river, but the prospect is still more interesting from the hills which rise at the back of the settlement. Between the buildings runs a small stream, with high banks, which rises from a pleasant valley, in which there are plantations of maize for the support of the inhabitants. Mr. Cabanné had planted fifteen acres of land with this invaluable grain, which yield, annually, 2,000 bushels of that corn, the land here being extremely fertile. Our vessel remained here the whole day, and we were besieged all the time by Indians, who caused a very disagreeable heat in our cabins. Mr. Bodmer made a sketch of the boy of an Omaha, whom the father first daubed with red paint. He took vermilion in the palm of the hand, spat upon it, and then rubbed it in the boy's face. The head of this boy was shaved quite smooth, excepting a tuft of hair in front, and another at the back. A number of men and women stood round, looking on with eager curiosity.

We spent a very pleasant evening with Mr. Cabanné; sitting in the balcony of his house, we enjoyed the delightful temperature and fine scene around us. The splendid sky was illumined by the full moon; silence reigned around, interrupted only by the noise of the frogs, and the incessant cry of the whip-poor-will, in the neighbouring woods, till the Indians assembled round the house, and, at the request of Mr. Cabanné, performed a dance. About twenty Omahas joined in it; the principal dancer, a tall man, wore on his head an immense feather cap composed of long tail and wing feathers of owls and birds of prey; in his hand he held his bow and arrows. He had a savage and martial appearance, to which his athletic figure greatly contributed. Another man, who was younger, of a very muscular frame—the upper part of whose body was naked, but painted white—had in his hand a war club, striped with white, ornamented at the handle with the skin of a polecat. He wore on his head a feather cap, like that already described. These two men, and several youths and boys, formed a line, opposite to which other Indians sat down in a row; in the middle of which row the drum was beat in quick time. Several men beat time with war clubs hung with bells; and the whole company (most of whom were painted white) sung, "Hi! hi! hi!" or "Hey! hey! hey!" They leaped opposite to each other, with great exertion, for about an hour; they perspired violently, till the usual presents, a quantity of tobacco stalks, were thrown on the ground before them. This dance was very interesting to me, especially in connection with the beautiful evening scene on the Missouri. The bright light of the moon illumined the extensive and silent wilderness; before us, the grotesque band of Indians, uttering their wild cry, together with the loud call of the night raven, vividly recalled to my mind scenes which I had witnessed in Brazil. We did not return to our vessel till late at night, after taking leave of our kind host, and of Major Pilcher; the former was on the point of returning to St. Louis, leaving the superintendence of the trading post in the hands of Major Pilcher.

Early in the morning of May 5 the *Yellowstone* resumed its journey northward into the territory of the Poncas and the Dakotas. There were the usual difficulties with snags and low water. Sometimes, in order to free the steamer from a sandbar, the entire ship's company would dash from one side of the deck to the other, trying to rock the steamer off the shoal. Maximilian, in his cabin, complained that this motion made it impossible to write in his journal. Violent storms with thundering lightning bolts whipped up stinging clouds of sand from the banks, reducing visibility to near-zero. Shortly the expedition passed the grave of Blackbird, a legendary chief of the once-powerful Omahas, now sadly depleted by the predations of the smallpox and the Sioux. Maximilian noted down the story of how Blackbird was buried according to his wishes in a mound, seated bolt upright on a live mule. On May 11 the *Yellowstone* overtook the Company steamboat *Assiniboin*, which had preceded it upriver and was now stranded by low water. Aided by a keelboat which lightered off portions of their cargoes, the two steamboats fought their way around and over the sandbars. [*See aquatint engraving on page 14.*] On May 17 the company sighted the first pronghorn antelope; and the next day, the first buffalo. Indians came aboard to receive gifts and were sketched by Bodmer. Woodcutters went ashore to cut cordwood for the boilers and manhandle it aboard. A few miles upstream they might have to unload it again so that the steamer, which drew five feet of water, could be cordelled over a sandbar. Hunting parties ranged the forests with indifferent success: ducks and a few geese, sometimes a rabbit, were bagged. Toward the end of the month, both steamboats were stranded for five days on a stretch of shallow water now engulfed by the reservoir above the Fort Randall Dam at the Nebraska–South Dakota border. At this point they were joined by a Company employee who had been traveling downstream from Fort Union since March, bringing the late winter casualty report. Three trappers, including the storied mountain man Hugh Glass, had been killed by a party of sixty Arikaras. Blackfeet had killed thirteen *engagés* in another action. Indian losses were not reported. The river finally rose, and on May 25 the steamboats passed the mouth of the White River and approached the Sioux Agency at Fort Lookout.

## MAY 25, 1833

On a point of land, at the left hand, round which the Missouri turns to the west, we saw the buildings of Sioux Agency; the *Yellowstone* saluted the post with several guns, and was welcomed to the fort by the hoisting of a flag, while the whole population, about fifty in number, chiefly consisting of Sioux Indians, were assembled on the beach. We proceeded a mile further, to an extensive forest, where we took in wood, and stopped for the night. In order to get acquainted with the Sioux, in whom I took so much interest, I returned, in a heavy rain, through the bushes and high grass, to the agency, where Major Bean [*who had preceded me there*] received me very kindly, though his dwelling, according to the fashion of the place, was rudely constructed, and he was incommoded by too many visitors.

Sioux Agency, or, as it is now usually called, Fort Lookout, is a square, of about sixty paces, surrounded by pickets, twenty or thirty feet high, made of squared trunks of trees, placed close to each other, within which the dwellings are built close to the palisades. These dwellings consisted of only three block-houses, with several apartments. Close to the fort, in a northern direction, the fur company of Mr. Sublette had a dwelling house, with a store; and, in the opposite direction, was a similar post of the American Fur Company. The fort is agreeably situated on a green spot, near the river. About ten leather tents of the Sioux were set up nearby.

The Dakotas, as they call themselves, or the Sioux of the French, are still one of the most numerous Indian tribes in North America. They are divided into several branches which all speak the same language, with some deviations. Three principal branches live on the Missouri, *viz.*, the Yanktons, the Tetons, and the Yanktonans.

The Yanktons live in Sioux Agency, or the furthest down the Missouri, among which tribe we now were. All these Dakotas of the Missouri, as well as most of those of the Mississippi, are only hunters, and, in their excursions, always live in portable leather tents. All these Indians have great numbers of horses and dogs, the latter of which often serve them as food. The Dakotas on the Missouri were formerly dangerous enemies to the Whites, whereas now, with the exception of the Yanktonans, they bear a very good character, and constantly keep peace with the Whites. Such of these Indians as reside near the Whites, are frequently connected with them by marriages, and depend on them for support. They then become negligent hunters, indolent, and, consequently, poor. This was partly the case at Sioux Agency, where they rarely possessed more than two horses. One of the most considerable men among them, wholly devoted to the Whites, was Wahktageli, called the Big Soldier, a tall, good-looking man, about sixty years of age, with a high aquiline nose, and large animated eyes.

## MAY 26, 1833

Mr. Bodmer having expressed a wish of painting a full-length portrait of Big Soldier, the latter arrived in his complete ceremonial dress. [*This portrait appears on page 45.*] Later, we paid a visit to Wahktageli in his tent, and had some difficulty in crawling through the narrow, low entrance, after pulling aside the skin that covered it. The inside of this tent was light, and it was about ten paces in diameter. Buffalo skins were spread on the ground, upon which we sat down. Between us and the side of the tent were a variety of articles, such as pouches, boxes, saddles, arms, &c. A relation of the chief was employed in making arrows, which were finished very neatly, and with great care. Wahktageli immediately, with much gravity, handed the tobacco pipe round, and seemed to inhale the precious smoke with great delight. His wife was present; their children were married. The conversation was carried on by Cephier, the interpreter kept by the agency, who accompanied us on this visit. It is the custom with all the North American Indians, on paying a visit, to enter in perfect silence, to shake hands with the host, and unceremoniously sit down beside him. Refreshments are then presented, which the Big Soldier could not do, as he himself stood in need of food. After this the pipe circulates. The owner of a neighbouring tent had killed a large elk, the skin of which the women were then busily employed in dressing. They had stretched it out, by means of leather straps, on the ground near the tent, and the women were scraping off the particles of flesh and fat with a very well-contrived instrument. It is made of bone, sharpened at one end, and furnished with little teeth like a saw, and, at the other end, a strap, which is fastened round the wrist. The skin is scraped with this instrument till it is perfectly clean. Among the peculiar customs of the Sioux is their treatment of the dead. Those who die at home are sewed up in blankets and skins, in their complete dress, painted, and laid with their arms and other effects on a high stage, supported by four poles, till they are decomposed, when they are sometimes buried. Those who have been killed in battle are immediately interred on the spot. Sometimes, too, in times of peace, they bury their dead in the ground, and protect them against the wolves by a fence of wood and thorns. There were many such graves in the vicinity of the Sioux Agency, among which was that of the celebrated chief, Tschpunka, who was buried with his full dress and arms, and his face painted red. Very often, however, they lay their dead in trees; and we saw, in the neighbourhood of this place, an oak, in which there were three bodies wrapped in skins. At the foot of the tree there was a small arbour, or shed, made of branches of poplar, which the relations had built for the purpose of coming to lament and weep over the dead, which they frequently do for several days successively. As a sign of mourning, they cut off their hair with the first knife that comes to hand, daub themselves with white clay, and give away all their best clothes and valuable effects, as well as those of the deceased, to the persons who happen to be present.

Mr. Bodmer finished his very capital likeness of Wahktageli. The elk, killed by the Indians, furnished us with fresh meat, and we considered ourselves very well off. In the afternoon, Messrs. Mc Kenzie and Sanford came from the *Yellowstone* to visit us, and we returned on board.

### May 27, 1833

Major Bean had the courtesy to present me with the complete dress of the Big Soldier, an interesting souvenir of the friendly reception we had met with in his house. The *Assiniboin* passed us rapidly in the afternoon, and we followed. A well-known Sioux chief, called Tukan-Haton, and, by the Americans, the Little Soldier, was on board with his family, intending to accompany us to Fort Pierre. [*Bodmer took his portrait. See page 46.*] These Indians were in mourning for some of their relations lately deceased; their dress was, therefore, as bad as possible, and their faces daubed with white clay. The Big Soldier also paid us a visit previous to our departure. He had no feathers on his head, but only a piece of red cloth. After receiving some food he took leave, and we saw the grotesque, tall figure stand for a long time motionless on the beach. As the vessel proceeded very quickly, our Indians laid down their heads as a sign that they were giddy,

but they were soon relieved, as the water became shallow. We lay to not far above the stream which Lewis and Clark call the Three Rivers.

### May 28, 1833

Part of the goods had been put into the keel-boat, to lighten the steamer, which was accomplished by eight o'clock. From this place to the Big Bend of the Missouri is fifteen miles, before reaching which we came to an island, which has been formed since Lewis and Clark were there. We soon overtook the *Assiniboin,* and reached the Big Bend which the Missouri takes round a flat point of land; following the course of the river, it is twenty-five miles round, while the isthmus is only one mile and a half across. The large peninsula, round which the Missouri turns, is flat, and bordered with poplars and willows; the opposite bank is higher, steep, and bare. A couple of antelopes were, in this place, frightened by the noise of our steamer; these animals are said to be very numerous here in the winter time. The Little Soldier sat by the fireside, smoking his pipe, in doing which, like all the Indians, he inhaled the smoke, a custom which is, doubtless, the cause of many pectoral diseases. The tobacco, which the Indians of this part of the country smoke, is called kini-kenick, and consists of the inner green bark of the red willow, dried, and powdered, and mixed with the tobacco of the traders.

### May 29, 1833

We were nearly at the end of the Big Bend, and stopped, at seven o'clock in the morning, to cut down cedars. Towards noon there appeared, on the western bank, steep, rocky walls, and, behind them, singularly-formed hills, some resembling pyramids, others, round towers, &c. At this place we suddenly espied a canoe, with four men in it, which touched at a sand bank; a boat was put out, and brought back two of the strangers, who proved to be Mr. Lamont, a member of the American Fur Company, and Major Mitchell, one of their officers, and Director of Fort Mc Kenzie, which is situated near the falls of the Missouri. They came last from Fort Pierre.

### May 30, 1833

Before six, in the evening, we reached the mouth of the Teton

River which the Sioux call the Bad River. The French Fur Company formerly had a fort just above the mouth of the Teton, which was abandoned when the companies joined, and another was built further up, which was called Fort Teton; this, too, was abandoned; and Fort Pierre (so called after Mr. Pierre Chouteau) was erected higher up, on the west bank, opposite an island. [*Present-day Pierre, South Dakota, lies just across the river from this site.*] The steamer had proceeded a little further, when we came in sight of the fort, to the great joy of all on board. The colours were hoisted, both on the steamer and on the fort, which produced a very good effect between the trees on the bank; a small village, consisting of thirteen Sioux tents, lay on the left hand. Our steamer first began to salute with its cannon, which was returned from the shore by a running fire of musketry, and this was answered from our deck by a similar very brisk fire. Before we reached the landing-place, we perceived an isolated, decayed old house, the only remains of Fort Tecumseh, and, ten minutes afterwards, landed at Fort Pierre, on the fifty-first day of our voyage from St. Louis. A great crowd came to welcome us; we were received by the whole population, consisting of some hundred persons, with the white inhabitants at their head, the chief of whom was Mr. Laidlaw, a proprietor of the fur company, who has the management at this place. There were many Indians among them, who had done their part to welcome us by firing their muskets, which they carried in their hands. There seemed to be no end of shaking hands; a thousand questions were asked, and the latest news, on both sides, was eagerly sought for.

Fort Pierre is one of the most considerable settlements of the fur company on the Missouri, and forms a large quadrangle, surrounded by high pickets. At the north-east and south-west corners there are block-houses, with embrasures; the upper story is adapted for small arms, and the lower for some cannon; each side of the quadrangle is 108 paces in length; the front and back, each 114 paces; the inner space eighty-seven paces in diameter. From the roof of the block-house, which is surrounded with a gallery, there is a fine prospect over the prairie; and there is a flag-staff on the roof, on which the colours are hoisted. The timber for this fort was felled from forty to sixty miles up the river, and floated down, because none fit for the purpose was to be had in the neighbourhood.

The situation of the settlement is agreeable; the verdant

Shudegacheh, chief of the Poncas, wore a beard and proudly displayed his silver medal, a gift from the whites.

prairie is very extensive, animated by herds of cattle and horses; of the latter, Fort Pierre possessed 150, and of the former, thirty-six, which afforded a sufficient supply of milk and fresh butter. Indians, on foot and on horseback, were scattered all over the plain, and their singular stages for the dead were in great numbers near the fort; immediately behind which, the leather tents of the Sioux Indians, of the branches of the Tetons and the Yanktons, stood, like a little village.

This time we visited the Indian tents uninvited; in that which we first entered there were several tall, good-looking men assembled; the owner of the tent was a man of middle-size; his complexion very light, and his features agreeable. His wives were dressed very neatly, and were remarkably clean, especially the one who appeared to be the principal; she wore a very elegant leather dress, with stripes and borders of azure and white beads, and polished metal buttons, and trimmed as usual at the bottom with fringes, round the ends of which lead is twisted, so that they tinkle at every motion. Her summer robe, which was dressed smooth on both sides, was painted red and black, on a yellowish-white ground. She estimated these articles of dress very highly. [*See page 47 for her portrait.*]

After we had conversed with the men, the pipe circulated. The pipes of the Dakotas are very beautiful, in truth the most beautiful of all the North American Indians, which they make, in various forms, of the red indurated clay, or stone. The pipe has a long, flat, broad wooden tube, which is ornamented with tufts of horse-hair, dyed red, yellow, or green, and wound round with strings of porcupine quills of divers colours.

We looked at the women as they were at work. For the shoes which they made they had softened the leather in a tub of water, and stretched it in the breadth and length with their teeth. In the middle of the hut was a fire, over which the kettle was suspended by a wooden hook; they now all use iron kettles, which they obtain from the traders. Before most of the tents poles were placed, leaning against each other, to which gaily-painted parchment pouches were hung, and like-wise the medicine-bags, as they are called, in which the medicine, or charms, are preserved, and which they open and consult only on solemn or important occasions, such as campaigns and the like. Here, too, were suspended the bow and quiver of arrows, spears, and a round shield of thick leather, with a thin cover, also of the same material. In another tent

the women were dressing the skins, either with a pumice-stone, or with the before-described toothed instrument, which was here entirely of iron. They then pulled the skin over a line, backwards and forwards, to make it pliable.

The Sioux, who live on Teton River, near Fort Pierre, are mostly of the branch of the Tetons; though there are some Yanktons here. The former are divided into five branches, and the latter into three. Like all the North American Indians, they highly prize personal bravery, and, therefore, constantly wear the marks of distinction which they have received for their exploits; among these are, especially, tufts of human hair attached to their arms and legs, and feathers on their heads. He who, in the sight of the adversaries, touches a slain or a living enemy, places a feather horizontally in his hair for this exploit. They look upon this as a very distinguished act, for many are often killed in the attempt, before the object is attained. He who kills an enemy by a blow with his fist, sticks a feather upright in his hair. If the enemy is killed with a musket, a small piece of wood is put in the hair, which is intended to represent a ramrod. If a warrior is distinguished by many deeds, he has a right to wear the great feather-cap, with ox-horns. This cap, composed of eagle's feathers, which are fastened to a long strip of red cloth, hanging down the back, is highly valued by all the tribes on the Missouri, and they never part with it except for a good horse.

The scalps taken in battle are drawn over small hoops, and hung on the top of the tent-poles. He who takes a prisoner wears a particular bracelet. These Indians frequently possess from thirty to forty horses, and are then reckoned to be rich. The tents are generally composed of fourteen skins, each worth two dollars. We were told, that wealthy people sometimes have eight or nine wives, because they are able to support them. The Sioux do not understand the treatment of diseases, but generally cure wounds very well. Before their death, they usually determine whether they will be buried, or be placed on a stage, or in a tree.

## June 2, 1833

Today, 7,000 buffalo skins and other furs were put on board the *Yellowstone*, which was to return to St. Louis. We took this opportunity of sending letters to Europe: the *Assiniboin* was assigned us for the continuation of the voyage. The weather, at this time, was very unfavourable; it rained at a temperature of 57°, and we were obliged to have a fire in our cabin throughout the day. The *Assiniboin* had already taken our baggage on board, but still lay on the east bank, for an attempt to bring it over to our side had failed, because the water was too low. In the afternoon, when we visited Mr. Laidlaw in the fort, six Sioux, from the prairie, arrived on horseback, whose horde, of 200 tents, was at the distance of a day's journey. They brought word that, two days' march from the fort, there were numerous herds of buffaloes.

## June 3, 1833

Mr. Lamont, who had taken leave of us today, to go by the steamboat to St. Louis, embarked with some of the Company's clerks; he was saluted with several cannon shot, and

before evening the *Yellowstone* rapidly descended the river.

## June 4, 1833

We received a visit from six or seven newly arrived Tetons, whom the interpreter, Dorion, introduced to us. They were particularly interested by the steam-boat, and, after they had very minutely examined it, they were served with dinner and pipes. The dinner chiefly consisted of bacon, which the Indians do not like; they, however, swallowed it, in order that they might not appear uncourteous. Among them was a Teton, named Wah-Menitu (the spirit, or god, in the water), and who had such a voracious appetite, that he devoured everything which the others had left; his face was painted red; he had a remarkably projecting upper lip, and an aquiline nose

Sioux encampment at Fort Pierre. The burial stage in foreground has a willow cage to protect the remains of a famous chief from the predations of carrion birds.

much bent. In his hair, which hung in disorder about his head, with a plait coming over one of his eyes or nose, the feather of a bird of prey was placed horizontally; but observe that he had a right to wear three. Mr. Bodmer, who desired to draw this man's portrait, gave him some vermilion, on which he spat, and rubbed his face with it, drawing parallel lines, in the red colour, with a wooden stick. Wah-Menitu stayed on board for the night; sung, talked, laughed, and joked without ceasing; and seemed quite to enjoy himself.

Low water delayed the departure of the *Assiniboin*, aboard which Maximilian and his party were ensconced in rather more spacious quarters than they had enjoyed on the *Yellowstone*. The important travelers were lodged in an airy stern cabin with eight beds. The rest of the ship's complement, which totaled about sixty, was split up among a larger cabin of twenty-four beds and quarters on the deck below. Maximilian reported himself well satisfied with his new arrangement, although he noted nervously that part of the cargo consisted of 200 barrels of gunpowder. Accompanied by two keelboats, the *Assiniboin* strove for several days to make headway through the sandbars just above Fort Pierre—without notable success. During this period McKenzie, Sanford, and Mitchell stayed behind at the fort, the prince commenting wryly in his journal that "they seemed yet unwilling for a separation from their Indian beauties." By June 8 the steamboat was at last free of the bars, and McKenzie and his companions rode overland to rejoin her. As the *Assiniboin* proceeded upriver, hunting parties were sent ashore, for game was becoming more plentiful. Elk, pronghorn antelope, deer, and occasionally buffalo were taken for the larder. Members of the party who stayed aboard blazed away at anything that moved on shore for the sheer sport of it. Wolves, swans, and beavers fell victim to their fire. Approaching the territory of the Arikaras, a notoriously fierce and hostile tribe, the ship's cannon and rifles were all loaded as a precautionary measure, but

no Arikaras were to be seen. On June 12 the *Assiniboin* passed two adjacent Arikara villages, totaling nearly 300 huts, that had been abandoned the year before because the tribe feared retribution from the whites in the wake of one of their periodic murder sprees. On June 15 a sharp rise in the river caused by the spring runoff in the Rockies enabled the steamboat to proceed swiftly into Mandan country. Two days later, there was an Indian scare:

### June 17, 1833

After we had passed, alternately, prairies, with their hills, steep clay banks, and stripes of forest, we prosecuted our voyage till dusk, and lay to near a large willow thicket, on the eastern bank, when some musket shots were suddenly heard, the flashes of which were seen as well. Mr. Mc Kenzie immediately supposed that it was an Indian war party, which people, in general, avoid, as they do not much trust them. We consulted what was to be done. Many shots followed, which made a very loud report, it being the custom of the Indians to use a great deal of powder; and we soon perceived, among the dark thickets, the figures of the Indians in their white buffalo robes. As nobody knew the intentions of these people, we looked forward to the meeting with some anxiety.

The Indians broke silence first, calling out that they were come with peaceable intention, and wished to be taken on board. Ortubize, the interpreter, telling us that they were Sioux, of the branch of the Yanktonans, we conferred some time with them, while a kind of bridge of planks was thrown across to the shore. Twenty-three, for the most part tall men, came on board, and were made to sit down, in a row, on one side of the large cabin. They came from a camp of the Yanktonans, consisting of 300 tents, which was in the neighbourhood; they generally lived on the banks of the Sheyenne, which falls into the Red River, near the Devils Lake. They had been hunting in the neighbourhood, and shot some buffaloes. The Yanktonans are represented as the most perfidious and dangerous of all the Sioux, and are stated frequently to have killed white men, especially Englishmen, in these parts. They generally come to the Missouri in the winter, but at this season it was a mere chance that we met with them. They were mostly robust, slender, well-shaped men, with long dishevelled hair, in which some wore feathers as indications of their exploits.

After we had smoked with these Yanktonans all round, the chief opened, before Mr. Mc Kenzie, a bag, with old pemmican (dry meat powdered), by way of present, and then rose to make a speech. After shaking hands, successively, with all persons present, he said, with much gesticulation, and in short sentences, between which he appeared to be reflecting, "that the whole body of the 300 tents was under the principal chief, Jawitschahka; that his people had been formerly on good terms with the Mandans, but had been at variance with them for about a year, on account of the murder of a Sioux, and now wished to make peace again; that with this view they had sent three of their people to the Mandan villages, but did not know the result; and, therefore, were very desirous of the mediation of Mr. Mc Kenzie; that they happened to be near the river, when they perceived their father's ship, and were come to visit him; that to be able to supply the fur company with more beaver skins, they wished to have liberty to hunt on the Missouri, and on that account peace with the Mandans was of importance to them. They hoped, therefore, that Mr. Mc Kenzie would intercede for them, and allow them to ac-company him." The answer was—"That if, like the other tribes of their nation, who lived constantly on the Missouri, they would, in future, conduct themselves properly, and never kill white men, he would attempt all that lay in his power; but he bade them consider what would be the best for them, whether to come on board with him, or to go alone by land to the Mandan villages, as he did not know how they might be received by the young men of the Mandan tribe." These Indians showed us a beautiful skin of a young, white, female buffalo, which they intended as a present for the Mandans, by whom such skins are highly valued. They had already sent them a white buffalo calf. Our visitors were afterwards taken into another apartment, where refreshments were set before them, and they were lodged for the night. The next morning, however, they went ashore, and proceeded to Fort Clark on foot.

JUNE 18, 1833

We left at an early hour the place of the meeting, from which it was twelve miles to Fort Clark. The Yanktonans, keeping in sight of us, walked through the prairie, where they

Wah-Menitu (the spirit in the water), a Teton Dakota, enjoyed a festive evening aboard the *Assiniboin* on June 4.

frightened a herd of ten or twelve wolves, which had long amused us by their gambols. At half-past seven we passed a roundish island covered with willows, and reached then the wood on the western bank, in which the winter dwellings of part of the Mandan Indians are situated; and saw, at a distance, the largest village of this tribe, Mih-Tutta-Hang-Kush, in the vicinity of which the whole prairie was covered with riders and pedestrians. As we drew nearer the huts of that village, Fort Clark, lying before it, relieved by the background of the blue prairie hills, came in sight, with the gay American banner waving from the flagstaff. On a tongue of land on the left bank were four white men on horseback; Indians, in their buffalo robes, sat in groups upon the bank, and the discharge of cannon and musketry commenced to welcome us.

The *Assiniboin* soon lay to before the fort, against the gently sloping shore, where above 600 Indians were waiting for us. Close to the beach, the chiefs and most distinguished warriors of the Mandan nation stood in front of the assembly of red men, among whom the most eminent were Charata-Numakschi (the wolf chief), Mato-Topé (the four bears), Dipauch (the broken arm), Berock-Itainu (the ox neck), Pehriska-Ruhpa (the two ravens), and some others. They were all dressed in their finest clothes, to do us honour. As soon as the vessel was moored, they came on board, and, after having given us their hands, sat down in the stern cabin. The pipe went round, and the conversation began with the Mandans, by the assistance of Mr. Kipp, clerk to the American Fur Company, and director of the trading post at Fort Clark, and with the Minnetarees, by the help of the old interpreter, Charbonneau, who had lived thirty-seven years in the villages of the latter people, near this place. Mr. Mc Kenzie caused the proposal of the Yanktonans to be submitted to these Indians, but the latter, after long deliberation, replied that they could not possibly accept these proposals of peace, because the Yanktonans were much too treacherous; that, however, no harm should now be done to them, and that they might depart unmolested. Most of the Indians in our cabin were stout, tall men, except Mato-Topé, who was of middle stature, and rather slim. I shall have occasion to say more of this brave and distinguished chief.

We soon went on shore, and examined the numerous assemblage of brown Indian figures, of whom the women and children, in numerous groups, were sitting on the ground; the men, some on horseback, some on foot, were collected around, and making their observations on the white strangers. Here we saw remarkably tall and handsome men, and fine dresses, for they had all done their utmost to adorn themselves. The haughty Crows rode on beautiful panther skins, with red cloth under them, and, as they never wear spurs, had a whip of elk's horn in their hand. These mounted warriors, with their diversely painted faces, feathers in their long hair, bow and arrows slung across their backs, and with a musket or spear in their hands, the latter of which is merely for show, were a novel and highly interesting scene. This remarkable assembly gazed at the strangers with curiosity, and we conversed with them by signs, but soon proceeded to the fort, which is built on a smaller scale, on a plan similar to that of all the other trading posts or forts of the Company. It is about the size of the Sioux Agency at Fort Lookout, but more rudely constructed. Immediately behind the fort there were, in the prairies, seventy leather tents of the Crows, which we immediately visited.

The tents of the Crows are exactly like those of the Sioux, and are set up without any regular order. On the poles, instead of scalps, there were small pieces of coloured cloth, chiefly red, floating like streamers in the wind. We were struck with the number of wolf-like dogs of all colours, of which there were certainly from 500 to 600 running about. They all fell upon the strangers, and it was not without difficulty that we kept them off by throwing stones, in which some old Indian women assisted us. We then proceeded about 300 paces in a north-west direction from the fort, up the Missouri, to the principal village of the Mandans, Mih-Tutta-Hang-Kush. This village consisted of about sixty large hemispherical clay huts, and was surrounded with a fence of stakes, at the four corners of which conical mounds were thrown up, covered with a facing of wickerwork, and embrasures, which serve for defence, and command the river and the plain. We were told that these cones or block-houses were not erected by the Indians themselves, but by the Whites. Three miles further up the river, and on the same bank, is the second village of the Mandans, called Ruhptare, consisting of about thirty-eight clay huts, which we could not then visit for want of time. In the immediate vicinity of the principal village, the stages on which these Indians, like the Sioux, place their dead, lay scattered. Around them were several high poles, with skins and other things hanging on them, as

offerings to the lord of life, Ohmahank-Numakshi, or to the first man, Numank-Machana. The three villages of the Minnetaree nation, whose language is totally different from that of the Mandans, are situated about fifteen miles higher up on the same side of the river, and most of their inhabitants had come on this day to the Mandan villages.

The view of the prairie around Fort Clark was at this time highly interesting. A great number of horses were grazing all round; Indians of both sexes and all ages were in motion; we were, every moment, stopped by them, obliged to shake hands, and let them examine us on all sides. This was sometimes very troublesome. Thus, for example, a young warrior took hold of my pocket compass which I wore suspended by a ribbon, and attempted to take it by force, to hang as an ornament round his neck. I refused his request, but the more I insisted in my refusal, the more importunate he became. He offered me a handsome horse for my compass, and then all his handsome clothes and arms into the bargain, and

Detail from a watercolor showing two abandoned Arikara villages that the expedition passed on the afternoon of June 12.

as I still refused, he became angry, and it was only by the assistance of old Charbonneau, that I escaped a disagreeable and, perhaps, violent scene. On returning to the steamer we there found a numerous company of Indians, some smoking, others wrapped in their blankets, and asleep on the floor.

Mr. Sanford, the sub-agent of the Mandans, Minnetarees, and Crows, had a conference with Eripuass (the rotten belly), the distinguished chief of the latter. We accompanied Mr. Sanford to this meeting. Eripuass, a fine tall man, with a pleasing countenance, had much influence over his people; being in mourning he came to the fort in his worst dress, his hair cut close, and daubed with clay. Charbonneau acted as interpreter in the Minnetaree language. Mr. Sanford recommended to the chief continued good treatment of the white people who should come to his territory, hung a medal round his neck, and, in the name of the government, made him a considerable present of cloth, powder, ball, tobacco, &c., which this haughty man received without any sign of gratitude; on the contrary, these people consider such presents as a tribute due to them, and a proof of weakness. The Crows, in particular, as the proudest of the Indians, are said to despise the Whites. They do not, however, kill them, but often plunder them.

At nightfall we visited Eripuass in his tent. The whole camp of the Crows was now filled with horses, some with their foals, all which had been driven in, to prevent their being stolen. This nation, consisting of 400 tents, is said to possess between 9,000 and 10,000 horses, some of which are very fine. The dogs were partly taken into the tents, and we were less exposed to their attacks than in the day time, yet still we had to fight our way through them. The interior of the tent itself had a striking effect. A small fire in the centre gave sufficient light; the chief sat opposite the entrance, and round him many fine tall men, placed according to their rank, all with no other covering than a breech-cloth. Places were assigned to us on buffalo hides near the chief, who then lighted his Sioux pipe, which had a long flat tube, ornamented with bright yellow nails, made each of us take a few puffs, holding the pipe in his hand, and then passed it round to the left hand. After Charbonneau had continued the conversation for some time in the Minnetaree language, we suddenly rose and retired, according to the Indian customs.

The Crows are a wandering tribe of hunters, who neither dwell in fixed villages, like the Mandans, Minnetarees, and Arikaras, nor make any plantations except of tobacco, which, however, are very small. About six years ago, the Crows are said to have had only 1,000 warriors, at present they are reckoned at 1,200. They roam about with their leather tents, hunt the buffalo, and other wild animals, and have many horses and dogs, which, however, they never use for food. They are said to possess more horses than any other tribe of the Missouri, and to send them in the winter to Wind River [in the Rockies], to feed on a certain shrub, which soon fattens them. The Crow women are very skillful in various kinds of work, and their shirts and dresses of bighorn leather, embroidered and ornamented with dyed porcupine quills, are particularly handsome, as well as their buffalo robes, which are painted and embroidered in the same manner. The men make their weapons very well, and with much taste, especially their large bows, covered with the horn of the elk or bighorn, and often with the skin of the rattle-snake.

In stature and dress these Indians correspond, on the whole, with the Minnetarees, both having been originally one and the same people, as the affinity of their languages proves. Long hair is considered as a great beauty, and they take great pains with it. The hair of one of their chiefs, called Long Hair, was ten feet long, some feet of which trailed on the ground when he stood upright. The enemies of the Crows are the Cheyennes, the Blackfeet, and the Sioux; their allies are the Mandans and Minnetarees. With the latter they bartered their good horses for European goods, but the American Fur Company has now established a separate trading post for them on the Yellowstone River, which is called Fort Cass.

Though the Crows look down with contempt upon the Whites, they treat them very hospitably in their tents, yet their pride is singularly contrasted with a great propensity to stealing and begging, which makes them very troublesome. They are said to have many more superstitious notions than the Mandans, Minnetarees, and Arikaras; for instance, they never smoke a pipe when a pair of shoes is hung up in their tent; when the pipe circulates none ever takes more than three puffs, and then passes it in a certain manner to his left-hand neighbour. They are skilful horsemen, and, in their attacks on horseback, are said to throw themselves off on one side, as is done by many Asiatic tribes. They have many bardaches [homosexuals] among them, and exceed all the other tribes in unnatural practices.

As among all the Missouri Indians, the Crows are divided into different bands or unions. A certain price is paid for admission into these unions and their dances, of which each has one peculiar to itself, like the other Missouri tribes; on which occasion the women are given up to the will of the seller in the same manner, as will be more particularly mentioned when speaking of the other tribes. Of the female sex, it is said of the Crows, that they, with the women of the Arikaras, are the most dissolute of all the tribes of the Missouri.

## June 19, 1833

The *Assiniboin* left Fort Clark, with a high, cold wind, and clouded sky; the thermometer, at nine in the morning, being at 60½°. The chiefs, and other Indians, had come on board, and also Kiasax, a Blackfoot Indian, who wished to return to his own people. The country, on the south bank, appeared to us to have some resemblance with many parts on the banks of the Rhine; but, on the right bank, there soon appeared those singular hills, resembling fortifications. At ten o'clock, we came to Ruhptare, the second Mandan village, on the south bank, which is situated in a plain a little higher than the river. All the inhabitants, in their buffalo dresses, were collected on the bank, and some had taken their station on the tops of their huts to have a better view: the whole prairie was covered with people, Indians on horseback, and horses grazing. In the low willow thickets on the bank, the brown, naked children were running about; all the men had fans of eagles' feathers in their hands. The village was surrounded with a fence of palisades; and, with its spherical clay huts, looked like a New Zealand Hippah. Here, too, there were high poles near the village, on which skins and other things were hung, as offerings to the lord of life, or the sun, and numerous stages for the dead were scattered about the prairie. As we proceeded, the whole population accompanied us along the steep bank on foot and on horseback, followed by many of their large wolf dogs.

[*Farther upstream*], the south bank of the river was animated by a crowd of Indians, both on foot and on horseback; they were the Minnetarees, who had flocked from their three villages to see the steamer and to welcome us. The appearance of this vessel of the Company is an event of the greatest importance to the Indians; they then come from considerable distances to see this hissing machine, which they look upon as one of the most wonderful medicines (charms) of the white men. The sight of the red-brown crowd collected on the river side, for even their buffalo skins were mostly of this colour, was, in the highest degree, striking. We already saw above a hundred of them, with many dogs, some of which drew sledges, and others, wooden boards fastened to their backs, and the ends trailing on the ground, to which the baggage was attached with leather straps.

The most attractive sight which we had yet met with upon this voyage, now presented itself to our view. The steam-boat lay to close to the willow thicket, and we saw, immediately before us, the numerous, motley, gaily-painted, and variously ornamented crowd of the most elegant Indians on the whole course of the Missouri. The handsomest and most robust persons, of both sexes and all ages, in highly original, graceful, and characteristic costumes, appeared, thronged together, to our astonished eye; and there was, all at once, so much to see and to observe, that we anxiously profited by every moment to catch only the main features of this unique picture. The Min-

netarees are, in fact, the tallest and best formed Indians on the Missouri, and, in this respect, as well as in the elegance of their costume, the Crows alone approach them, whom they, perhaps, even surpass in the latter particular.

The expression of their remarkable countenances as they gazed at us, was very various; in some, it was cold and disdainful; in others, intense curiosity; in others, again, good-nature and simplicity. The upper parts of their bodies were, in general, naked, and the fine brown skin of their arms adorned with broad, bright bracelets of a white metal. In their hands they carried their musket, bow, and battle-axe; their quivers, of otter skin, elegantly decorated, were slung over their backs; their leggins were trimmed with tufts of the hair of the enemies whom they had killed, with dyed horse-hair of different colours, and with a profusion of leather fringe, and beautifully embroidered with stripes of dyed porcupine quills, or glass beads, of the most brilliant colours.

Several tall, athletic men were on horseback, and managed their horses, which were frightened by the noise of the steam-boat, with an ease which afforded us pleasure. Urging them with their short whips in the manner of the Cossacks, with the bridle fastened to the lower jaw, they, at length, pushed the spirited animals through the willow thicket, till they reached the river, where these fine bold horsemen, resembling the Circassians, with their red-painted countenances, were regarded with great admiration. Many of them wore the large valuable necklace, made of long bears' claws, and their handsomely-painted buffalo robe was fastened round the waist by a girdle.

Among the young women we observed some who were very pretty, the white of whose sparkling hazel eyes formed a striking contrast with the vermilion faces. I regret that it is impossible, by any description, to give the reader a distinct idea of such a scene, and there was not sufficient time for Mr. Bodmer to make a drawing of it.

The chiefs of the Minnetarees came on board for a short time; among them were old Addih-Hiddisch (the road maker), Pehriska-Ruhpa (the two ravens), Lachpitzi-Sihrish (the yellow bear), and several others, and with them the Blackfoot Kiasax, in his best dress, who was to make the voyage along with us. He was accompanied by his Minnetaree wife, who carried a little child, wrapped in a piece of leather, fastened with straps. She wept much at parting from her husband, and the farewell scene was very interesting. While this was going on, an Indian, on the shore, was employed in keeping off the crowd with a long willow rod, which he laid about the women and children with a right hearty good will, when, by their curiosity, they hindered our *engagés* and crew in loosening the vessel from the shore. The vessel, however, was ready to start; Mr. Kipp, Charbonneau, the interpreter, and the Minnetaree chiefs, took leave, and hastened to land, on which the *Assiniboin* proceeded rapidly up the Missouri.

The Indians followed us, for a time, along the bank; about thirty of them formed an interesting group on horseback, two sometimes sitting on the same beast. As the willow thickets on the banks ceased, we had a good view of the prairie, where many Indian horsemen were galloping about; herds of horses fled from the noise of the vessel. The friends and relations of Kiasax and Matsokui—for we had taken another Blackfoot on board—followed the vessel longer than any of the others; they frequently called to them, and nodded farewell, to which Kiasax answered with a long wooden pipe, upon which he played a wretched piece of music.

## June 21, 1833

In the morning, we found that the river had risen considerably and brought down trunks of trees, branches &c., which covered the surface, and gave our vessel some violent shocks. On the southern bank we came to a green spot at the mouth of the Little Missouri, which is reckoned to be 1,670 miles from the mouth of the Great Missouri. Before noon we reached the territory of the Assiniboins, and were, at this time, at Wild Onion Creek. Kiasax (l'ours gauche—left-handed or awkward bear) had permitted Mr. Bodmer to take his portrait, without making any objection, whereas Matsokui (beautiful hair) was not to be persuaded to do so, affirming that he must then infallibly die. As it turned out, he was to die, and Kiasax to return, unhurt by the enemy. The latter had adopted the costume of the Minnetarees, but at the same time wrapped himself in a Spanish blanket, striped blue, white, and black, which, as well as a metal cross, which he wore suspended round his neck, was a proof of the intercourse between the Blackfoot Indians and the Spaniards near the Rocky Mountains. [*For Kiasax's portrait, see page 65.*] These two Indians appeared to be very quiet, obliging men. Thus, for instance, they never returned from an excursion on shore, without bringing me some handfulls of plants, often, it is true, only

common grass, because they had observed that we always brought plants home with us.

## June 22, 1833

About ten o'clock we had an alarm of fire on board: the upper deck had been set on fire by the iron pipe of the chimney of the great cabin. We immediately lay to, and, by breaking up the deck, the danger was soon over, which, however, was not inconsiderable, as we had many barrels of powder on board. We had scarcely got over this trouble, when another arose; the current of the swollen river was so strong, that we long contended against it to no purpose, in order to turn a certain point of land, while, at the same time, the high west wind was against us, and both together threw the vessel back three times on the south coast. The first shock was so violent, that the lower deck gallery was broken to pieces. Our second attempt succeeded no better; part of the paddle-box was broken, and carried away by the current. We were now obliged to land forty men to tow the vessel, for which purpose all on board voluntarily offered their services; even the two Blackfeet overcame their natural laziness. Beyond this dangerous place, we took on board the hunters whom we had sent out. They were covered from head to foot with blood, and hung about with game, having killed two elks. The effect of the current and the wind upon our vessel continued for a long time. It was often thrown against the alluvial bank, so that the deck was covered with earth, and the track of our vessel clearly marked along the sand bank.

In the afternoon we saw in the prairie of the north bank a large grizzly bear, and immediately sent Ortubize and another hunter in pursuit of him, but to no purpose. Soon after, we saw two other bears, one of a whitish, the other of a dark colour, and our hunters, when they returned, affirmed that they had wounded the largest. Harvey had shot an elk, and brought the best part of it from a great distance, and with considerable exertion, to the river. From this place upwards, the grey bear became more and more common; further down the river it is still rare.

## June 23, 1833

On our further progress up the river, we saw, for the first time, the animal known by the name of the bighorn, or the

Rocky Mountain sheep, the *Ovis montana* of the zoologists. A ram and two sheep of this species stood on the summit of the highest hill, and, after looking at our steamer, slowly retired. These animals are not frequent hereabouts, but we afterwards met with them in great numbers.

### June 24, 1833

Following the numerous windings of the Missouri, from one chain of hills to another, we reached, at seven o'clock in the evening, the mouth of the Yellowstone, a fine river, hardly inferior in breadth to the Missouri at this part. A little further on lay Fort Union, on a verdant plain, with the handsome American flag, gilded by the last rays of evening, floating in

Reaching Fort Clark on June 18, the travelers encountered a band of Crow Indians, some of whom Bodmer hastened to sketch.

the azure sky, while horses animated the peaceful scene.

As the steamer approached, the cannon of Fort Union fired a salute, with a running fire of musketry, to bid us welcome, which was answered in a similar manner by our vesel. When we reached the fort, we were received by Mr. Hamilton, an Englishman, who, during the absence of Mr. Mc Kenzie, had performed the functions of director, as well as by several clerks of the Company, and a number of their servants (*engagés* or *voyageurs*), of many different nations, Americans, Englishmen, Germans, Frenchmen, Russians, Spaniards, and Italians, about 100 in number, with many Indians, and half-breed women and children. It was the seventy-fifth day since our departure from St. Louis, when the *Assiniboin* cast anchor at Fort Union.

The first stages of Maximilian's upstream voyage consisted primarily of a struggle against the snags and sandbars of the Missouri. Game and Indians were scarce, and it was not until the party reached the Sioux Agency at Fort Lookout on May 26 that Bodmer got down to the serious business of painting the detailed ethnographic Indian studies that Maximilian desired. Even then his time was severely limited, as the steamboats pressed urgently forward in order to deliver their goods to the upriver posts in time for the annual trading sessions. At Fort Clark, where the *Assiniboin* was welcomed on June 18 by hundreds of Mandans and Minnetarees dressed in their finest ceremonial attire, the party paused only overnight before continuing the voyage to Fort Union. Not until November, on the downstream voyage, would Bodmer have the opportunity to paint these two tribes that Maximilian found to be the most interesting of all Plains Indians.

---

*Opposite:* Struggling upstream on April 25, Maximilian noted that ". . . we met with many difficulties, so that we were even obliged to back for some distance." Bodmer's watercolor indicates the nature of the "difficulties." *Overleaf:* Skirting a sandbar in an open channel along the western bank of the Missouri in this detail from a watercolor made on May 15, the *Yellowstone* is shown passing under a chain of high hills that Maximilian described as "rising one above the other; some covered with verdure, some of a yellowish colour, mostly without life and variety."

On May 3 the *Yellowstone* reached Bellevue, a few miles above the mouth of the Platte River at the present-day site of Omaha, where Major John Dougherty maintained his government agency for the Otos, Pawnees, and Omahas. *Opposite:* Wahktageli (the gallant warrior), called Big Soldier by the whites. Bodmer painted this portrait of one of the principal men of the Yankton Sioux on May 26 at Fort Lookout, the Sioux Agency. Big Soldier posed patiently in his ceremonial attire exquisitely ornamented with dyed porcupine quills and the hair of a Mandan scalp he had taken, pausing now and then to smoke the pipe tomahawk that he holds in his hand. Major Bean, the Sioux agent, later made Maximilian a present of this costume. *Overleaf, left:* Tukan-Haton (the horned toad), a Sioux chief who was also known as Little Soldier, boarded the steamboat with his family on May 27 for the trip from Fort Lookout to Fort Pierre. As he was in mourning, his only adornment was his tattoos. *Overleaf, right:* Chan-Cha-Nia-Teuin, a woman of the Teton Sioux, whom Bodmer painted on June 1 at Fort Pierre. She valued her leather dress too highly for Maximilian's purse, but he did succeed in buying her buffalo robe.

Fort Union, bastion of the American Fur Company's trading operations on the Upper Missouri, as seen from the north.

PART II

# Sojourn at Fort Union

## June 24-July 6, 1833

Assiniboins sketched during the upstream sojourn at Fort Union.

Fort Union, located some 1,800 miles upstream from St. Louis, a bit west of what is now Williston, North Dakota, at the Montana border, was the principal trading post and upriver supply depot of the American Fur Company. From this wilderness stronghold Kenneth McKenzie directed the Company's operations in the imperious style that had earned him the sobriquet "King of the Missouri." Although Maximilian did not seem overly impressed, McKenzie did himself pretty well, at least during the summer months, considering the remoteness of his post. The leading Company men decked their Indian wives in St. Louis fashions, dressed formally for dinner themselves, and laid a bounteous table for their guests. There was milk, butter, and cheese from the dairy herd, all kinds of game and fowl, and beef and mutton as well. Brandies and imported wines flowed freely on social occasions. Life in the wilderness had its compensations, provided one belonged to the ruling elite. Maximilian had no more than set foot ashore before he began setting down a history and description of the fort and the Assiniboin Indians in whose territory it was located:

June 24, 1833

The erection of Fort Union was commenced in the autumn of 1829, by Mr. Mc Kenzie, and is now completed, except that some of the edifices which were erected in haste are under repair. The fort is situated on an alluvial eminence, on the northern bank of the Missouri, in a prairie, which extends about 1,500 paces to a chain of hills, on whose summit there are other wide-spreading plains. The river runs at a distance of scarcely fifty or sixty feet from the fort, in the direction from west to east; it is here rather broad, and the opposite bank is wooded. The fort itself forms a quadrangle, the sides of which measure about eighty paces in length, on the exterior. The ramparts consist of strong pickets, sixteen or seventeen feet high, squared, and placed close to each other. On the south-west and north-east ends, there are block-houses, with pointed roofs, two stories high, with embrasures and cannon, which, though small, are fit for service.

In the front of the enclosure, and towards the river, is the well-defended principal entrance, with a large folding gate. Opposite the entrance, on the other side of the quadrangle, is the house of the commandant; it is one story high, and has four handsome glass windows on each side of the door. The roof is spacious, and contains a large, light loft. This house is very commodious, and, like all the buildings of the inner quadrangle, constructed of poplar wood, the staple wood for building in this neighbourhood. In the inner quadrangle are the residences of the clerks, the interpreters, and the *engagés*, the powder magazine, the stores, or supplies of goods and bartered skins, various workshops for the handicraftsmen, smiths, carpenters, &c., stables for the horses and cattle, rooms for receiving and entertaining the Indians; and in the centre is the flag-staff, around which several half-breed Indian hunters had erected their leathern tents. A cannon was also placed here, with its mouth towards the principal entrance. The fort contains about fifty or sixty horses, some mules, and an inconsiderable number of cattle, swine, goats, fowls, and domestic animals. The cattle are very fine, and the cows yield abundance of milk. The horses are driven, in the day time, into the prairie, guarded and exercised by armed men, and, in the evening, brought back into the quadrangle of the fort, where the greater part of them pass the night in the open air. Mr. Mc Kenzie has, however, lately had a separate place, or park, provided for them.

Fort Union is one of the principal posts of the fur company, because it is the central point of the two other trading stations, still higher up, towards the Rocky Mountains, and having the superintendence of the whole of the trade in the interior, and in the vicinity of the mountains. One of these two trading stations, called Fort Cass, is 200 miles up the Yellowstone River, and is confined to the trade with the Crow tribe; the other, Fort Piegan, or, as it is now called, Fort Mc Kenzie, is 650 miles up the Missouri, or about a day's journey from the falls of this river, and carries on the fur trade with the three tribes of the Blackfoot Indians. The latter station has been established about two years, and, as the steamers cannot often go up to Fort Union, they dispatch keel-boats, to supply the various trading posts with goods for barter with the Indians. They then pass the winter at these stations, and in the spring carry the furs to Fort Union, whence they are transported, during the summer, to St. Louis, by the steamers. The Company maintains a number of agents at these differ-

ent stations; during their stay they marry Indian women, but leave them, without scruple, when they are removed to another station, or are recalled to the United States. The lower class of these agents, who are called *engagés* or *voyageurs,* have to act as steersmen, rowers, hunters, traders, &c., according to their several capabilities. They are often sent great distances, employed in perilous undertakings among the Indians, and are obliged to fight against the enemy, and many of them are killed every year by the arms with which the Whites themselves have furnished the Indians. Some of the agents of the fur company winter every year in the Rocky Mountains.

Wild beasts and other animals, whose skins are valuable in the fur trade, have already diminished greatly in number along this river, and it is said that, in another ten years, the fur trade will be very inconsiderable. As the supplies along the banks of the Missouri decreased, the Company gradually extended the circle of their trading posts, as well as enterprises, and thus increased their income. Above 500 of their agents are in the forts of the Upper Missouri, and at their various trading posts; and, besides these individuals, who receive considerable salaries (for it is said that the Company yearly expend 150,000 dollars in salaries), there are in these prairies, and the forests of the Rocky Mountains, beaver and fur trappers, who live at their own cost; but whose present wants, such as horses, guns, powder, ball, woollen clothes, articles of clothing, tobacco, &c. &c., are supplied by the Company, and the scores settled, after the hunting season is over, by the furs which they deliver at the different trading posts. Many of these, when not employed in hunting, live at the Company's forts. They are, for the most part, enterprising, robust men, capital riflemen, and, from their rude course of life, are able to endure the greatest hardships.

During the summer the Company send out, under the direction of an experienced clerk, a number of strong, well-armed, mounted men, who convey the necessary goods and supplies, on pack-horses, to the trading stations, at a distance from the river; they always observe and enforce the required conditions of the Indians, and not unfrequently come to blows with them. These expeditions have to support themselves by the chase, consequently the men must be good hunters, as they subsist almost exclusively on what they procure by their guns. Besides the forts which I have so often named, the Company has also small winter posts, called log-houses, or block-houses, among the Indians, quickly erected, and as quickly abandoned. To these the Indians bring their furs, which are purchased, and sent, in the spring, to the trading posts. The American Fur Company has, at present, about twenty-three, large and small, trading posts. In the autumn and winter the Indian tribes generally approach nearer to these posts, to barter their skins; while in the spring and summer they devote themselves especially to catching beavers, for which they receive every encouragement from the merchants, who lend or advance them iron traps for the purpose.

The animals, whose skins are objects of this trade, and the annual average of the income derived from skins, may be pretty well ascertained from the following statement:

1. Beavers: about 25,000 skins. They are sold in packs of 100 lbs. weight each, put up separately, and tied together. There are, generally, about sixty large skins in a pack; if they are smaller, of course there are more skins. A large beaver skin weighs about two pounds—sometimes more. The usual price is four dollars a pound.
2. Otters: 200 to 300 skins.
3. Buffalo cow skins: 40,000 to 50,000. Ten buffalo hides go to the pack.
4. Canadian weasel: 500 to 600.
5. Martin (pine or beech martin): about the same quantity.
6. Lynx: the northern lynx: 1,000 to 2,000.
7. Lynx: the southern or wild cat: 1,000 to 2,000.
8. Red foxes: 2,000.
9. Cross foxes: 200 to 300.
10. Silver foxes: 20 to 30. Sixty dollars are often paid for a single skin.
11. Minks: 2,000.
12. Musk-rats: from 1,000 to 100,000. (At Rock River, which falls into the Mississippi, the Indians caught, in 1825, about 130,000 musk-rats; in the following year about half that number; and, in about two years after, these animals were scarcely to be met with.)
13. Deer (*Cervus Virginianus* and *macrotis*): from 20,000 to 30,000.

Below Council Bluffs, scarcely any articles are bartered by the Indians—especially the Iowas, Kansas, and the Osages —except the skins of the *Cervus Virginianus,* which is found in great abundance, but is said to have fallen off there likewise very considerably.

The elk is not properly comprehended in the trade, as its skin is too thick and heavy, and is, therefore, used for home consumption. The buffalo skin is taken, as before observed, from the cows only, as the leather of the bulls is too heavy. The wolf skins are not at all sought by the company, that is to say, they do not send out any hunters to procure them; but, if the Indians bring any, they are bought, not to create any dissatisfaction, and then they are sold at about a dollar a-piece. The Indians, however, have frequently nothing to offer for barter but their dresses, and painted buffalo robes.

The support of so large an establishment as that at Fort Union requires frequent excursions into the prairie; and Mr. Mc Kenzie, therefore, maintained here several experienced hunters of a mixed race, who made weekly excursions to the distance of twenty or more miles into the prairie, sought the buffalo. herds, and, after they had killed a sufficient number, returned home with their mules well laden. The flesh of the cows is very good, especially the tongues, which are smoked in great numbers, and then sent down to St. Louis. The colossal marrow-bones are considered quite a delicacy by the hunters and by the Indians. The consumption of this animal is immense in North America, and is as indispensable to the Indians as the reindeer is to the Laplanders, and the seal to the Esquimaux.

It is difficult to obtain an exact estimate of the consumption of this animal, which is yearly decreasing and driven further inland. In a recent year, the fur company sent 42,000 of these hides down the river, which were sold, in the United States, at four dollars a-piece. Fort Union alone consumes about 600 to 800 buffaloes annually, and the other forts in proportion. The numerous Indian tribes subsist almost entirely on these animals, sell their skins after retaining a sufficient supply for their clothing, tents, &c., and the agents of the Company recklessly shoot down these noble animals for their own pleasure, often not making the least use of them, except taking out the tongue. Whole herds of them are often drowned in the Missouri; nay, I have been assured that, in some rivers, 1,800 and more of their dead bodies were found in one place. Complete dams are formed of the bodies of these animals in some of the morasses of the rivers; from this we may form some idea of the decrease of the buffaloes, which are now found on

A solemn young Assiniboin warrior posed proudly for this water-color portrait at Fort Union on June 29.

the other side of the Rocky Mountains, where they were not originally met with, but whither they have been driven.

Besides the buffalo, the hunters also shoot the elk, the deer, and, occasionally, the bighorn. The former especially are very numerous on the Yellowstone River. All other provisions, such as pork, hams, flour, sugar, coffee, wine, and other articles of luxury for the tables of the chief officers and the clerks, are sent from St. Louis by the steamer. The maize is procured from the neighbouring Indian nations. Vegetables do not thrive at Fort Union, which Mr. Mc Kenzie ascribes to the long-continued drought and high winds.

The climate about Fort Union is very changeable. We had often 76° Fahrenheit, and storms of thunder and lightning alternating with heavy rains. Other days in the month of June were cold, the thermometer falling to 56°. Winds prevail here the greater part of the year, and therefore the temperature is usually dry. The weather, while we were there, was uncommonly rainy. Spring is generally the wettest season; the summer is dry; autumn the finest time of the year; the winter is severe, and often of long continuance. The snow is often three, four, or six feet deep in many places, and the dog sledges are used, and the Indians wear snow shoes. In general, however, the climate is said to be very healthy. There are no endemic disorders, and the fine water of the Missouri, which, notwithstanding the sand mixed with it, is light and cold, does not a little contribute to make the inhabitants attain an advanced age. There are no physicians here, and the people affirm they have no need of them. Persons, whom we questioned on the subject, said, "We don't want doctors; we have no diseases." In the preceding spring, however, there had been more sickness than usual on the Missouri, and at the time of our visit, the approach of the cholera was feared. Colds are, probably, the most frequent complaints, the changes in the temperature being sudden, the dwellings slight and ill built, and the people exposing themselves without any precaution.

Fort Union is built in the territory of the Assiniboins, of whom a certain number generally live there. At this time they had left, because the herds of buffaloes were gone to a distant part of the country. The Assiniboins are real Dakotas, or Sioux, and form a branch which separated from the rest a considerable time ago, in consequence of a quarrel among them. They still call themselves by that name, though they seem generally to pronounce it Nakota. They parted from

the rest of the tribe, after a battle which they had with each other on Devils Lake, and removed further to the north. The tribe is said to consist of 28,000 souls, of whom 7,000 are warriors. They live in 3,000 tents; the territory which they claim as theirs, is between the Missouri and the Saskatchewan, bounded by Lake Winnipeg on the north, extending, on the east, to Assiniboine River, and, on the west, to Milk River. The English and Americans sometimes call them Stone Indians, which, however, properly speaking, is the name of only one branch.

Most of the Assiniboins have guns, the stocks of which they ornament with bright yellow nails, and with small pieces of red cloth on the ferrels for the ramrod. These are the common Mackinaw guns, which the fur company obtain from England at the rate of eight dollars a-piece, and which are sold to the Indians for the value of thirty dollars. Like all the Indians, they carry, besides, a separate ramrod in their hand, a large powder-horn, which they obtain from the fur company, and a leather pouch for the balls, which is made by themselves, and often neatly ornamented, or hung with rattling pieces of lead, and trimmed with coloured cloth. All have bows and arrows; many have these only, and no gun. The case for the bow and quiver are of the skin of some animal, often of the otter, fastened to each other; and to the latter the tail of the animal, at full length, is appended. The bow is partly covered with elk horn, has a very strong string of twisted sinews of animals, and is wound round in different places with the same, to strengthen it. The bow is often adorned with coloured cloth, porcupine quills, and white strips of ermine, but, on the whole, this weapon does not differ from that of the Sioux. Most of them carry clubs in their hands, of various shapes, and the fan of eagles' or swans' wings is indispensable to an elegant dandy.

The Assiniboins being hunters, live in movable leather tents, with which they roam about, and never cultivate the ground. Their chief subsistence they derive from the herds of buffaloes, which they follow in the summer, generally from the rivers, to a distance in the prairie; in the winter, to the woods on the banks of the rivers, because these herds, at that time, seek for shelter and food among the thickets. They are particularly dexterous in making what are called buffalo parks, when a tract is surrounded with scarecrows, made of stones, branches of trees, &c., and the terrified animals are driven into a narrow gorge, in which the hunters lie concealed. There was such a park ten miles from Fort Union, where I was told there were great numbers of the bones of those animals. On such occasions the Indians sometimes kill 700 or 800 buffaloes. Of the dried and powdered flesh, mixed with tallow, the women prepare the well-known pemmican, which is an important article of food for these people in their wanderings. These Indians frequently suffer hunger, when the chase or other circumstances are unfavourable; this is particularly the case of the northern nations, the Crees, the Assiniboins, the Chippewas, and others. In the north, entire families perish from hunger. They eat every kind of animals, except serpents; horses and dogs are very frequently killed for food, which is the reason why they keep so many, particularly of the latter.

In comparison with the other nations, the Assiniboins have not many horses; their bridles and saddles are like those of the Minnetarees. The rope of buffalo hair, which is fastened to the lower jaw as a bridle, is always very long,

and trails on the grass when the animal is not tied up. Many have large parchment stirrups in the shape of shoes, and all carry a short whip in their hand, generally made of the end of an elk's horn, and gaily ornamented. Their dogs are of great help to the women in their heavy work; and they are loaded with the baggage in the same manner as among the Minnetarees.

In general, the Assiniboins have the customs as well as the superstitious notions of the Sioux. They keep on good terms with the fur company, for their own interest; they are, however, horse stealers, and not to be trusted; and when one meets them alone in the prairie, there is great danger of being robbed.

Many games are in use among the Assiniboins; one of these is a round game, in which one holds in his hand some small stones, of which the others must guess the number, or pay a forfeit. This game is known also to the Blackfeet. Another is

Abundant growths of cacti were encountered in the prairie near Fort Union, to the considerable discomfort of the travelers.

that in which they play with four small bones and four yellow nails, to which one of each sort is added; they are laid upon a flat wooden plate, which is struck, so that they fly up and fall back into the plate, and you gain, or lose, according as they lie together on one side; the stake is often very high.

Among the amusements and festivities are their eating feasts, when the guests must eat everything set before them, if they will not give offence. If one of the guests is not able to eat any more, he gives his neighbour a small wooden stick, and the plate with food, the meaning of which is that he will make him a present of a horse, on the next day, if he will undertake to empty the plate; and the young men do this in order to gain reputation. The Assiniboins are brave in battle, and often very daring. They frequently steal into the villages of the Mandans and Minnetarees, shoot the inhabitants in or near their huts, or steal their horses.

They believe in a creator, or lord of life (Unkan-Tange), and also in an evil spirit (Unkan-Schidja), who torments people with various disorders, against which their sorcerers or physicians (medicine men) use the drum and the rattle (schischikué) to expel the evil spirit. Like the Crees and several other tribes, they believe that thunder is produced by an enormous bird, which some of them pretend to have seen. Some ascribe lightning to the Great Spirit, and believe that he is angry when the storm is violent. They believe that the dead go to a country in the south, where the good and brave find women and buffaloes, while the wicked or cowardly are confined to an island, where they are destitute of all the pleasures of life. Those who, during their lives, have conducted themselves bravely, are not to be deposited in trees when they die, but their corpses are to be laid on the ground, it being taken for granted that, in case of need, they will help themselves. Of course they are generally devoured by the wolves, to secure them from which, however, they are covered with wood and stones. Other corpses are usually placed on trees, as among the Sioux, and sometimes on scaffolds. They are tied up in buffalo hides, and three or four are sometimes laid in one tree.

The language of the Assiniboins is, on the whole, the same as that of the Sioux, altered by their long separation, and the influence of time and circumstances. Like them, they have many gutturals and nasal tones; in general, however, it is an harmonious language, which a German pronounces without difficulty.

---

Noapeh (a troop of soldiers) was painted on June 27.

Mr. McKenzie had given us a comfortable lodging in his house, and we lived here very pleasantly, in a plain style, suitable to the resources of so remote a place; for we could not hope to meet with so good a table as we had had on board the steamer. We had, every day, fresh or dried buffalo flesh, bread made of flour, and also a good supply of coffee and wine. The first days passed rapidly in examining the fort and the immediate environs, while, on board the steamer, they began already to unload and convey the provisions and goods to the fort, so that all was bustle and activity. Eight hundred packs of buffalo hides, each consisting of ten, were immediately embarked, amid a heavy fall of rain, which did much injury to these hides, which are tanned by the Indians. It was, therefore, necessary to open every one of the packs, and dry them again. The furs in the interior of North America are free from a nuisance so common among us, I mean insects, especially moths, which are unknown on the Upper Missouri. Besides the buffalo hides, many beaver, bear, wolf, lynx, fox, and other skins were embarked. Of the wolf and lynx, sixty-two packs, each consisting of 100 skins.

Some of the Indians were very troublesome while this was doing, continually asking and begging for various things, particularly tobacco, which they were too indolent to prepare, or to get from the forest for themselves. The tobacco which the fur company sells to them, to mix with their leaves or bark, is strong, clammy, and black, and is in twists, six or eight inches long. Most of the Indians now present looked wretchedly poor, and many of them had not even a pipe of their own. Several apartments in the fort were assigned to these visitors, where they cooked and slept.

After we had made ourselves acquainted with the fort, we made excursions into the prairie, especially to the chain of hills, and Mr. Bodmer took many views of the country. In all such excursions it is not usual to go alone, at least not without being well armed, because the Indians, especially war parties, can never be trusted.

JUNE 26, 1833

The *Assiniboin* having taken in its cargo, was to depart in the afternoon, and return to St. Louis; the company, therefore, assembled once more on board, to dine together. About three o'clock, when the whole population of the place was assembled on the beach, we took leave of our travelling companions, Messrs. Sanford and Pratte, with whom some of the Company's clerks had embarked to return to the United States. In order to turn, the *Assiniboin* first went a little way up the river, and then passed the fort with the rapidity of an arrow, while a mutual salute of a discharge of cannon and musketry was re-echoed from the mountains, and handkerchiefs were waved till a bend of the river hid the vessel, which we had so long inhabited, from our view. On this day the Assiniboins had left the fort to go into the prairie; others, in part much better dressed, had arrived, but only as harbingers of a great number of their people, and of Crees, who, in fact, came on the 27th of June, singly, and in companies.

JUNE 27, 1833

The Crees did not much differ, in appearance, from the Assiniboins; they are robust, powerful-looking men, with lank hair falling over their shoulders, and a broad flat lock, cut off straight over their eyes; one man, however, had it hanging down to his mouth. Some had their long hair plaited in several tails; many wore skin caps adorned with feathers, and one had the whole tail of a prairie hen; several of them wore the leather cases of their bows wound round their heads, like a turban. Their faces were painted red, some with black stripes, and their dress was like that of the Assiniboins. Several of them wore long wolf skins over their shoulders, with the head of the animal on the breast, and the tail trailing on the ground. Their leggins had a quantity of long leather fringe; the men are said to be often much tattooed.

The chief of the Crees was Maschkepiton (the broken arm), who had a medal with the effigy of the President hung round his neck, which he had received on a visit to Washington. The present intention of these people, who had no skins to sell, was to welcome Mr. McKenzie, who is much beloved by the Indians, and frequently receives presents from them; and, on many occasions, they have carried him about, as in triumph, to do him honour, and prove their attachment to him. The Crees live in the same territory as the Assiniboins, that is, between the Saskatchewan, the Assiniboine, and the Missouri. They ramble about in small bands with the others, are poor, have many dogs, which carry their baggage, but only a few horses. They live, like the Assiniboins, in leather tents, and follow the herds of buffaloes, of which they sometimes kill great numbers in their parks. The Crees are reckoned at 600 or 800 tents; consequently, assuming the usual number of three men for each, there will be from 1,800 to 2,400 men for this tribe. Their customs, games, and religious opinions, are said to agree with those of the Assiniboins. Their language has an affinity with that of the Ojibways, but entirely different from that of the Assiniboins, or Sioux, though many of the Crees learn the latter.

In the early afternoon, the arrival of a numerous band of Assiniboins was announced to us by several messengers; they intended to compliment Mr. Mc Kenzie, who had long been absent. All on a sudden we heard some musket-shot, which announced a very interesting scene; and all the inhabitants of the fort went out of the gate to witness the arrival of this savage horde. Towards the north-west, the whole prairie was covered with scattered Indians, whose numerous dogs drew the sledges with the baggage; a close body of warriors, about 250 or 300 in number, had formed themselves in the centre, in the manner of two bodies of infantry, and advanced in quick time towards the fort. The Indian warriors marched in close ranks, three or four men deep, not keeping their file very regularly, yet in pretty good order, and formed a considerable line. Before the centre, where, in a European battalion, the colours are carried, three or four chiefs advanced, arm in arm, and from the ranks of this motley, martial, painted mass, loud musket-shot were heard. The whole troop of these warriors now commenced their original song, consisting of many abrupt, broken tones, like those of the war-whoop, and having some resemblance to the song which we heard, in the years 1813 and 1814, from the Russian soldiers. The loaded dogs, guided by women and children, surrounded the nucleus of warriors, like the sharp-shooters that hover about the line. Thus this remarkable body advanced towards us, and many interesting features appeared the nearer they approached.

All these Indians were wrapped in their buffalo robes, and dressed out in the most diverse and highly fantastical manner. Most of them had their faces painted all over with vermilion; others, quite black. In their hair they wore the feathers of eagles, or other birds of prey. Some had wolf-skin caps, notwithstanding the great heat, and these caps were partly smeared with red paint. Others had fastened green leaves round their heads; long wolves' tails were hanging down at their heels, as marks of honour for enemies they had killed, and the part of their dress made of leather was new and

handsome. They had their guns in their arms, their bows and arrows on their shoulders, and, in this manner, these robust men, who were, for the most part, five feet eight or nine inches, and many six feet high, advanced with a light, quick step, in an upright posture, which gave them a perfectly military air; and this impression was heightened by the song which sounded from their ranks, and the loud beating of their drums. They advanced to within about sixty paces, then halted at a fosse running from the Missouri past the fort, and waited, the chief standing in front, for our welcome.

Mr. Mc Kenzie had sent two interpreters, Halero and Lafontaine, to meet them, who shook hands with the chiefs, and then led them to the gate of the fort, which was shut as usual, and a guard set before it, for too many Indians are never admitted at the same time, because they can never be implicitly trusted. On this occasion, only the chiefs and about thirty of the principal warriors were admitted, who sat down around the apartment which was allotted to such meetings. All the other Indians went first to the Missouri to drink, and then sat down to rest in the shade.

It was natural that we, as strangers, constantly remained with the assembled Indians, for there were many interesting subjects for our observation. The thick stone pipes, with long flat tubes, were handed round, and they showed us a remarkably handsome one, ornamented with yellow horsehair, which was intended as a present for Mr. Mc Kenzie. The whole company received something to drink; and many Indians, before they raise the vessel to their lips, dip the fore finger of their right hand into it, and sprinkle some of the liquid five or six times in the air, doubtless as an offering to the higher powers. They gazed on us with much curiosity, and the interpreter gave them an account of the singular strangers, who hunted after animals, plants, and stones, and prepared the skins of the former, of which they, of course, could not see the use.

While tranquillity was gradually restored within the fort, a new and very interesting scene took place without. On the west side of the fort the Indian women were engaged in erecting temporary travelling or hunting huts, composed of poles, fixed in the ground, and the dog sledges set up against them, and covered with green boughs, as they had brought only a part of their baggage. Horses were everywhere grazing, dogs running in all directions, and groups of the red men dispersed all round. The scene was highly entertaining; and the various occupations of cooking, gaming, and making preliminary arrangements, diffused life and activity over the prairie. I was particularly struck with one Assiniboin on account of his head-dress, which I frequently saw afterwards, and the interpreter called him to us. He wore, across his head, a leather strap, to each side of which a horn was fixed, and between them, black feathers cut short. The horns, which were cut out of those of an antelope, had, at their point, a tuft of horse-hair dyed yellow, and on the side hung leather strings, with feathers at the end, and bound with yellow porcupine quills. Mr. Bodmer made a very faithful drawing of this man, as he wished to be taken in his full dress. His name was Noapeh (a troop of soldiers), and his countenance and whole figure were characteristically Indian.

We visited several of the newly erected huts, where the fire was already burning in the centre; we were everywhere asked for whiskey and tobacco, of which only the last was here and there given. If we wished to obtain anything by barter, brandy was always demanded in payment, and, therefore, very little could be done. Late in the evening, the singing and the drum of this restless multitude were heard in the fort, and the noise and tumult continued the whole night.

### June 28, 1833

We were early in motion, that we might lose no part of the new scenes around us. Noapeh was brought at an early hour, and stood with unwearied patience to the painter, though his relations frequently endeavoured to get him away. He had put on his best dress, and had, on his breast, a rosette of dyed porcupine quills, eight or ten inches in diameter.

### June 29, 1833

The expected arrival of more Assiniboins was delayed; they do not willingly travel with their leather tents in wet weather, because their baggage then becomes very heavy; several Indians, however, soon appeared, wet through and through, and covered with mud up to their knees, which, however, they did not mind. A sketch was taken of a tall young warrior, who preserved a most inflexible gravity of countenance till Mr. Bodmer set his musical snuff-box agoing, on which he began to laugh.

Another interesting young man of the branch of the Stone

Assiniboin cradle, made of buffalo hide and slung from lodge poles.

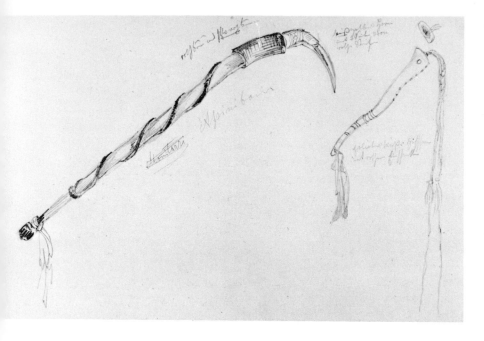

Indians, whose name was Pitatapiu, had his portrait taken. His hair hung down like a lion's mane, especially over his eyes, so that they could scarcely be seen; over each of them a small white sea shell was fastened with a hair string; in his hand he carried a long lance, such as they use only for show, to which a number of slips of the entrails of a bear were fastened, and smeared with red paint. This slender young man had his painted leather shield on his back, to which a small packet, well wrapped up, his medicine or amulet in horse-stealing, was fastened, and which he greatly prized. These people will not part with such things on any terms. The handle of his whip was of wood, with holes in it like a flute. [*See page 67 for Pitatapiu's portrait.*] He and several Indians brought word that his countrymen, from the environs of the Fort des Prairies, on the Saskatchewan River, would shortly visit us, to dispose of all their beaver skins. It made us shiver to see the Indians, in the damp, cold weather, run about barefoot the whole day in the deep mud, while we, in our room, sat constantly by the fire-side. They, too, greatly enjoyed the warm room, and a number of them were always sitting with us, to smoke their pipes, while Mr. Bodmer was drawing Pitatapiu's likeness. We took care that their pipes should be constantly filled, and, in general, tried every means to amuse them, that they might not lose their patience during the operation.

### JUNE 30, 1833

Shortly after noon a band of Assiniboins appeared in the distance. To the west, along the wood by the river side, the prairie was suddenly covered with red men, most of whom went singly, with their dogs drawing the loaded sledges. The warriors, about sixty in number, formed a close column. They came without music, with two chiefs at their head, and proceeded towards the gate of the fort. Among them there were many old men, one, especially, who walked with the support of two sticks, and many who had only one eye. The first chief of this new band was Ayanyan, generally called General Jackson, because he had made a journey to Washington. He was a handsome man, in a fine dress; he wore a beautifully embroidered black leather shirt, a new scarlet blanket, and the great medal round his neck.

The whole column entered the fort, where they smoked, ate, and drank; and, meantime, forty-two tents were set up.

Assiniboin riding implements. At left, a crop, or goad. At right, a quirt with a decorated elkhorn handle.

The new camp had a very pretty appearance; the tents stood in a semicircle, and all the fires were smoking, while all around was life and activity. [*For Bodmer's watercolor of this encampment, see pages 70–71.*] We witnessed many amusing scenes; here, boys shot their arrows into the air; there, a little, brown, monkey-like child was sitting alone upon the ground, with a circle of hungry dogs around it. In one of the tents there was a man very ill, about whom the medicine men were assembled, singing with all their might. Many people had collected about this tent, and were peeping through the crevices. After the conjuration had continued some time, the tent was opened, and the men who had been assembled in it went away by threes, the one in the middle always stepping a little before the others, and they continued singing till they reached their own tents.

## July 1, 1833

In the morning, we heard that Matsokui, the young Blackfoot Indian, who had come here with us, had been shot, during the night, in the Indian camp. Berger, the Blackfoot interpreter, who was charged to have a watchful eye over this young Indian, had frequently warned him to keep away from the Assiniboins and the Crees, or some mischief would certainly befall him; but he had suffered himself to be deceived by their apparently friendly conduct, and had remained in a tent till late at night, where he was shot by a Cree, who had immediately made his escape. We saw the dead body of our poor travelling companion, laced up in a buffalo's skin, lying in the fort, and it was afterwards buried near the fort, in a coffin made by the carpenter. Kiasax had been more prudent; he had not trusted the Assiniboins, and had returned with the steamboat to his family. Mr. Mc Kenzie told us, that he had witnessed a similar incident the year before. A Blackfoot whom he brought with him, was shot by the Crees at their departure, though he had been many times in their camp.

After the perpetration of this deed, a dead silence prevailed in the Indian camp; but about noon, two of the chiefs, attended by other Indians in procession, singing aloud, and among them General Jackson, came as a deputation to make their excuses to Mr. Mc Kenzie for this murder. They brought, by way of present, a horse, and a couple of very beautiful pipes, one of which was a real calumet, adorned with feathers and green horse-hair. They made an address to Mr. McKenzie,

in which they solemnly asserted their innocence of the death of the Blackfoot, saying that the deed had been done by a Cree, who had immediately fled, and whom they had pursued, but in vain. Ayanyan is said to have spoken remarkably well on this occasion.

In the afternoon we again heard the Indian drum beating very loud in the tent of the sick man, and we went there to see their conjurations. We looked cautiously through the crevices in the tent, and saw the patient sitting on the floor, his head, covered with a small cap, sunk upon his breast, and several men standing around him. Two of the medicine men were beating the drum in quick time, and a third rattled the schischikué, which he waved up and down. These people were singing with great effort; sometimes they uttered short ejaculations, and were in a violent perspiration; sometimes they sucked the places where the patient felt pain, and pretended they could suck out or remove the morbid matter. Such jugglers are very well paid by the patients, and always regaled with tobacco. Many of the Indians went away this afternoon, because they could not find sufficient subsistence. Among others, General Jackson had taken leave. It was reported that some of the Crees had said they would take up the body of the Blackfoot that was shot, because there had not been time to scalp him; but such expressions were quite usual, and the grave was not disturbed.

## July 4, 1833

The keel-boat from Fort Cass had arrived, on board of which we were to go to Fort Mc Kenzie. We had, therefore, a numerous company, but we were in no want of provisions, as our hunters had brought home, from their last excursion, the flesh of nineteen buffaloes. It was exactly a year today, July 4th, since we had landed at Boston. Mr. Mc Kenzie sent Berger, the interpreter, and one Harvey, by land, to Fort Mc Kenzie, to which they proceeded on horseback, before us, along the north bank of the river. They had no baggage but their arms, their beds of buffalo skin, and blankets. They took some dried meat with them, but they chiefly depended for subsistence on their rifles. While the people were employed in loading the keel-boat with the goods and provisions for the tribes living higher up the river, we made use of our time for excursions into the neighbouring woods on the river side, and to the prairie.

*Fort Union den 2. Juli 1833.*

Like most of the Company's trading posts, Fort Union was situated on a low, flat prairie suitable for the encampment of large numbers of Indians during the trading sessions. Since buffalo herds seldom ventured close to an inhabited fort, no large body of Indians could sustain itself for long at a trading encampment. Hence, there was a constant coming and going of successive bands of Indians during the late summer, as indicated in this rather faint sketch that Bodmer made on the upstream journey. The view is from the north looking south across the Missouri which flows behind the fort at a distance of some sixty feet from the palisades. This sketch was used to make the aquatint engraving that appears on page 48. Maximilian gives a detailed description of Fort Union in his entry for June 24.

At Fort Union, Maximilian and his party spent nearly two weeks awaiting the arrival of the keelboat *Flora* that was to carry them to Fort McKenzie. During this time large bands of Assiniboins made their successive ceremonial arrivals and set up camp near the fort. With the aid of interpreters, Maximilian was able to interview leading men of the Assiniboins and their allies, the Crees, while Bodmer made his paintings. By the time the *Flora* was ready to sail, the Europeans had been able to satisfy their curiosity about many matters ranging from religious superstition to Indian migratory habits. They also witnessed an example of the sort of endemic treachery that was part of the Plains Indian tradition. As reported at some length in Maximilian's entry for July 1, a young Blackfoot named Matsokui, who had wangled passage upstream on the *Assiniboin* in order to rejoin his tribe at Fort McKenzie, was gratuitously murdered by a Cree.

*Opposite:* Kiasax (the awkward bear), a Piegan Blackfoot who had been living among the Minnetarees near Fort Clark but wanted to pay a visit to his own people at Fort McKenzie. Maximilian described Kiasax's leave-taking from his Minnetaree wife and child in his entry for June 19. In Bodmer's watercolor Kiasax wears a Spanish blanket and a silver cross (trade goods from Santa Fe) and holds the flute on which he played "a wretched piece of music" when departing Fort Clark. Sensing the hostility of the Assiniboins and Crees, Kiasax gave up his plans of continuing on to Blackfoot country and turned back downstream at Fort Union, returning safely to Fort Clark on the steamboat. His companion Matsokui was not so prescient.

Bodmer found several of these strange monuments in the hills behind Fort Union on June 25. They were erected by the Assiniboins to invoke the approach of buffalo herds. *Opposite:* Pitatapiu, an Assiniboin of the Stone band, posed for his portrait on June 29. The bundle on his shield contains his highly treasured horse-stealing medicine.

The Crees were lesser allies of the large Assiniboin nation and roamed the same general territory in what is now northern Montana and southern Saskatchewan. *Above:* The Cree hunter Piah-Sukah-Ketutt (the speaking thunder), who brought Maximilian a piece of mastodon tooth and had his portrait painted on October 24, during the prince's second visit to Fort Union. *Opposite:* The Cree wife of Dechamp, a half-breed Cree who was one of the Company's best hunters. The marks on her chin are tattoos. Nearly all the Plains Indians painted their faces with vermilion, obtained from the Company at a price of ten dollars per pound.

*Opposite:* An Assiniboin encampment at Fort Union. In the foreground is the tepee of Ayanyan, a chief whom the whites called General Jackson and whose arrival at Fort Union was described by Maximilian on June 30. In his field journal the prince wrote of the tepee, "on each of its sides, a large grizzly bear was painted in a black color, at the head of which a small scarlet pennant was fluttering in the wind—probably a talisman or medicine." Three travois are pitched near the tepee. *Below:* In early October, shortly after returning to Fort Union on the downstream voyage, Bodmer made this painting of a young Blackfoot girl who was being raised among the Assiniboins. Since the Assiniboins and Blackfeet were enemies, she was undoubtedly a war captive. This practice was followed by many tribes in order to maintain population.

Dangerous encounter between the keelboat *Flora* and an encampment of Gros Ventres des Prairies below Fort McKenzie.

PART III

# Fort Union to Fort McKenzie

July 6-August 9, 1833

Although in years to come steamboats would eventually venture farther upstream on the Missouri, in 1833 Fort Union was the head of steamboat navigation on the river. Cargoes destined for posts farther west had to be transported either overland by pack train or upriver by keelboat, the method most often employed by the Company. Keelboats were stoutly built barges fitted with a keel, a mast, and a large rudder so that they could be sailed when conditions permitted. The rest of the time they were propelled with long sweep oars, pushed with iron-shod poles, or dragged along by the cordelle. In times of shallow water, such as the summer of 1833, the cordelle became the prime means of locomotion. The keelboat *Flora* that carried Maximilian and his party upstream measured sixty feet overall and had a beam of sixteen feet. David D. Mitchell, the Company manager for Fort McKenzie, was in command. In addition to him and the three Europeans, forty-eight others crowded aboard for the trip. Among these were the clerk

Alexander Culbertson; Henry Morrin, the helmsman; a carpenter; and two Indian women, one of them Mitchell's wife. The rest were mostly *engagés* whose function was to haul the heavily laden boat upstream by the cordelle. A number of hunters were also aboard. As there was little room for provisions, the ship's company would live off the land. First-class passengers slept in the rear cabin, where there were two bunks. One was assigned to Maximilian; Mitchell and his wife used the other. Culbertson, Bodmer, and Dreidoppel slept on the floor. Most of the *engagés* generally spent the night ashore, under the stars, when the weather permitted. Mitchell divided the crew into watches and issued powder and ball to all hands, accompanied by the threat of a five-dollar fine for unauthorized discharge of firearms after sunset, since this might attract Indian war parties. Later on, he would threaten the same penalty for the practice among the crew of kicking overboard the animal skulls and other specimens that Maximilian deposited

Above Fort Union the terrain along the riverbanks became increasingly rugged: eroded clay hills backed by sandstone mountains.

on the deck to bleach. Maximilian noted sadly that his ukase seemed to have little effect.

At seven o'clock on the morning of July 6 the *Flora*'s *engagés* shouldered the cordelle, and, to the accompaniment of the usual cannon salutes, the voyage began. For the first ten days the crew had to contend with shallow water and a swift current. The cordellers sloshed through waist-deep mud and willow thickets. They climbed hills and skirted high bluffs. The *Flora* ran aground, was freed, and ran aground again. Riverbanks collapsed under the feet of the *engagés*, putting the boat in danger of being crushed by the fall of immense trees. More than once the crew had to saw through a forest of underwater snags to cut a channel. Clouds of mosquitoes tormented the travelers, and a violent storm thoroughly soaked the baggage through the leaky roof of the cabin. The cordelle broke, and the boat was nearly lost in a whirlpool. Veteran Company men swore that it was the most difficult passage within memory. The only thing that improved was the victuals. Two days' distance from the fort, game became plentiful and the hunters were sent out. Soon the foredeck of the *Flora* was festooned with the carcasses of deer, elk, and buffalo. It was primarily buffalo cows that were sought after, for as Maximilian observed, "the mating season of the buffalo is beginning now, and the bull becomes very lean, malodorous and inedible." By July 17 the expedition had reached a particularly dangerous stretch of water where the keelboat *Beaver* had been lost in a severe windstorm during the previous year:

### July 17, 1833

The place where the *Beaver* was wrecked was about 200 steps from our night's quarters, and we went to look at it. At that time the *Beaver* had lain about 300 paces further up the river, but in a dark night was loosened from its moorings by a storm, driven down the river, and thrown upon a sand bank. Two men were drowned, and Mr. Mitchell had escaped by an immense leap from the deck to the shore. The greater part of the cargo, worth 30,000 dollars, was lost: the crew then built a small fort, or log-house, about forty paces in length, in which they remained till part of the goods were saved, and another boat came up to fetch them. In this melancholy situation they were in danger of a quarrel with a band of Blackfoot Indians. These Indians were returning by land from Fort Union, to which they had been invited, on account of the conclusion of a treaty of peace. The presents made to them by the traders were on board the *Beaver*, and the greater part was lost, which much incensed the Indians. The disputants had already taken up and cocked their pieces, and it was entirely owing to the resolute conduct of Mr. Mitchell that the matter was amicably settled. Since that time the bank of the river, at this place, has undergone a considerable change. Only the pickets, at the back of the log-house, were still standing; all the rest had been swept away. At that time the whole place was bare sand; now, it was covered with willows, five feet high, and the river had carried away the bank for the breadth of, at least, 100 paces.

### July 18, 1833

During our voyage today I could not help making comparisons with my journeys on the Brazilian rivers. There, where nature is so infinitely rich and grand, I heard, from the lofty, thick, primeval forests on the banks of the rivers, the varied voices of the parrots, the macaws, and many other birds, as well as of the monkeys, and other creatures; while here, the silence of the bare, dead, lonely wilderness is but seldom interrupted by the howling of the wolves, the bellowing of the buffaloes, or the screaming of the crows. The vast prairie scarcely offers a living creature, except now and then, herds of buffaloes and antelopes, or a few deer and wolves. These plains, which are dry in summer, and frozen in winter, have certainly much resemblance, in many of their features, with the African deserts. Many writers have given them the name of savannahs, or grassy plains; but this expression can be applied, at most, to those of the Lower Missouri, and is totally inapplicable to the dry, sterile tracts of the north-west, where a more luxuriant growth of grass may be expected, at best, only in a few moist places, though various plants, interesting to the botanist, are everywhere to be found.

After our hunters had returned, with the flesh of a buffalo, we had a favourable wind, which allowed us to use our sail.

At a turn of the river we suddenly saw a couple of bears running backwards and forwards on a sand bank before the willow thickets. One of them at length went away, and the other ran along the strand, and fell on the dead body of a buffalo cow, which was half buried in the mud. While the keel-boat sailed against the stream in the middle of the river, a boat was put out, into which Messrs. Mitchell and Bodmer, and the hunters, Dechamp and Dreidoppel, threw themselves, and rowed along the bank towards the ravenous animal. The sight of this first bear chase was interesting, and we that remained as spectators on deck awaited the result with impatience.

Dechamp, a bold and experienced hunter, and an excellent marksman, was put on shore, and crept unperceived along the strand, till he got to the branch of a tree, about eighty paces from the bear, in order, in case of need, to intercept his retreat to the thickets. The ravenous bear sometimes raised his colossal head, looked around him, and then greedily returned to his repast; doubtless, because the wind was in our favour, and these animals are not remarkably quick-sighted. The boat had got to within fifty paces, when the pieces were levelled. Mr. Mitchell fired the first mortal shot, behind the shoulder blade. The other shots followed in quick succession, on which the bear rolled over, uttered fearful cries, tumbled about ten steps forwards, scratched the wounded places furiously with his paws, and turned several times completely over. At this moment Dechamp came up, and put an end to his misery by shooting him through the head. The huge beast lay stretched out: it was fastened by ropes to the boat, and conveyed in triumph to the ship, where it was measured, and a drawing made of it. I much regretted that I had not taken part in the sport; but I had not believed that it was possible, in such an open, unprotected spot, to get so near the bear.

This grizzly bear was a male, about three years old, and, therefore, not of the largest size: he was six feet two inches and two lines in length, from the nose to the tip of the tail; the latter being eight inches. His colour was dark brown, with the point of the hair of a rusty colour, but new hair already appeared of a lighter grey, with yellow tips. This bear is known to be a very dangerous beast of prey, and is willingly avoided by the hunters: if fired at, he very frequently attacks, even if not wounded, when they suddenly come too near him. If he perceives a man in time, he generally gets out of the way, especially when he has the wind.

Almost all the hunters of the prairie relate their adventures with the bears, and whole volumes might be filled with such stories. It is certain that many white men and Indians have been torn to pieces by these dangerous animals, especially in former times, when they were very numerous, and lived to a great age, as may be seen in Lewis and Clark's Travels. Even last year, five of Mr. Mitchell's hunters, who had wounded one of these animals, were so quickly pursued by him, that they were obliged to take refuge in the Missouri.

This species of bear cannot climb, and therefore a tree is a good means to escape their attacks. The true country of these animals on the Missouri, where they are at present the most numerous, is the tract about Milk River. Here there is no wood of any extent in which they are not found, but they are likewise seen everywhere in a north-westerly direction. In these solitudes, the long claws of this bear serve to dig up many kinds of roots in the prairie, on which he chiefly subsists, but he is especially fond of animal food, particularly the flesh of dead animals. There is no other species of bear on the Upper Missouri, for the black bear is not found so high up. At the place where we had killed the bear, it would have been easy to shoot many of these animals, by posting ourselves near the dead buffalo cow: the whole sand bank was covered with the prints of bears' footsteps, and trodden down like a threshing-floor; but our time was too short and too precious: we, therefore, proceeded on our voyage till a violent thunder-storm threatened us, and we lay to, by the high bank of the prairie, where our bear was skinned. During the night, torrents of rain fell, which wetted our books and plants in the cabin.

JULY 19, 1833

We had another chase after a colossal bear, which swam through the Missouri to a dead buffalo; but our young hunters were this time too eager, and fired too soon, so that the animal escaped, though probably wounded, as fifteen rifles were discharged at him. Afterwards we saw several beaver lodges. The people towed the keel-boat in the afternoon, making their way along the bank, through a dense willow thicket. All on a sudden they cried that there were bears close to them; on which the hunters immediately leaped on shore. Mr. Mitchell had scarcely arrived at the head of the towers, when he perceived a she bear with two cubs. Dechamp came to his

aid, and in a few minutes the three animals were in our power. Mr. Mitchell had killed the mother, which was of a pale yellowish-red colour; one of the cubs, which was brought alive on board, was whitish about the head and neck, and brownish-grey on the body; the other was dark brown. The females of these animals are generally of a lighter colour than the males, which is the case with many beasts of prey, particularly the European fox. The cub was in a great rage, and growled terribly; it was impossible for me to save his life.

After this successful chase we were detained by a high contrary wind, and it was, therefore, late when we reached the mouth of Milk River, on the north bank. This river comes down in many windings, and constitutes the western frontier of the territory of the Assiniboins. Its waters are generally muddy and mixed with sand, whence it has its name.

Approaching the Mauvaises Terres, the party encountered naked gray mountains totally lacking in vegetation.

## July 20, 1833

Early in the morning we reached the place where the Missouri makes a great bend of fifteen miles, the distance across by land being only 400 or 500 paces. At this place the ice drives in spring over the flat land, or sandy point, and the tall poplars at the end of it were rubbed smooth, on the lower part, to half the thickness of their trunks. This bend is called Le Grand Detour, and there are several such in this river. The wind, in many of these bends, being too strong for the efforts of the towers, and the masses falling from the bank, often endangering our vessel, we lay to under the protection of the hills on the north bank of a narrow prairie covered with bushes, where I found the blue-grey butcher-bird, the magpie, and several common birds, many of which we shot; we also caught a great many butterflies, which were hovering about the flowers in the burning rays of the sun. Henry Morrin, our pilot, a very good marksman, brought in a large male antelope. The other hunters had killed, on the opposite bank, twelve buffaloes, *viz.,* four bulls, five cows, and three calves, but brought away only the flesh of the cows, leaving all the rest to the wolves, the bears, and the vultures: they had missed a large bear.

## July 21, 1833

We came to the place where the buffaloes were killed the day before: part of the flesh of the animals, which had not been touched, was taken away, and a full grown young bald eagle was shot down from the nest. It was now the dry season, which, in these parts, continues from the middle of July to the end of autumn. The whole prairie was dry and yellow; the least motion, even of a wolf crossing it, raised the dust. We could recognise the vicinity of the herds of buffaloes at a distance, from the clouds of dust which they occasioned. All the small rivers were completely dried up. Even the Missouri was very shallow, which it always is in summer and autumn.

Continuing our way but very slowly, we perceived, on one of the hills of the bank, some elks, and, by the aid of our telescopes, saw that they were large males with immense horns; and at this same moment, a black bear came from the thicket on the north bank, and began to swim across the river. The hunters immediately divided into two parties; the one, including Messrs. Mitchell and Bodmer, going by land along the bank of the river; the other in the boat, rowing after the bear. Unluckily our boat got aground, by which the bear got the start, and came too near to the hunters, who were posted behind the bank. As soon as he set foot on land, he was killed by several shot. He was not so large as the one lately killed, of a dark brown colour, and we contented ourselves with carrying off as trophies only his head and fore paws. On account of the high wind we did not leave this spot today, and the chase gave us much employment. Scarcely was the bear killed, when buffalo bulls came into the river in several places, which we should certainly have killed, if our young men had known how to restrain their ardour. In the artemisia bushes of the prairie, a porcupine was caught alive, which was not killed till it was on board the keel-boat, our *engagés* declaring that it was a great delicacy. This animal is of great importance to the Indians, on account of its quills, which they dye, and use to embroider their clothing, and for other ornamental purposes.

## July 22, 1833

We made a considerable progress today because a favourable wind had allowed us to use our sails. While the wind allayed the heat of the day, we rambled through the prairies on the bank; as far as the eye could reach there were the bleached bones of the buffaloes and elks, and their immense horns. A couple of sparrow-hawks, a kind of lark, and a flock of wild geese, which had made an excursion from the river into the prairie, were the only large living creatures that we met with here. Thousands of grasshoppers, many of them of beautiful colours, were hopping and flying about: numerous butterflies, but only three or four species, were hovering about the shrubs in these dry clay steeps, which were bare of grass. There were a great many ant hills, and mosquitoes, and several other kinds of troublesome stinging insects.

As we looked around on an eminence, whence we perceived our boat sailing with a fair wind, we saw an immense buffalo bull, which approached us slowly, not suspecting any danger: we quickly hid ourselves behind some bushes on the edge of a deep cleft, and, as the majestic animal passed through it, we killed it with three well-directed shots. The magnificent creature lay stretched out about forty paces above the ravine, and only the advance which our boat had gained obliged us to leave our prize. At length, however, by firing some shot on the steep bank of the river, we succeeded in drawing the attention of our people, and they dispatched a boat for us. We took advantage of the interval to make a second attempt at buffalo hunting, and Dreidoppel, who was endeavouring to drive some of these animals towards me, killed a young bull, on which the boat arrived, the crew of which took away the tongues and part of the flesh of the buffaloes which we had killed. Much fatigued and heated, we reached our vessel at four o'clock in the afternoon, after having been exposed, since eight o'clock in the morning, without a drop of water, to the heat of the sun in the barren prairies.

## July 25, 1833

Some of our hunters returned with two black-tailed deer and a young fawn; and, soon afterwards, two buffalo bulls were killed, a great part of the flesh of which we brought away, because we were approaching the part of the country called Mauvaises Terres, where we could not expect to find much large game. In the afternoon we saw some Indian huts under high poplars on the bank; and, on the northern bank, sketches were taken of singular mountain tops. In general, the bare grey masses of the eminences on the bank were so singularly formed that it was impossible not to wish that an able geologist might make a minute investigation of the chain. Their tops, like towers, pillars, &c., were contrasted with the clear blue sky, and the sun caused them to cast deep shadows. As we were sailing with a fair wind, I was obliged to submit to the necessity of rapidly passing these highly interesting scenes.

A thunder-storm, with high wind, suddenly caused our vessel to be in great danger; but the same wind which had at first thrown us back, became all at once very favourable when we reached a turn in the river, and sailed, for some time, rapidly upwards. This brought us to a remarkable place, where we thought that we saw before us, two white mountain castles. On the mountain of the south bank, there was a thick, snow-white layer, a far-extended stratum of a white sand-stone, which had been partly acted upon by the waters. At the end where it is exposed, being intersected by the valley, two high pieces, in the shape of buildings, had remained standing, and upon them lay remains of a more compact, yellowish red, thinner stratum of sand-stone, which formed the roofs of the united building. On the façade of the whole building, there were small perpendicular slits, which appeared to be so many windows. These singular natural formations, when seen from a distance, so perfectly resembled buildings raised by art, that we were deceived by them, till we were assured of our error. We agreed with Mr. Mitchell to give to these original works of nature the name of "The White Castles." Mr. Bodmer has given a very faithful representation of them. [*See pages 92–93 for this painting.*]

There were similar formations on the north bank likewise; but the increasing storm did not allow us time to contemplate these wonders: our sail rent, and we were obliged to seek for shelter at the prairie of the south bank. We took advantage of the halt to explore the adjacent country, while the trees bent under the fury of the storm, and the thunder pealed in the very sultry air.

For the next ten days the *Flora* was poled, cordelled, and (occasionally) sailed along a difficult stretch of river that is now inundated by the Fort Peck Reservoir in eastern Montana. As the party struggled westward, the terrain became increasingly mountainous and desolate. Veins of sandstone began to appear in the eroded clay mountains that bordered the river,

In the Mauvaises Terres the weirdly eroded mountaintops had split into columns topped by "kidney" formations of harder sandstone.

26.

25.

B. B.

Sandstone formations of the Mauvaises Terres and Stone Walls.

indicating a transition to a rocky geologic area. Hunting parties ranged the sere prairies but game was scarce. Maximilian was able to add only the skins of an eagle, several prairie dogs, and a rattlesnake to his zoological collection. The creek beds were dry. No Indians were to be seen. The keelboat was poled past the mouth of the Musselshell and entered the heart of the badlands section known as the Mauvaises Terres. Maximilian described it thusly:

> The mountains here presented a rude wilderness, looking in part like a picture of destruction; large blocks of sand-stone lay scattered about. . . . Some spots were covered with a low plant with white flowers and there are several species of grasses on which the mountain sheep, or bighorn, is said chiefly to feed. A few pines and junipers appear here and there, and on the declivities small patches of grass, like Alpine meadows, so that we could fancy ourselves now in Switzerland, now in the valley of the Rhine. But the naked, rude character of the Mauvaises Terres seems to be unique in its kind, and this impression is strengthened when you look up and down the river. Only the croaking of the raven was heard in this desolate waste, which even the Indian avoids. . . .

Bighorn sheep were sighted on the peaks and rapids were encountered in the river. The *Flora* sprang a leak in one of them and had to be offloaded so that the hull could be repaired. Finally the river made a sweeping turn to the north and the travelers beheld "beautiful, medium sized mountains and, at their foot, fresh green forests, a gratifying aspect since we had seen nothing but naked, whitish mountains for so long." The Mauvaises Terres were behind them.

AUGUST 5, 1833

At half-past seven, when we lay to, to give our people time to get their breakfast, we saw five Indians coming round a hill on the south bank, whose fire-arms glistened in the bright light of the morning sun. They fired their pieces, and sat down on the bank, on which Mr. Mitchell and Dechamp immediately rode over to them. Several women, with their dogs drawing travois, soon joined them, and the boat brought four men and a woman, who had a thick club in her hand, on board. They were tall and well made, and very different from the Assiniboins; they belonged to the tribe of the Gros Ventres, called by the English, Fall Indians. They had no covering on the upper part of the body, except buffalo skins. They sat down in the cabin, where they smoked their pipes, and had some refreshment. A troop of Indians now appeared on the bank, whom we saluted with a cannon shot, on which our visitors desired to be taken on shore. The boat brought back a chief and medicine man, called Niatohsa (the little French man, or the French child), of whom Mr. Bodmer immediately took a very good likeness. [*For this portrait, see page 128.*] This man wore his hair together in a thick bunch over the forehead, which only people of his description are allowed to do. As he spoke the Blackfoot language, Doucette was able to converse with him, while we proceeded rapidly, with a fair wind, and twenty-seven men towing us.

Meantime, a number of Indians, on foot and horseback, had assembled on the bank, who hastened before to inform their countrymen of the approach of the traders, which is an event highly interesting to them. The sight of the Indians, all in motion, sometimes stopping to look at the vessel, and firing their pieces, gave great animation to the prairie. Being detained by a violent thunder-storm, it was one o'clock before we reached the place where the Missouri flows through a rather narrow gorge, from the remarkable sand-stone valley, called the Stone Walls.

In the front of the eminences the prairie declined gently towards the river where above 260 leather tents of the Indians were set up; the tent of the principal chief was in the foreground, and, near it, a high pole, with the American flag. The whole prairie was covered with Indians, in various groups, and with numerous dogs; horses of every colour were grazing round, and horsemen galloping backwards and forwards, among whom was a celebrated chief, who made a good figure on his light bay horse. While this was passing, several Indians had been on board, many of whom swam across to us; among them, a tall man came on board in this manner, shook off the water, and went without ceremony into the cabin, but

Mr. Mitchell drove him out, and gave him to understand that none but the chiefs could be admitted there; he then had the Indians told to go back to their camp, where he would visit them.

While the camp was saluted at intervals with cannon shot, and the Indians answered with their guns, the keel-boat, which had hoisted its flag, was anchored on the north bank, opposite to the tents, a very necessary precaution to prevent our coming directly into contact with all the Indians at the same time. About forty Indian warriors, drawn up on the bank, having made a running fire, and our cannon again saluted, Mr. Mitchell, with the interpreter, Doucette, took the boat and rowed across. He alone had pistols, the others were unarmed. On the summit of the bank, all the Indians formed a long red line, and immediately below, on the water's edge, sat the chiefs, in a detached small body. After Mr. Mitchell had seated himself by them, and had some conversation with them, he invited them to accompany him on board, and brought us eight of these chiefs, who sat down in the cabin to smoke their pipes. Among them were several men of a good open character; but one was a very bad man, Mexkemanastan (the iron that stirs), whom Mr. Mitchell had turned out of doors the year before, at Fort Mc Kenzie, on account of his bad conduct. We were now entirely in the power of these people, and had every reason to fear the vengeance of this man. Prompted, doubtless, by his own interests, he behaved, to our astonishment, in a most friendly manner; shook hands with us, and, like his comrades, gratefully accepted the presents which were made him. He wore his hair in a thick knot on the forehead, and had a deceitful, fawning countenance. [*See page 129 for a portrait of Mexkemanastan.*] While we were engaged with these chiefs, we saw a number of men and women, from all parts of the bank, swim through the river, or cross over to us in their round boats, made of buffalo skin, and our keel-boat was suddenly entered on every side and crowded with them. Tall, slender men covered the deck, thrust themselves into the apartments, and we were really overwhelmed with them. They all demanded brandy, powder, and ball, and brought to exchange with us, skins, leather, and dried and fresh meat. The leather boats, laden with their articles for barter, were brought alongside the keel-boat, drawn by one swimmer, and pushed by another, and in this manner we were soon hemmed in, so that it was necessary to ask the chiefs to clear the vessel; they, indeed,

Passing through the Stone Walls, Bodmer sketched this massive outcropping which is today known as La Barge Rock.

induced the greater part of the young men to leap into the water, though only to enter the boat again on the other side.

Our situation was everything but agreeable, for these same Indians had entirely demolished a fort, on the frontiers of Canada, two years before, killed a clerk, and eighteen other persons, besides murdering several other white people in those parts; they had, in addition to this, had a quarrel with Lewis and Clark, and no confidence could we therefore place in them, though Mr. Mitchell affirmed that he always transacted business with them with pleasure, and had never had any proofs of the treachery imputed to them. If it was their intention to treat us in a hostile manner, there was no way for us to escape; and how easily might the most trifling dispute with these rude men lead to a breach, by which fifty Whites, in the power of eight or nine hundred Indians, would have had no chance. They were therefore treated with much apparent confidence and familiarity, and everything went off very well.

A favourable wind for using our sail was very welcome, in assisting us to escape from this perilous situation. Doucette had been sent on shore with some goods, and instructions to barter with the Indians, and thus, in some measure, to satisfy their desires. We on board saw our people on shore closely surrounded by a great mass of Indians; the noisy traffic was long continued, though Mr. Mitchell had repeatedly given orders for the return of the boat. We were obliged to wait a long time, and already began to be apprehensive for the safety of our dealers, when we at length saw the boat, overloaded with Indians, put off from the bank, on which orders were given to proceed immediately on our voyage. About fifty robust Indians joined our men in towing, and we were drawn along very rapidly; our keel-boat was so crammed with people, that it drew much water.

In this singular company we began to pass through the most interesting part of the whole course of the Missouri, namely, the Stone Walls; but we could not breathe freely enough duly to appreciate the surrounding scenery, before we were quit of our troublesome visitors. The chiefs were repeatedly informed that the boat was ready to carry them on shore, and they had all received presents, with which, however, some of them were not satisfied; at length they were all sent off, with an intimation that they might go to Fort Mc Kenzie, to their allies, the Blackfeet, where the goods would be landed, and the barter conducted as they desired. We lay to for the night, on the right bank, at the fore part of the Stone Walls, and a number of Indians, especially women, who were found concealed in the vessel, and turned out, kindled fires near us. Many articles were missing, and we had given much more than we received, yet we were truly glad at having come off as well as we did. A strong watch, with an officer, was set for the night.

AUGUST 6, 1833

At break of day the weather was extremely cool and disagreeable; the thermometer at half-past seven was only at 58°, and a bleak wind prevailed, which enabled us to use our sails. The part of the country called the Stone Walls, which now opened before us, has nothing like it on the whole course of the Missouri; and we did not leave the deck for a single moment the whole forenoon. Lewis and Clark have given a short description of this remarkable tract, without, however, knowing the name of Stone Walls, which has since been given it. In this tract of twelve or fifteen miles, the valley of the Missouri has naked, moderately high mountains, rounded above, or extending like ridges, with tufts of low plants here and there, on which the thick strata of whitish coarse-grained friable sand-stone, which extends over all this country, are everywhere visible. This sand-stone formation is the most striking when it forms the tops of more isolated mountains, separated by gentle valleys and ravines. Here, on both sides of the river, the most strange forms are seen, and you may fancy that you see colonnades, small round pillars with large globes or a flat slab at the top, little towers, pulpits, organs with their pipes, old ruins, fortresses, castles, churches, with pointed towers, &c. &c., almost every mountain bearing on its summit some similar structure.

Towards nine o'clock the valley began to be particularly interesting, for its fastastic forms were more and more numerous; every moment, as we proceeded along, new white fairy-like castles appeared, and a painter who had leisure might fill whole volumes with these original landscapes. As proofs of this we may refer to some of these figures, which Mr. Bodmer sketched very accurately. All these eminences are inhabited by numerous troops of the wild mountain sheep, of which we often saw thirty or fifty at a time climbing and springing over the sand-stone formation. These harmless animals often stood on a lofty peak, far beyond the reach of our rifles, while the outlines of their forms were clearly defined against the bright blue sky.

Early in the afternoon we came to a remarkable place where the Missouri seems to issue from a narrow opening, making a turn round a dark brown rugged pointed tower-like rock on the south, to which the traders have given the name of the Citadel Rock. We had, however, not yet taken leave of the extraordinary sand-stone valley; on the contrary, we now came to a most remarkable place. The stratum of sand-stone, regularly bedded in low hills, runs along both banks of the river, which is rather narrow, like a high, smooth, white wall, pretty equally horizontal above, with low pinnacles on the top. At some distance before us, the eye fell on an apparently narrow gate, the white walls in the two banks approaching so near to

each other, that the river seemed to be very contracted in breadth as it passed between them, and this illusion was heightened by the turn which the Missouri makes in this place to the south-west. Looking backwards, the high, black, conical rock rose above the surrounding country; and on our right hand, there were, on the bank, dark perpendicular walls, seemingly divided into cubes, in the form of an ancient Gothic chapel with a chimney. [*Bodmer's watercolor of this scene is to be found on pages 94–95.*]

## AUGUST 7, 1833

We looked with impatience to reach what is called the Gate of the Stone Walls. We soon came to a dark brown rock, like

Bodmer's notation on the sketch reads: "Quite like a wall erected from squared blocks. The background formation, pale sand-stone."

a tower, rising in the middle of the white wall, the front of which had fallen down, and had a great number of boulders about it. From this tower it is between 600 and 800 paces to the place which appeared to us yesterday to form a narrow gate. A mile further up, we saw, to the south, in the direction of the river, the foremost chain of the Rocky Mountains, looking like a distant blue range, which was soon hid behind the naked, sterile banks of the river.

### August 8, 1833

Turning round a point of land, we saw before us a long table-formed range of hills, behind which is Fort Mc Kenzie, which we might have reached by land in half an hour. In the front of these hills, on the north bank, is the mouth of Marias River. After we had passed it, we saw, about six o'clock, on the same bank, the ruins of the first fort, or trading post, which Mr. Kipp, clerk of the American Fur Company, had built, in the year 1831, in the territory of the Blackfeet. This fort was abandoned in 1832, and the present Fort Mc Kenzie built in its stead, and this, too, is soon to be abandoned. In this manner the fur company continues to advance, and firmly establishes itself among nations that are but little known, where the fur trade is still profitable.

At twilight we lay to under the high clay wall of the southern bank. We were much surprised that no notice had yet been taken of us by the fort, which was so near, though, in the two preceding years, the boat had been welcomed by the Blackfeet further down the river; and as we were now so close to the fort, we might expect to see the white inhabitants of the post. Besides this, the Minnetarees had told us that the garrison of Fort Mc Kenzie had had a dispute with the Indians, and Dechamp affirmed that he had heard today some cannon-shot. All these considerations, taken together, excited in Mr. Mitchell—who was well aware of the little reliance that could be placed on the Indians—some apprehensions for the safety of the fort and our expedition. Small parties of Whites, at a distance from the Missouri, are generally murdered, or at least plundered, by the Blackfeet. We had, therefore, reason to proceed with much caution. Accordingly, Major Mitchell resolved to reconnoitre the fort in person, and, meantime, a strong night watch was ordered on board the vessel. Mr. Mitchell chose four of our hunters, who were thoroughly acquainted with the country, and well armed, to accompany him. The boat landed them on the north bank of the river, where it remained in safety.

They set out on their expedition at nightfall, the moon shining brightly. It was agreed that, in case of a misunderstanding with the Indians, we should drop down the river if Mr. Mitchell had not returned before midnight. The people on board the vessel remained on the alert, awaiting the result. The night was exceedingly fine, warm, and serene, but the moonlight did not last long. We plainly heard the drums of the Indians in the direction of the fort, and, on the opposite bank of the river, the loud howling of the wolves. At half-past ten o'clock Mr. Mitchell returned with two of his men. He had ascended the hills, but had lost his way, and came to the mouth of the Marias River, from which he now returned. The other two had again proceeded towards the fort. The feet of our wanderers had suffered severely by the thorns of the cactus plants. As we had no information of the state of the fort, we had nothing to do but patiently to wait for daylight.

As Maximilian and his companions waited for whatever adventure the dawn might bring, they had ample time to reflect upon the progress of their expedition thus far. It was almost four months to the day since they had departed St. Louis. During those months they had covered more than 2,500 miles of river and witnessed many strange sights. Still stranger and more vivid experiences lay ahead. In the thirty-three days that the *Flora* had required for the trip from Fort Union to the vicinity of Fort McKenzie the ship's complement of fifty-two had lived almost exclusively from the product of the hunt. Hauling a sixty-foot keelboat up a river is hard work, and a healthy appetite, both for meat and diversion, was one of the results, as Maximilian's tally for the upstream hunt affirms:

Buffaloes—54; Elks—18; Blacktailed deer—13; Common deer—26; Antelopes—2; Bighorns—2; Bears—9; Wolves—1; Skunk—1; Porcupines—1; Hares—2; Eagles (bald)—6; Horned owls (big)—5; Prairie hens—3; Wild geese—10; Prairie dogs—10; Rabbits—1.

On August 6, approaching the Stone Walls, the *Flora* passed Citadel Rock and lay to. Bodmer ran out of paper for his sketch.

On the keelboat voyage from Fort Union to Fort McKenzie—a journey that lasted thirty-four days and covered 650 miles of river—Maximilian and Bodmer encountered the most spectacular scenery of the entire trip. Clay hills gave way to eroded sandstone mountains and narrow canyons of fantastic aspect. The names given to the succeeding stretches of river tell the story: Mauvaises Terres; White Castles; Stone Walls.

---

*Opposite:* By July 9, the fourth day out of Fort Union, the terrain had become increasingly mountainous. Maximilian remarked upon a "strange chain of clay hills with conical peaks and red and black markings." Bodmer promptly executed a watercolor. *Overleaf:* Two days above Fort Union, on July 7, the river was bordered by high bluffs that had been weathered into strange formations. Since there was no wind, the cordelle was in use. As Maximilian described it, "the towers had much labour at this part of our voyage, the current of the river being very strong; they were sometimes obliged to climb, in a long row, up the hills, where we saw them suspended, like chamois, in dangerous positions."

In late July, Maximilian and Bodmer came to a prospect that astounded them: two white castles perched above the mountainous valley through which the keelboat sailed. They proved to be eroded outcroppings of a vein of white sandstone. But the illusion was a powerful one, as described in Maximilian's text for July 25. These formations are now inundated by the reservoir lake behind Fort Peck Dam. *Overleaf:* The Stone Walls of the Missouri, the most spectacular vista of the voyage, passed before the astonished eyes of Maximilian and his companions in early August. The Gate of the Stone Walls may be identified in the near background. For Maximilian's description, see his detailed text entry for August 6.

A celebrated Indian battle: Assiniboins and Crees attack a small encampment of Blackfeet outside the stockade of Fort McKenzie.

# PART IV

# Sojourn at Fort McKenzie

August 9–September 14, 1833

Bodmer began his ethnographic reportage at Fort McKenzie with these studies of Blackfoot hairstyles.

The morning of August 9, 1833, the thirty-fourth day of the voyage upstream from Fort Union, found Maximilian and his companions moored to the river-bank a dozen or so miles downstream from Fort McKenzie. A heavy rain that was to continue inter-mittently throughout the day did little to buoy the spirits of the travelers, who waited anxiously for news about conditions at the fort. Proceeding cautiously upstream they were soon met by a small mounted party from the fort bringing word that all was well: a large and relatively peaceful encampment of Black-feet waited for the commencement of trade.

In the days ahead, Maximilian would witness how this most difficult and dangerous aspect of the fur business was conducted. Operating out of a make-shift fort set deep in the heart of Blackfeet country, a relative handful of whites would have to deal with bands of excitable Indian warriors that outnumbered them sometimes by as many as ten to one. Fort McKenzie was the spearhead of the American Fur Company's invasion of the Rockies, where the Rocky Mountain Fur Company and the Hudson's Bay Com-pany had long fought over the rich harvest in pelts. The ever-increasing competition between these three organizations had driven the price of beaver to ruin-ous levels by 1833. Pelts were being purchased in the field for twice and more what they would bring in St. Louis. Thus the object of this year's trade was not to turn a profit but to bankrupt the competition. The Indians, sensing that for once in their dealings with the whites they held the upper hand, were more than usually irascible and capricious. The fact that whiskey was employed as one of the chief items of trade did not make things any easier. Much of the trouble with the Indians over the next weeks was fueled by alcohol. To handle this delicate business required men with the combined skills of a diplomat, a politician, and a psychologist. McKenzie had assigned three of his best men to the task. David Mitchell, a resolute and imaginative leader, had already made a great name for himself in the trade. Alexander Culbertson, although still in his mid-twenties, was to succeed Mitchell at Fort McKenzie and remain in command until just before the post was abandoned. Jacob Berger, the interpreter who was already on the scene, was an old mountain hand. It was he who had opened the Company's trade with the Blackfeet in 1830.

The arrival of the *Flora* would swell the number of whites at the fort from twenty-seven to nearly eighty, barely enough for comfort when one considered that the Blackfeet had a well-earned reputation as the most warlike of all the Plains tribes. At the time of Maximilian's visit, the population of the Blackfeet nation was estimated at between 18,000 and 20,000. The nation was divided into three tribes that spoke a common language but were not adverse to making war on each other, given proper provocation—which was often very slight. Maximilian identified the tribes as: (1) the Siksika, or the proper Blackfeet; (2) the Kahna, or Blood Indians; (3) the Piegan. These tribes inhabited the same general area in the Rockies and their western slopes to the north of Fort McKenzie. The Bloods were accounted to be the fiercest, with the Siksika running a close second. Maximilian gives a better report of the Piegans' proclivities than do other authorities, but he noted that all the tribes were highly dangerous:

> They are always dangerous to white men who are hunting singly in the mountains, especially to beaver hunters, and kill them whenever they fall into their hands; hence the armed troops of the traders keep up a constant war with them. It was said that in the year 1832, they shot fifty-eight Whites and, a couple of years before that time, above eighty.

After entertaining the welcoming committee from the fort with a hurried breakfast on board the *Flora*, the travelers pushed on upriver toward their destination. Fort McKenzie had been hastily thrown up the previous year under the direction of David Mitchell. It replaced an even more primitive establishment that was built by James Kipp in 1831 after the conclusion of a peace treaty, signed by chiefs of the Blackfoot nation, the Assiniboins, and Kenneth McKenzie. In view of what was to happen during the 1833 trading session, this treaty possesses a certain poignancy:

> We send greetings to all mankind! Be it known unto all nations, that the most ancient, most illustrious, and most numerous tribes of the red skins, lords of the soil from the banks of the great waters unto the tops of the mountains, upon which the heavens rest, have entered into solemn league and covenant to make, preserve, and cherish a firm and lasting peace, that so long as the water runs, or grass grows, they may hail each other as brethren and smoke the calumet in friendship and security.
>
> On the vigil of the feast of St. Andrew, in the year eighteen hundred and thirty one, the powerful and distinguished nation of the Blackfeet, Piegan, and Blood Indians, by their ambassadors, appeared at Fort Union, near the spot where the Yellow Stone River unites its current with the Missouri, and in the council-chamber of the Governor Kenneth M'Kenzie met the principal chief of all the Assiniboin nation, the Man that holds the Knife, attended by his chiefs of council, le Brechu, le Borgne, the Sparrow, the Bear's Arm, la Terre qui Tremble, and l'Enfant de Medicine, when, conforming to all ancient customs and ceremonies, and observing the due mystical signs enjoined by the grand medicine-lodges, a treaty of peace and friendship was entered into between the high contracting parties, and is testified by their hands and seals hereunto annexed, hereafter and for ever to live as brethren of one large united happy family; and may the Great Spirit, who watcheth over us all, approve our conduct and teach us to love one another.

Maximilian was to discover how these lofty sentiments were observed in practice, but now, after a dozen miles of soggy sailing, beset by rain and clouds of mosquitoes, the *Flora* approached its goal:

AUGUST 9, 1833

We passed the last winding of the river, and a most interesting scene presented itself. A prairie extends along the north bank, at a point to which, projecting towards the river, we saw Fort Mc Kenzie, on which the American flag was displayed. [*See color plate on pages 122–123*]. A great number of Indian tents was erected in the plain, which was covered with the red population in various groups, all of whom hastened to the bank. Near to the fort, the men (about 800 Blackfeet) were drawn up in a close body, like a well-ordered battalion. They formed a long dark brown line, with a black stripe at the top, which was occasioned by their black hair. The palisades and the roof of the fort, as well as the neighbouring trees, were occupied by Indian women and their children, singly, or in groups, and the whole prairie was covered with them. The smoke of the powder rose in the fort, and the thunder of the cannon re-echoed from the banks.

The fire of musketry among the mass of the Indian warriors was uninterrupted, and their war cry sounded over to us, while our vessel, in spite of the rain, kept up a brisk fire. In front of the Indians we saw three or four chiefs in red and blue uniforms, trimmed with lace, and wearing round hats with plumes of feathers. The most distinguished among them was Mehkskehme-Sukahs (the iron shirt), dressed in a scarlet uniform, with blue facings and lace, with a drawn sabre in his hand; riding without stirrups, he managed, with great dexterity, his light bay horse, which was made very restiff by the firing of the musketry. The most respected chief among the Blackfeet, at this time, was the Spotted Elk, who, after a successful battle with the Flatheads, had changed his name, and was now called Ninoch-Kiaiu (chief of the bears).

We approached the landing-place, and at length set foot on shore, amidst a cloud of smoke caused by the firing of the Indians and of the *engagés* of the fort, who were drawn up in a line on the bank. Here we were received by the whole population, with the Indian chiefs at their head, with whom we all shook hands. The Chief of the Bears was quite an original: his countenance, which was not very handsome, with a large crooked nose, was partly hid by his long hair. On his head he had a round felt hat, with a brass rim, and a silver medal on his breast. We were led through a long double line of the red men, the expression of whose countenances and their various dresses greatly amused us. When we arrived at the fort there

Blackfeet at leisure, during a respite in the trading session.

was no end of the shaking of hands; after which we longed for repose, and distributed our baggage in the rooms.

AUGUST 10, 1833

Having made our arrangements on the first day of our arrival, and viewed the Indian camp, with its many dogs, and old dirty brown leather tents, we were invited, together with Mr. Mitchell, to a feast, given by the Blackfoot chief, Mehkskehme-Sukahs (the iron shirt). We proceeded to a large circle in the middle of the camp, enclosed with a kind of fence of boughs of trees, which contained part of the tents, and was designed to confine the horses during the night, for the Indians are so addicted to horse-stealing that they do not trust each other. The hut of the chief was spacious; we had never before seen so handsome a one; it was full fifteen paces in diameter, and was very clean and tastefully decorated. We took our seats, without ceremony, on buffalo skins, spread out on the left hand of the chief, round the fire, in the centre of the tent, which was enclosed in a circle of stones.

Our host was a tall, robust man, who at this time had no other clothes than his breech-cloth; neither women nor children were visible. A tin dish was set before us, which contained dry grated meat, mixed with sweet berries, which we ate with our fingers, and found very palatable. After we had finished, the chief ate what was left in the dish, and took out of a bag a chief's scarlet uniform, with blue facings and yellow lace, which he had received from the English, six red and black plumes of feathers, a dagger with its sheath, a coloured pocket-handkerchief, and two beaver skins, all which he laid before Mr. Mitchell as a present, who was obliged to accept these things whether he liked or not, thereby laying himself under the obligation of making presents in return, and especially a new uniform. When the chief began to fill his pipe, made of green talc, we rose and retired (quite in the Indian fashion) in silence, and without making any salutations. We crept through the small door, which was besieged by numerous dogs, and stepped over the foremost, who grinned at us maliciously. Mr. Mitchell was immediately invited to three or four similar feasts, an honour which can only suit an Indian stomach. [*For a portrait of Mehkskehme-Sukahs, see page 134.*]

In the afternoon the *engagés* of the fort gave us what they call baptism; namely, a welcome on our happy arrival in this remote wilderness by firing several salutes in the court-yard of the fort, for which it is usual to give them something to drink, or else a present. Our entertainment for the evening was the noise of the drum of the Indian camp, which is employed not only to drive the evil spirit out of the sick, but in their dances and other amusements, and is, therefore, heard almost every day and every hour. We were likewise much entertained by the antics of three young bears, which ran about in the court-yard. Another very pretty animal had been brought up in the fort: this was a young prairie fox, which Mr. Mitchell made me a present of, and which, by its tameness and vivacity, helped to amuse us during the following winter. Our new lodging swarmed with mice, which ran over our feet while we were writing, and kept the traps set for them continually in motion. We trained my pretty little fox to this sport, which was new to him, and he soon became a capital mouser.

Also on this day preparations were made for the solemn reception of the Indians, which always precedes the opening of the trade, and which is considered by the Indians as a matter of great importance. The flag being hoisted, two small cannon, placed in the middle of the court-yard, fired signals for the commencement of the trade. It was full half an hour before a noise arose in the Indian camp: we heard singing, firing of guns, and saw the mass of the Indians advancing on all sides. When Ninoch-Kiaiu (the bear chief) approached the gate, it was opened, and the two cannon were again fired. He entered, followed by three or four chiefs, who approached Mr. Mitchell with their heads inclined; and, after shaking hands with him, were made to sit down in the Indian apartment. Soon afterwards another body appeared, and Mr. Mitchell went out of the gate to meet them. They advanced in small parties, headed by their chiefs, who always bring a present consisting either of some beavers' skins or of a horse. The first horses that we received in this manner were two greys and a light bay, which were variously painted with red, chiefly on the forehead, the shoulders, and the haunches, and marked on the legs with transverse stripes like a zebra.

The chiefs and about thirty of the principal warriors were admitted, and, after being seated on buffalo hides in the dining apartment, they refreshed themselves by drinking and smoking. In this manner three or four different bands advanced with rapid strides, repeatedly discharging their guns, and singing their rude songs. We observed some remarkable, martial-looking physiognomies among these men, painted in the strangest manner, marching with a very warlike air. The chiefs wore, for the most part, the uniform received from the Company, made in the fashion of a great coat, with round hats and tufts of feathers, on which they prided themselves greatly, but which disfigured them most lamentably. Their faces, painted of a bright red, surrounded with their thick, lank hair, and surmounted by a round hat with a tuft of feathers, such as our German post-boys used to wear, had such a ridiculous appearance, that we could not refrain from laughing.

After three or four bands of the Blackfeet had been received, they were followed by one of the dangerous Blood Indians, under their chief and medicine man, Natohs (the sun), and these, too, were admitted; after which a detachment of from sixty to eighty of the Gros Ventres des Prairies arrived, who, having likewise brought a horse and some beaver skins as a present, were treated like the others. The chiefs were always welcomed by firing the cannon, and then delivered up their colours, most of which they had received from English merchants, and which were carried before them on long ensign staffs, quite in military style. Mr. Mitchell had attempted, in the preceding year, to dispense with these salutations, but the Indians immediately took offence and were even going to part without transacting any business; for they are extremely punctilious in points of honour.

While the company of Indians were employed in smoking, Mr. Mitchell took Ninoch-Kiaiu (who had always been very faithful and devoted to the Whites and the fur company), into his own room, and presented him with a new uniform, half red and half green, with red and green facings, and trimmed with silver lace; a red felt hat, ornamented with many tufts of feathers; in short, a complete dress, and a new double-barrelled percussion gun. Mr. Mitchell wished particularly to distinguish this man, because he had never been to the north to trade with the Hudson's Bay Company. When he had equipped himself in his new uniform, which was worth 150 dollars, and entered the assembly of the chiefs in the court-yard of the fort, it immediately became evident that the distinction conferred upon him made no favourable impression on them; some chiefs who had made presents to Mr. Mitchell, and had not yet received anything in return— for instance, Mehkskehme-Sukahs, could not conceal their feelings; the latter hid his head behind the person who sat next to him, while others hung down their heads, and seemed lost in thought. When Mr. Mitchell perceived this, he caused it to be intimated to the chiefs, that "they saw how the American Fur Company distinguished its faithful friends; that they, on the contrary, had generally taken their beaver skins to the English; that he, therefore, could not give them much now, but would make every chief a present. That it would be their interest to deal with him in future, like Ninoch-Kiaiu, and then it would be in his power to make them more considerable presents."

Several Indians rose, among whom was Haisikat (the stiff foot, formerly the old head), who, with violent gesticulations, made a long speech. He was brother-in-law to the Bear Chief, and plainly advised him to go home, and keep himself sober, because otherwise something serious might happen. The Blood Indians were offended; they spoke loudly of shooting Ninoch-Kiaiu, between whom and his friends long conferences took place. While this was passing, we saw all the other Indians sit down in half circles before the gate of the fort. The warriors sat on the ground, and, while liquor and tobacco were distributed among them, they sang without ceasing, and sometimes fired their guns. At six in the evening, when we were relieved from these troublesome guests, and hoped to have some repose after the fatigues of the day, a violent dispute arose among the *engagés,* which might have had serious consequences. Blows had been exchanged, and the example which the Whites gave the Indians was not very creditable to them.

AUGUST 11, 1833 [FIELD JOURNAL]

Bartering had gone on late into the previous night and we saw most interesting and comic scenes. Those of the Indians who had drunk too much whiskey became exceedingly affectionate, shaking hands without end and even embracing and kissing us heartily. They traded their furs for whiskey and clamoured for it incessantly. Most entertaining was the sight of a wizened old Indian who was painted grey and had brought a very tame female bear to the fort in order to sell her. He sat down on the ground with his charge, played with her and kissed her repeatedly. The animal was charming and completely tame. Today I bought her for whiskey. Mr. Mitchell then made me the present of a very nice young male to serve as her mate.

In the afternoon at the fort the scenes of bartering and

bacchanals were soon repeated. The Indians came with a small cask and with everything serviceable they owned and gave everything to get their favourite drink. Many came singing and dancing and offered their wives and daughters in exchange for whiskey. Others brought horses, beavers, and other skins, and we saw indescribable scenes. The young as well as the old got something to drink, and even very small children here and there could neither stand nor walk.

AUGUST 12, 1833

About noon, the Blackfoot chief Kutonapi arrived in the fort with his band, firing their guns, and was received with the usual discharge of the cannon. The cheerfulness that then prevailed among us was immediately interrupted by discord and mourning. Some Blood Indians had stolen three horses belonging to the fort, and search was made in vain after the thieves, when, in the afternoon, a much more serious event occurred. Mr. Bodmer had just begun to paint the portrait of Hotokaneheh (the head of the buffalo skin), with his large, handsomely ornamented calumet, when we heard a shot in an adjoining room, and immediately saw the people running together. A Blood Indian, who had often been in the fort, and had, till that time, always conducted himself well, had shot, with a pistol, one of our young men named Martin. All the people were assembled round the perpetrator, and nobody knew the cause of this event. The Indian seemed, indeed, to be rather confounded, and affirmed that his pistol had gone off by accident. Many of the young men were for having him shot, because, as they said, he had doubtless committed the murder designedly; but Mr. Mitchell decided with more moderation, considering the occurrence as an unfortunate accident. When the first moments of exasperation were past, he forbade the murderer the fort, but at the same time strictly enjoined the *engagés* to refrain from all acts of violence towards this Indian.

Ninoch-Kiaiu, who was present, did not take the matter so easily. Though he had been offended in the forenoon, because brandy was refused him, he warmly took part with the Whites, and was going to shoot the murderer; but being prevented in this, he beat him with the butt-end of his gun, and drove him, as well as several Gros Ventres des Prairies, who happened to be present, with blows, out of the fort. Kutonapi, who was likewise present, stepped forward, and made a violent speech,

Rough sketch of a Blackfoot woman seated outside Fort McKenzie.

in which he described, in lively colours, the offences of the Blood Indians against the Whites, and exhorted us to take vengeance for them. Mr. Mitchell thanked him, but persevered in the more temperate course, which, in his situation, was the most judicious.

AUGUST 13, 1833 [FIELD JOURNAL]

Martin was buried this morning. Most of the Indians are now departing, but new ones are expected any day now.

AUGUST 14, 1833 [FIELD JOURNAL]

Only some twenty-three tents of the Indians remained around the fort. Niatohsa, the Gros Ventres chief, paid a visit and was well-received, as Mr. Mitchell has a high opinion of these Indians. He wanted to get whiskey for himself and some of his men. The morning passed with entertainment of various Indians. We could see many drunken persons everywhere. Whole families came and begged incessantly for whiskey. I saw a couple of men riding, both on the same horse, and both intoxicated. The man in front rattled his schischikué, singing loud and shouting all the time. Behind him was an old man who had recently made a long speech in the fort. He was slumped down and heavily drunk. A woman led the horse, accompanied by several children. Several Indians brought us women and girls in order to barter them, as usual, against whiskey.

AUGUST 15, 1833 [FIELD JOURNAL]

The big oars of our keel-boat were sawed into pieces today. They are made of hickory and will be used for axe handles, as it is not possible to obtain wood here that may be used for such purposes. Dreidoppel returned from hunting. He had shot a kingfisher and a yellow oriole. Our residence was besieged all day long by Indians who were attracted by our drawing and writing. They said about Mr. Bodmer, after he had executed a portrait, that he could "write" well. In the evening, we went to the tents of the Indians, where we saw at least six women whose noses had been cut off. This is the way in which the Piegans and other Blackfeet punish the infidelity of their women, a hideous disfigurement.

[*This practice was apparently widespread among the Black-feet, as Maximilian noted elsewhere in his journal:*

Bodmer made this formal watercolor portrait of Homachseh-Kakatohs (the great star) primarily because of his remarkable nose.

Many of the men have six or eight wives, whom they are very ready to give up to the Whites; even very young little girls are offered. On the other hand, they generally punish infidelity in their wives very severely, cutting off their noses in such cases; and we saw, about Fort Mc Kenzie, a great many of these poor creatures, horribly disfigured. When ten or twelve tents were together, we were sure to see six or seven women mutilated in this manner. The woman whose nose is cut off, is immediately repudiated by her husband; nobody will take her as his wife; and such women generally work for their subsistence in other. tents; attend on the children, tan hides, or perform other household work. There have been frequent instances of a husband immediately killing his wife when she has had intercourse with others; often he avenges himself on the paramour, takes away his horse or other valuable property, to which the latter must submit quietly.

[*The actual mutilation was often inflicted by members of the husband's band or union:*

If a woman, whose husband is in one of the unions, has had any intercourse with another, the union meets in one of the tents where they smoke and, in the evening, when all around are buried in sleep, they penetrate into the woman's tent, drag her out, ill-treat her as they please, and cut off her nose. The husband cannot make any opposition; he must repudiate such a woman.]

### August 16, 1833

Mr. Mitchell thought now of building a new fort, for which he endeavoured to choose the most suitable situation. We rode out for this purpose, ascended the chain of hills behind the fort, where the little prairie dogs retreated into their burrows, and then perceived two armed Indians, who, as soon as they observed us, turned their horses, and galloped up to us. They had not noticed our double-barrelled guns, and doubtless came up to frighten us, and to try their fortune with us; for, as soon as they came near, and saw our arms, they turned round and trotted away.

We had scarcely set out on our return to the fort, and reached the shady spot on the bank, when Dauphin, one of our people, came galloping on an Indian horse, quite out of breath, and told Mr. Mitchell that Ninoch-Kiaiu desired to

inform him that his nephew had been murdered by the Blood Indians—that he should immediately attack them, and, therefore, advised us to return as speedily as possible.

On reaching the fort we learned that the nephew of the Bear Chief, a very quiet, well-disposed Indian, had ridden out in the morning to look for a horse which had been stolen from him, and had been murdered not far off, on the hills, by the Blood Indians, who had attacked him with their guns, knives, and clubs. Ninoch-Kiaiu was furious, and he now came to Mr. Mitchell to consult with him what was to be done. A sensible old Indian advised that this matter should not be treated as a concern of the whole tribe, but as a private affair, and, consequently, they should wait patiently for an opportunity when they might take vengeance on some member of the murderer's family. The chief, who felt that his honour was deeply wounded, was silent, and lost in thought. As a sign of mourning, he had put on his worst clothes, but not cut off his hair, saying that "his head was too great and strong to do this." [*A portrait of Ninoch-Kiaiu in mourning is on page 139.*] He had loaded with ball the double-barrelled gun which he had lately received, and suddenly hastened away without saying a word. He afterwards sent word to Mr. Mitchell, that he must go to revenge his kinsman, whose dead body he would not see; but, that it might fall into good hands, he would make a present of it to Mr. Mitchell, whom he requested to bury it. As the murder of the Indian was a consequence of the offence which Ninoch-Kiaiu had offered to the Blood Indians, on the occasion of Martin's death, the present could not well be refused.

### August 17, 1833

Early in the morning, the howling and lamenting of the Indians in the camp was heard; and, soon afterwards, the corpse of the murdered man was brought into the fort. It was wrapped up very tightly in buffalo skins, and tied to a travois drawn by one horse. An old man, with a multitude of women and children, his relations, followed the body with loud lamentations. An aged woman in the train had just cut off one joint of her little finger as a sign of mourning, and held the bleeding stump wrapped in a handful of wormwood leaves. When our people had taken the body from the travois between the two gates of the fort, and carried it into the Indian apartment, a young man, the brother of the Bear Chief, made a speech to the weeping relatives, saying—"Why do you lament and cry?—see, I do not cry: he is gone into the other country, and we cannot awaken him; but, at least, two Blood Indians must accompany him and wait upon him there." An infant, and a boy, the brother of the deceased, died on the same night; and the Indians said that the murdered brother had called the others away. [*In his field journal Maximilian identifies the dead infant as a child of David Mitchell, the issue of a liaison with an Indian woman. The infant was buried in the same grave with the murdered Blackfoot and his dead brother.*]

Thus we had three dead bodies in the fort. As that of the Indian had long been exposed to the air and the sun, it was necessary to make haste to get it out of the way; and Berger, the interpreter, had the disagreeable office of painting, putting on its best clothes, and ornamenting it in the Indian fashion. The two Indians were laid in the same grave, wrapped in a red blanket and buffalo skin, over which was laid a piece of coloured stuff, given by Mr. Mitchell. The bottom and sides of the grave were lined with boards; the body, too, was covered with wood; his bridle, whip, and some other trifles were thrown in, and the grave filled up.

## August 18, 1833

Ninoch-Kiaiu now continually talked of going to a little camp of the Blood Indians, on the other side of the river, to take vengeance. His brother, who likewise made a great noise, walked about the fort with a loaded pistol, and, at last, begged Mr. Mitchell to have him conveyed over the river, because it was thought that two Blood Indians had been seen, whom he wanted to shoot; to which Mr. Mitchell very calmly replied, that "if he intended to kill any body, he would not assist him." With an expression of violent passion, the Indian, on this, mounted his horse and galloped away, "in order," as the chief said, "to quiet his heart for the present, by the death of a Blood, as they might, at some future time, shoot the real murderer." The chief's aged uncle, Natoie-Poochsen (the word of life), was one of the principal mourners. He had cut off his hair, and besmeared it, as well as his feet and legs, with whitish clay. Mr. Bodmer made a good portrait of him in this dress. [*For this likeness, see page 138.*] He went about howling and crying, while the Bear Chief thought only of procuring brandy. He had in his hand a little mustard-glass filled

with this precious liquor; and one of his friends, who also possessed some brandy, sipped a small quanity, and, embracing the chief, discharged it into his mouth, which is considered, among the Blackfeet, as the highest possible proof of friendship.

## August 19, 1833

The *engagés* of the Company were now employed in packing up the skins obtained by barter from the Indians, for which purpose there is a particular machine. It consists of a frame of laths, which mark the size of the packages, and in which the skins are laid. In putting up small, light furs, a couple of planks are passed through the frame-work, on each end of which a man stands to press the skins together, and then to cord them. The buffalo hides, which are much thicker, are pressed together by means of a thick beam; in this operation six or eight men are required. Others of our people were engaged in sawing plank, burning charcoal, and the like; they had, however, much leisure time, which they spent in various amusements. They fired at a mark with their rifles, at which Papin and Morrin were very expert.

## August 20, 1833

In the evening we generally had an interesting sight, when the great number of horses belonging to the fort returned from the hills. Eight armed men rode behind and at the sides, and as many Indians, who, for the sake of safety, had joined with their horses. The whole body was very numerous, and presented a striking appearance when, in a cloud of dust, they galloped down the hills with a thundering noise, and entered the fort.

## August 21, 1833

In order to obtain a handsome, large mountain sheep, Mr. Mitchell gave me the services of Papin, with whom my own hunter, Dreidoppel, joined to make an excursion. Papin went very unwillingly, though, for the sake of security, a Blackfoot was sent with them. He affirmed that he would not undertake this dangerous enterprise for 100 dollars, if he had not bound himself to the Company. They made arrangements to stay out a couple of nights, and took a pack-horse with them. Other hunters were sent out with the Indians, and we soon received information that a good many buffaloes had been killed.

AUGUST 22, 1833 [FIELD JOURNAL]

The afternoon was very hot and the Indians bathed in the river in great numbers, including women, girls, and children. They swam to the keel-boat and sprang from it into the river. The noise from all this was very great. In our rooms, three to five Indians sat incessantly, for whom one had to stuff the pipe constantly. They were too lazy to rise and fetch fire themselves, so I had to light even my own pipe for them. It was not different in the other rooms of the fort, either,

whiskey to the Indians, whereby they become bad, dissolute, lazy, and, therefore, dangerous. They omit, because of this, to sell good furs and merchandise to the Whites. The women, who know quite well that they profit nothing from their labour since the men barter it for whiskey immediately and bring nothing home, tan the skins only half-way and badly. In 1816, the government issued a regulation that prohibited the sale of spirits to the Indians and allowed the importation of only a sufficient quantity to provide a half-pint per day to each man engaged in the service of the fur companies. Recently an amendment has been made that no whiskey at all may be imported. The Indian agents, who should be living permanently among the Indians, are entrusted, along with military personnel, the task of monitoring the importation of

particularly in the quarters of Berger, the old interpreter. Dreidoppel and Papin returned late. They had shot a bighorn sheep this morning and brought the skin back with them. On the first day they had ridden until nine at night and had seen a great many antelope, had shot at some but did not get any. They also saw a herd of seventy elk. During the night they slept in a place where we had made an excursion recently with Mr. Mitchell. From there they rode onward and shot this sheep. The Indian cut open the animal immediately and ate the kidneys and half of the liver raw. Then they grilled the meat. In the evening Papin shot a buffalo bull, and the Indian immediately ate his heart arteries in the raw state.

AUGUST 24, 1833 [FIELD JOURNAL]

In the cool of the evening, sitting in front of our doors, we had a long talk with Mr. Mitchell about the abuse of selling

spirits. But not only do they not live amongst the Indians—they come out only once each year—they tolerate everything to happen without reprimand. (Some of them are related to leading men of the fur companies as well.) Nonetheless, they receive high salaries from the government, which bestows every year considerable gifts upon the Indians through them. Should these gentlemen carry out their obligations, the harmful consumption of whiskey among the Indians might be effectively controlled. In the surroundings of Fort Mc Kenzie it might be difficult to carry out this regulation of the government of the United States, as all the Indians who live in these northern regions may get as much whiskey as they want from the English. Consequently, should they not get whiskey from the American Fur Company, all trade would withdraw completely from here and be turned to the English. At the Mandans and Minnetarees there is no whiskey, and Mr. Mc Kenzie has no stock there of it at all.

Medicine cane of a Piegan Indian, used for lighting his pipe.

The dogs of the Indians howled terribly during the night. Hundreds of voices of all kinds were heard at the same time, and in this concert there was no difference at all from the howling of the wolves that we had heard so often of an evening in the lonely wilderness along the Missouri. It was Sunday, and people were wearing clean clothes. Two Indians brought a horse and sold it to the Company for a cask of whiskey, a blanket, powder, and shot. In the afternoon, when

we were entertaining ourselves with our three young bears, Mr. Mitchell had the notion of letting them swim in the river. I advised against it immediately, fearing that they would surely try to escape, but he insisted, and before we knew it, they were already on the other side of the river. There, they ran far downstream and swam still further, and it was very difficult to follow them in the skiff and bring them back again to the river bank. Before we got them back to the fort, after half an hour, I had thought that these splendid, strong young animals were lost.

Tomeksih-Siksinam (the white buffalo) came tonight to the fort bringing a nice Flathead bow that he had taken as a prize in his last battle. It was adorned with many ermine strips at the ends, and when I asked him if he would sell it, he replied that he "liked it very much." At this point one has not to question an Indian any more, as he will continuously elevate his price. This Indian, by the way, is a very reliable and good man, and much attached to the Whites. He is a gallant warrior and jealous of his honour. He shot dead his married sister who was having intercourse with another man, although he had sought to dissuade her from it.

The *engagés* bound and shot a fine big dog in the yard of the fort, in order that they could eat him afterwards. They singed him in the fire. He was very fat and was a gift to them from Mr. Mitchell. The hunters Papin and Loretto who could be heard shooting beyond the river brought back an antelope and a deer. For many days we have had nothing more to eat than hard, dried buffalo meat. An Indian sold us a beaver today and we ate its meat for supper. It was tender and even though a bit stale, not bad to eat. As some of the Indians were suffering from hunger, Mr. Mitchell gave them a portion of our tainted dried meat for which the women and children happily scrambled. The Indians who arrived today told us that a big tribe of about 200 tents would arrive at the fort the day after tomorrow at the latest.

An elaborately decorated Blackfoot calumet, or ceremonial pipe.

Last night just as we were going to bed, we were invited to the quarters of Mr. Mitchell. The occasion was the marriage of Mr. Culbertson to an Indian woman. According to the local custom, he had paid to the value of 100 dollars for her and his Piegan wife had brought him a rifle. A horse was to follow. She was of the family of the White Buffalo. An Indian woman who lives in the fort said yesterday that she had been told that the Indians intended to ask a double price for their beavers and that should this be refused they would kill all the Whites. Even if such talk is without foundation, it is indicative of an evil frame of mind among the Indians. When the band of Piegans arrive we will be very weak because the expedition to the country of the Kutenai Indians will depart tomorrow and this will take from us two interpreters and some of our best men. We will have then only a few men who have little knowledge of the Blackfoot language and will be embarrassed in making ourselves understood, particularly in the trading sessions. Mr. Bodmer's musical box made a great impression on all those who heard it. They deem that this box is great medicine and, next to the steam-boat, probably one of the greatest. Towards evening a number of new Indians arrived, and many received whiskey. We saw very sedate men offer, in exchange for a little whiskey, things that they would not part with for any price yesterday. The White Buffalo offered a good rifle and a beautiful quiver of panther fur for a small quantity of whiskey. Nobody was found, however, who would profit from his drunkenness.

## August 28, 1833

At break of day, we were awakened by musket-shot, and Doucette entered our room, crying, "Levez-vous, il faut nous battre," on which we rose in haste, dressed ourselves, and loaded our fowling-pieces with ball. When we entered the court-yard of the fort, all our people were in motion, and some were firing from the roofs. On ascending it, we saw the whole prairie covered with Indians on foot and on horseback, who were firing at the fort; and on the hills were several detached bodies. About eighteen or twenty Blackfoot tents, pitched near the fort, the inmates of which had been singing and drinking the whole night, and fallen into a deep sleep towards morning, had been surprised by 600 Assiniboins and Crees. When the first information of the vicinity of the enemies was received from a Blackfoot, who had escaped, the engagés immediately repaired to their posts on the roofs of the buildings, and the fort was seen to be surrounded on every side by the enemy, who had approached very near. They had cut up the tents of the Blackfeet with knives, discharged their guns and arrows at them, and killed or wounded many of the inmates, roused from their sleep by this unexpected attack. Four women and several children lay dead near the fort, and many others were wounded. The men, about thirty in number, had partly fired their guns at the enemy, and then fled to the gates of the fort, where they were admitted. They immediately hastened to the roofs, and began a well-supported fire on the Assiniboins.

In the fort itself all was confusion. If the men had been mustered and inspected, it would have been found that the engagés had sold their ammunition to the Indians; they were, therefore, quite unprepared to defend themselves, and it was necessary, during the combat, to distribute powder as well among the Whites as the Indians. Mr. Mitchell and Berger, the interpreter, were employed in admitting the Blackfeet women and children, who were assembled at the door of the fort, when a hostile Indian, with his bow bent, appeared before the gate, and exclaimed, "White man, make room, I will shoot those enemies!" This exclamation showed that the attack was not directed against the Whites, but only against the Blackfeet. Mr. Mitchell immediately gave orders to his people to cease firing; notwithstanding this, single shots continued to be fired, and our Blackfeet were not to be restrained, nay, ten or twelve of our people, among whom were Doucette and Loretto, went into the prairie, and fired in the ranks of the Blackfeet, who were assembling, and every moment increasing in numbers. Loretto had shot, at the distance of eighty-six paces from the pickets, the nephew of the Assiniboin chief, Minohanne (the left-handed), and this was the only one of the killed whom the enemy were unable to carry away, for we saw them lay many others on their horses, and take them off. In the fort itself only one man was wounded, having had his foot pierced by an arrow, and likewise a horse and a dog. If the enemy had occupied the heights on the other side of the river, they might, from that position, have killed all our people in the fort.

When the Assiniboins saw that their fire was returned, they retreated about 300 paces, and an irregular firing continued, during which several people from the neighbourhood joined the ranks of the Blackfeet. While all this was passing, the court-yard of the fort exhibited very singular scenes. A number of wounded men, women, and children, were laid or placed against the walls; others, in their deplorable condition, were pulled about by their relations, amid tears and lamentations. The White Buffalo, whom I have often mentioned, and who had received a wound at the back of his head, was carried about, in this manner, amid singing, howling, and crying: they rattled the schischikué in his ears, that the evil spirit might not overcome him, and gave him brandy to drink. He himself, though stupefied and intoxicated, sung without intermission, and would not give himself up to the evil spirit. Otsequa-Stomik, an old man of our acquaintance, was wounded in the knee by a ball, which a woman cut out with a penknife, during which operation he did not betray the least symptom of pain. Natah-Otann, a handsome young man, with whom we had become acquainted, was suffering dreadfully from severe wounds. Several Indians, especially young women, were likewise wounded. We endeavoured to assist the wounded, and Mr. Mitchell distributed balsam, and linen for bandages, but very little could be done; for, instead of suffering the wounded, who were exhausted by the loss of blood, to take some rest, their relations continually pulled them about, sounded large bells, rattled their medicine or amulets, among which were the bears' paws, which the White Buffalo wore on his breast. A spectator alone of this extraordinary scene can form any idea of the confusion and the noise, which was increased by the loud report of the musketry, the moving backwards and forwards of the people carrying powder and ball, and the tumult occasioned by above twenty horses shut up in the fort.

When the enemy were still very near the fort, Mr. Mitchell had given orders to fire the cannon of the right-hand front block-house among them; but this had not been done, because the Blackfeet were partly mixed with the Assiniboins; no use, therefore, had been made of them, of which the Indians complained bitterly. The enemy gradually retreated, and concentrated themselves in several detachments on the brow of the hill, and this gave us an opportunity to open the gate, with due precaution, and view the destroyed tents and the bodies of the slain. The Indian who was killed near the fort especially interested me, because I wished to obtain his skull. The scalp had already been taken off, and several Blackfeet were engaged in venting their rage on the dead body. The men fired their guns at it; the women and children beat it with clubs, and pelted it with stones; the fury of the latter was particularly directed against the privy parts.

Before I could obtain my wish, not a trace of the head was to be seen. Not far from the river there was a melancholy scene; old Haisikat (the stiff foot) was lamenting over his grown-up daughter, who had concealed herself in the bushes near the fort, and had been shot in mistake by Dechamp, who thought she was an enemy.

At the very beginning of the engagement, the Blackfeet had dispatched messengers on horseback to the great camp of their nation, which was eight or ten miles off, to summon their warriors to their aid, and their arrival was expected every moment. Meantime, Ninoch-Kiaiu came and called on Mr. Mitchell for assistance, for they had been attacked by another party of the enemy. Hotokaneheh likewise came to the fort, and made a long and violent speech, in which he reproached the Whites with being inactive while the enemy were still in the vicinity; they ought not to confine themselves to the "defence of the fort, if they seriously desired the alliance of the Blackfeet, but endeavour to attack the common enemy in the prairie," &c. All these reproaches hurt Mr. Mitchell, and he resolved to show the Indians that the Whites were not deficient in courage. With this view he made the best hunters and riflemen mount their horses, and, in spite of our endeavours to dissuade him from this impolitic measure, he proceeded to the heights, where 150 or 200 Blackfeet kept up an irregular fire on the enemy.

We who remained in the fort had the pleasure of viewing a most interesting scene. From the place where the range of hills turns to the Missouri, more and more Blackfeet continued to arrive. They came galloping in groups, from three to twenty together, their horses covered with foam, and they themselves in their finest apparel, with all kinds of ornaments and arms, bows and quivers on their backs, guns in their hands, furnished with their medicines, with feathers on their heads; some had splendid crowns of black and white eagles' feathers, and a large hood of feathers hanging down behind, sitting on fine panther skins lined with red; the upper part of their bodies partly naked, with a long strip of wolf's skin thrown across the shoulder, and carrying shields adorned with feathers and pieces of coloured cloth. A truly original sight! Many immediately galloped over the hill, whipped their tired horses, in order to take part in the engagement, shouting, singing, and uttering their war-whoop; but a great part of them stopped at the fort, received powder and balls, and, with their guns and bows, shot at the disfigured remains of the Assiniboin who was slain, and which were now so pierced and burnt as scarcely to retain any semblance of the human form. As the Indians near the fort believed themselves to be now quite safe, they carried the wounded into the leather tents, which were injured and pierced through and through by the enemy's balls, round which many dead horses and dogs were lying, and the crying and lamenting were incessant.

About one o'clock Mr. Mitchell and his people returned, much fatigued by the expedition, and the great heat, the thermometer being at 84°. Mr. Mitchell's horse had been shot through the withers; he himself fell off and hurt his arm; another horse was shot through the neck, and captured by the enemy; Bourbonnais, its rider, had escaped. All our people, however, had returned safe. The enemy had been driven back to Marias River, where, from the want of bravery in the Blackfeet, they were able to maintain their ground behind the trees; nay, they had sometimes advanced and repulsed their enemies. They were plainly heard encouraging each other, on which they came forward in parties of twenty or thirty, and renewed the attack. It was generally observed that the Assiniboins fought better than the Blackfeet, many of whom did not leave the fort during the whole day. Mr. Mitchell, with his people, had always been in advance of the Blackfeet, and nearer to the enemy. He had often shamed the Blackfeet, whose numbers had increased to 500 or 600, calling out, "Why did they lag behind? They had reproached the Whites with cowardice, but now it was seen who were the most cowardly. Now was the time to show their courage." The hunter, Dechamp, had especially distinguished himself by his bravery and well-directed fire at the enemy, of whom he had killed or wounded several.

The Indians had fired quite at random, otherwise the loss must have been much greater on both sides. We learnt, later, that the Assiniboins had three killed, and twenty severely wounded. Many Indians took Mr. Mitchell by the hand, welcomed him as their friend and ally, and offered him several horses, which he did not accept. We visited the wounded in their tents, had the blood washed from their wounds, and their hair, which was clotted with it, cut off; and gave them medicines and plaster, and, instead of brandy, which they asked for, sugar and water to refresh them. A child had died of its wounds; they had daubed its face with vermilion.

A Crow war shield, ornamented with two white weasels and other medicine bundles. Made from the thick hide of an old buffalo bull, it had been presented to the Blackfeet as a peace offering.

Camp der Piekan-Indianer
bei Fort Mac-Kenzie

The main body of the Piegan Blackfeet arrived a day or two after the battle fought outside the Fort McKenzie stockade on August 28. At its height, the encampment numbered some 400 tepees pitched on the prairie surrounding the fort. In Bodmer's hasty pencil sketch, the Missouri is located behind the encampment, running along at the foot of the high bluffs to the south. After three or four days of trade and revelry, most of the tribe departed as swiftly as it had arrived.

## August 29, 1833

In the morning a part of the Blackfeet came to us, fatigued and hungry, and reported that they had pursued the enemy, and fired at them on both flanks, and had found one killed; but the enemy had not returned the fire, without doubt, for want of ammunition. During the night we had lodged the principal chiefs in the fort; among them were Tatsiki-Stomik (the middle bull), Penukah-Zenin (the elk's tongue), Kuto-napi, and Ihkas-Kinne (the low horn); the latter was a chief of the Siksika, or proper Blackfeet. Most of the Indians of the great horde went away, promising to return soon, with their tents and baggage, and begin the trade. The tents, with the wounded, were all removed, except a few, to better positions higher up the river. [*Indians were no more eager to report their casualties than are modern armies, and no completely authoritative report of losses on both sides has come down to us. Maximilian totaled the Blackfeet dead at fourteen (seven men, five women, and two children) with many more wounded. Other sources placed Blackfeet losses much higher and gave Assiniboin casualties as six dead and twenty or more seriously wounded. In October, Dechamp was told by Assiniboins at Fort Union that the war party had numbered 588, of whom 100 were Crees, and that their losses were three dead and twenty wounded. Although it was extremely rare for whites to witness a battle between rival Indian tribes (most firsthand reports of Indian warfare involve white attacks upon Indians or vice-versa), the fracas at Fort McKenzie was typical of Indian battle tactics. As Maximilian remarks in his essay on Mandan Ethnology (see pages 241–252), Plains Indians ideas of valor were quite different from those of the whites. To willfully expose themselves to enemy fire would, in the eyes of the Indians, be folly rather than bravery. Plains Indians relied on stealth and cunning as their principal strategies. They also liked substantial numerical superiority whenever possible. Once the initial assault had been carried out, they generally retreated, carrying away their trophies or licking their wounds, as the case might have been. North American Indians had little taste for pitched battles between large numbers of warriors. Considering the role that warfare played in their culture, it could hardly have been otherwise. Total war, or a series of major battles would have wiped them all out long before the whites nearly succeeded by various means, including warfare.*]

## August 30, 1833

The expedition to the Kutenais, projected by Mr. Mc Kenzie, set out from Fort Mc Kenzie today. The object of it was to trade with that people, and especially to obtain skins of the white mountain goat. It consisted of Doucette, Isidore Sandoval, with his Indian wife, four *engagés,* and two Kutenai Indians, one of whom was Homach-Ksachkum, all mounted, and with nine pack-horses, which carried the goods, the kitchen utensils, and the beds. [*For portraits of Homach-Ksachkum and his son, see pages 124–125.*] They had to proceed two days' journey along the banks of the Teton River, and then to strike directly to the north, to the mountains; and, if the Kutenai were found in their usual places of abode, they expected to be able to reach them in twelve days. They did not think that they could be back before the next spring. This enterprise was very dangerous; and we, in fact, learnt, in the sequel, that Doucette had been shot by a Blood Indian, and that the expedition had proved a complete failure.

They had scarcely vanished from our sight behind the heights, when a great number of Blackfeet arrived, and among them many who were quite strangers to us, and who gazed on us with astonishment, as they had been but little accustomed to the sight of white men. They had put on their handsomest dresses, and were much dissatisfied when they learnt that the trade could not begin that day, because Mr. Mitchell was indisposed. The fort was crowded with them; we saw them smoking in every corner; and they were so idle, or so proud, that they gave their pipes to the first white man they saw to light them, though they were close to the kitchen fire. The gate was besieged by Indians who were by no means all permitted to enter, and we ourselves all refrained from going out, because the great assemblage of these people inside could not be trusted. The number of chiefs at this time in the fort was small, in comparison with the preceding year, when fifty-four of them were there at one time.

Among the Blackfeet who visited us there was an old man, called Homachseh-Kakatohs (the great star), who had a remarkable hooked nose. He wore the round felt hat with a tuft of feathers, which Mr. Bodmer made him take off, and then drew his portrait, which was an excellent likeness. When the drawing was finished, and he had received some tobacco, he rose, went into the court-yard, and delivered, with good address, a long speech, the tenor of which was: "The chief below (Mr. Mc Kenzie) had sent his children hither, and recommended them to the Blackfeet; they ought, therefore, to treat them well, to bring them good meat, that they might not lament and complain, but be merry, and always have their bellies full." [*The likeness of Great Star is on page 104.*]

Soon after the arrival of the Great Star, Tatsiki-Stomik and Ihkas-Kinne came to the fort; they all asked for brandy, which seemed to be the main subject for their thoughts. Ihkas-Kinne was a tall, well-looking man, with a very marked countenance. He wore an otter's skin over his shoulders, with the tail hanging down before, and which was ornamented all over with pieces of shell. [*For a portrait of Ihkas-Kinne, see page 141.*] This man had rendered some services to the fort, and was to be depended on. On this occasion he stepped forward, with a noble, manly air, and delivered a long speech. "The French," he said, "must have hearts ill-disposed towards the Indians; for, on the evening after the battle, they had not given the Blackfeet (he would not say a word of himself) anything to drink; even the chiefs had received nothing. They had come to the fort hungry and thirsty, and so they had left it, though they were fatigued by their exertions in fighting for the Whites. He was just this moment come from an expedition against the Crows, in which they had lost two of their people, and had no articles to trade with. They had traversed, without shoes, great tracts of prairie; their feet were sore, and tired, yet he had taken part in the action, and neither he nor others had received any present from the Whites."

Mr. Mitchell answered that "he would make the chiefs some presents tomorrow; though he thought that he had done enough, as he had distributed among them, on the preceding day, a great quantity of powder and ball, and received those that were in need into the fort. Though it was true that the Whites possessed many medicines which they could employ to the ruin of the Indians, he had no such thoughts. He would, however, show them such a one today, to give them an idea of the power of the Whites. When a cannon was fired, they should pay attention. Tomorrow he would have the colours hoisted, and a gun fired as a signal for the solemn reception of the chiefs." One of the Blackfeet chiefs had before observed, that "he was much surprised that the Whites always appeared in their common every day clothes, whereas they (the chiefs) put on their handsomest dresses. They had never seen the fine clothes of the Whites."

The chiefs having left us about six in the afternoon, the gate of the fort was shut, and, as soon as it was dark, Mr. Mitchell caused a gun to be fired, and then some skyrockets to be successively thrown up, which, as it happened, succeeded extremely well, rising to a great height, and bursting into stars. Most of the Indians, however, did not betray much astonishment at this exhibition, having already seen the same at the English posts. The Indians before the fort had already

The leader of one of the Siksika Blackfoot war parties that arrived too late to wreak its vengeance on the Assiniboins posed for his portrait in early September, after the excitement died down.

been dancing and singing to the sound of their drum; they now retired, rejoicing, to their tents. It was a still, moonlight night, but the noise of the Indians continued, and a watch was kept in the fort.

AUGUST 31, 1833                 [FIELD JOURNAL]

The White Buffalo, still suffering from his head wound, came last night to the fort with his wives and children and asked for quarters, as the smell of the dead women and children who had been buried hurriedly in a shallow trench was so intolerable that he could not sleep in his tent. Mr. Mitchell complied with his wish, and today he left early. At nine o'clock, when the cannon was fired as a signal for the Indians, it began to rain heavily. About twenty-four chiefs and most distinguished warriors of the Piegans advanced at a slow pace from the camp, all the other men staying behind. Women and children were gathered as spectators, crowding round the fort. Mr. Mitchell went out to meet the chiefs, and at that moment we could see on the brim of the hills beyond the Missouri the Blood Indians who had previously been in the neighbourhood. They wanted to camp at the fort. But Ninoch-Kiaiu now appeared and declared that if these Indians were permitted to approach, he would be inclined to shoot at them, even if entirely sober, and would be particularly so inclined in the event of intoxication. So word was sent to the Bloods not to come over.

The chiefs of the Piegans were beautifully attired, some even exquisitely so. But the heavy rain drove them singly to the fort, and since not all of them were known, some of them were not properly greeted with cannon fire. They were led to the dining quarters where they occupied the last room. Here they smoked and drank whiskey. Some of the chiefs, among them Tatsiki-Stomik in exquisite regalia, were in Mr. Mitchell's room. He made a long speech in which he said that we should not think that they were taking their skins to the north. It is quite in their interest to maintain good relations with the fort, as the other one is much too far for them. The angry heart against them should be calmed and all should believe that when some of them talked about going to the Hudson's Bay Company, this was merely an attempt to obtain merchandise on better terms. [*A portrait of Tatsiki-Stomik is on page 121.*]

All the chiefs demanded whiskey, and each was allotted a

A war bonnet or "feather cap," as Maximilian called them.

small barrel, but as we had not enough vessels, they received the whiskey partly in open kettles and tin pots. They were very seldom satisfied and all wanted more. Some were insulted and departed. It was impossible to satisfy all their demands, even though Mr. Mitchell distributed more than two [*large*] barrels as a gift, before the beginning of trade.

Towards noon, an attempt was begun to ease the chiefs out, one by one. Only Penukah-Zenin remained when a quarrel suddenly erupted at the gate. An Indian struck the gate keeper, who defended himself, and they scuffled fiercely. A knife was pulled, but fortunately Penukah-Zenin and another Indian restored peace by pushing the offender out the gate. We had hardly finished lunch when singing, shouting, and scuffling at the gate revealed the effects of the whiskey among the Indians. Soon shots were fired near the fort and the Piegans then fired at the Blood Indians, who returned the fire. Mr. Mitchell mounted a strong armed guard at the gate. The Blood Indians were lying on the high river bank across from the fort where we could see only their heads. We were shut in like prisoners. The gates were rigorously guarded, and outside one could hear the formidable noise of a frenzied throng. The Indians were given passage between the double gates and through a neighbouring room into the room where the trading was carried on. Here there was continuous pushing, high words, and fighting. Towards evening the Blood Indians retired to their camp, and by eight o'clock it had become rather quiet.

### SEPTEMBER 1, 1833

The trade continued today and we saw in the fort the wife of the chief of the Blood Indians, who had lately passed by the fort, and who much regretted the misunderstanding that had arisen between the Piegans and her tribe. They had entered into a negotiation with the Piegans, to atone by presents for their blood-guiltiness, which might lead to an amicable arrangement.

### SEPTEMBER 2, 1833

During the night some Indians had broken a hole through the clay wall of the Indian magazine, and stolen several articles, among which were some dresses of the chiefs; and it was evident that the thief must have kept himself concealed in the fort during the night. Towards seven in the morning we heard some musket-shot fired in the fort, and the band of our friend Kutonapi, about sixty or seventy in number, advanced to the fort, headed by three chiefs, who were admitted. All the principal chiefs of the Piegans arrived afterwards, whom Mr. Mitchell clothed in red uniforms, calico shirts, and every other article of dress—hung about their necks round looking-glasses, or silver medals with the bust of the President. The most amusing was when he put on them the new red felt hats, with red plumes of feathers. Their prodigious, long, thick hair was too large for the hat, and the whole was, therefore, made into a great bunch, and stuffed into the hat before it could be put on their heads. They suffered themselves to be dressed like children, and received other presents, such as powder, ball, tobacco, knives, &c. The dress of every chief might be estimated at ninety dollars.

In the meantime, a newly-arrived band of the Siksika had pitched their tents, and the fort was again surrounded by a multitude of dangerous men. Sometimes they threatened to fire at our people when they appeared on the pickets, and several things were stolen in the fort, because many men were still admitted on account of the trade. The chiefs were constantly begging, as well as the meanest Indians, and this may be justly stated as a most troublesome habit of the Blackfeet. In this respect the other tribes have much more delicacy. The Crows, in their visits and negotiations, presented the Blackfeet with valuable articles, costly feather caps, shields, horses, &c., but received nothing at all when they came to the latter, by which all the other Indian nations are incensed against the Blackfeet.

As the Indians became very troublesome towards evening, Mr. Mitchell had all the arms loaded with ball. Three detachments, each consisting of nine men and an officer, were commanded to keep guard, and he gave orders to fire from the pickets the instant an Indian attempted to climb over. All the chiefs were made acquainted with this order, that they might communicate it to their people. A new report being spread, that a thousand Assiniboins were approaching, the guards were doubled, and the officers divided, from which we strangers were not excepted.

During this state of imprisonment our horses suffered from want of food, as they could not be driven into the meadows, and there was but little hay in the fort. The Indians had used or burnt the hay that was in the prairies higher up on the

Missouri, and we were, therefore, much embarrassed about the horses.

## SEPTEMBER 3, 1833

In the morning, some shots were fired, and soon afterwards a new body of the Siksika, consisting of between thirty and forty men, arrived, of whom two of the principal warriors were admitted. They were tall and handsome, in costly new dresses. The name of the leader was Makuie-Kinn (the wolf's collar). The other carried in his hand the sign of the prairie dogs—a long crooked staff wound all round with otter's skin, and adorned with bunches of feathers. He told us that this medicine had the effect of rallying the warriors who were dispersed in the prairie. They told us that the greater portion of their people were in the north, but that two strong parties of warriors were coming; and, in fact, one of them, consisting of 150 men, soon appeared on the heights, where it halted, and afterwards came down to the fort. The chiefs were admitted, but soon dismissed, because they had no articles to trade with. The proper Blackfeet (Siksika) and the Blood Indians catch but few beavers, being chiefly engaged in war parties, and especially selling meat to the Hudson's Bay Company. The Piegans, on the other hand, catch the most beavers. Beaver traps (which are lent them) were distributed among them today, and many Indians went away to hunt.

## SEPTEMBER 4, 1833

Early in the morning, the band of the Blood Indians, who had lately been sent away, were seen approaching the fort, because the trade with the Piegans was concluded. Their old chief, Stomik-Sosak (the bull's hide), and a medicine man, Pehtonista (who calls himself the east), entered the fort. The first, a very good old man, had saved the life of Mr. Mitchell the year before, when an Indian was going to run him through with his spear. He is a great friend to the Whites, and resolved, with his small band, to remain faithful to the fort. He greatly regretted the late unfortunate occurrence, when his son had shot, by accident, as he affirmed, young Martin; and spoke much of his attachment to the French, as he called them. He called Mr. Mitchell his son, and added that, "to his great sorrow, he had been obliged to see the fort every day, without daring to come near it, on account of the unhappy difference with Ninoch-Kiaiu." [*For a portrait of Stomik-Sosak, see page 136.*]

One of the Siksika took off all his clothes, and laid them down as a present before Mr. Mitchell, on which Stomik-Sosak lent him his robe to cover him. On such an occasion these people do not hesitate to sit down quite naked. This was again a very unpleasant day to us, for the press of the savage Siksika was very violent. There was no end of their importunate begging, and dangerous men forced their way into the fort.

During the night Mr. Mitchell sent all the good horses belonging to the fort, about twenty in number, to Fort Union, by land, because we were not able to feed them any longer. Dechamp and his brother, with Papin and Vachard, were charged with this business, and arrived safe at Fort Union. The speedy removal of the horses was the more necessary, as the Indians intended to steal them, and so advantage was taken of the fine moonlight night to send them away.

## SEPTEMBER 5, 1833

It was my intention to pass the winter in the Rocky Mountains, and I had the execution of this project much at heart; but circumstances had arisen which rendered it very difficult, nay, impossible. A great number of the most dangerous Indians surrounded us on all sides, and had in particular occupied the country towards the Falls of the Missouri, which was precisely the direction we should have to take. They had obliged Mr. Mitchell to send away all the serviceable horses; so that, with the best will in the world, he could not have supplied us with these animals, which were indispensably necessary. Without an interpreter we could not undertake a journey which was very difficult for a few persons, and, Doucette having been sent away, Mr. Mitchell had not one left; at the same time, a long stay, which would be absolutely necessary for our researches in natural history, was quite out of the question, as we should be obliged, in some sort, to make our way by stealth. We had before asked old Tatsiki-Stomik whether we should encounter much danger in such an undertaking. His answer was, that "the Piegans might, perhaps, rob us, but would not probably treat us as enemies; but that the Bloods and the Siksika were fools, and we must be on our guard against them"; and, in truth, we might judge of the intentions of the latter, since they had fired with ball at the Piegans, though of their own nation.

For all these reasons, I therefore found myself compelled to give up my plan of going further up the Missouri, and therefore asked Mr. Mitchell for a vessel to return down the rivers; but, as he had not one to spare, he promised to have a new one built for me. As we might any day be attacked by the Assiniboins, and such an attack might have proved more serious than the preceding, much valuable time would be lost by our being again imprisoned in the fort. Autumn being already far advanced, a longer delay promised us a very unpleasant voyage and I endeavoured to have the work hastened as much as possible, in which Mr. Mitchell willingly co-operated. We had, besides, got pretty well acquainted with the Blackfeet Indians, and collected a great number of interesting portraits of them, and could not hope to observe anything new during the winter, or to add to our collection. As the Assiniboins were our enemies, to whom our scalps would doubtless have been a very welcome acquisition, I intended, in case of need, to make use of the night also, and I had therefore no time to lose.

Planks were cut for my new Mackinaw boat, and the carpenter or shipwright immediately set to work in the courtyard of the fort. The weather was rather cool, and the Gros Ventres des Prairies, who visited us early in the morning, came with their teeth chattering with cold, the nights being already frosty. A sign of autumn was, that the locusts sought their food on the shrubs, there being nothing more in the prairies, and the crows began to take their flight in large flocks to the south.

## September 11, 1833

During the day twenty-one men, belonging to the fort, took the boat, which had been built for me by the carpenter, Saucier, to the Missouri: the necessary arrangements for our voyage were made; large cages were made for my two live bears; and kitchen utensils and beds were procured. The cases, containing my collections, filled a great part of the boat, which, unfortunately, proved too small. I had received from the Company, Henry Morrin as steersman, and, besides him, three young, inexperienced Canadians, Beauchamp, Urbin, and Thiebaut, who were ill qualified for such a voyage, and did not even possess serviceable fire-arms. Thus, there were only seven persons in the boat, but time was most valuable. I fixed my departure for September 14.

Blackfoot drinking vessel made from the horn of a bighorn sheep.

The commencement of trading at Fort McKenzie that began on August 10 and continued for nearly a month brought thousands of Indians to the fort. Amid the tumult of the trading, Maximilian and Bodmer set about recording the ethnology of the various tribes. Most of the arriving guests were Piegans, Bloods, and Siksika of the Blackfoot nation, but there was also a large contingent of Gros Ventres des Prairies and a war party of uninvited guests—Assiniboins and Crees who made the attack on August 28. The two Europeans tracked down representatives of other tribes as well, and by the time the last beaver plew had been bartered they had completed an unsurpassed description of a fur-trading session.

---

*Opposite:* Tatsiki-Stomik (the middle bull), the principal chief of the Piegan Blackfeet, made a long speech of friendship at the formal opening of trade with his tribe on August 31. Maximilian was distressed that he posed in ordinary attire rather than in his splendid ceremonial regalia. To decorate their faces, Blackfeet warriors used a blue earth found in the foothills of the Rockies, in addition to the vermilion of the traders. *Overleaf:* Fort McKenzie was hastily erected in 1832 on the north bank of the Missouri, surrounded by a level plain suitable for the encampment of Indian trading parties. It was built in the same manner as the other Company forts and was about the same size as Fort Clark (forty-five paces square). Immediately across the river on the southern bank was a high clay bluff capped by a layer of sandstone. As the whites were soon to realize, this bluff could be easily mounted by hostile Indians who could then fire down into the stockade, placing the fort in serious jeopardy. Plans had been made to move it to a more secure location some miles upstream.

Different tastes in dress were displayed by a father and son. *Opposite:* Homach-Ksachkum (the great earth), a Kutenai Indian, wears an elkskin shirt and unadorned buffalo robe. His lower face is tattooed. *Above:* His son Makuie-Poka (the son of the wolf), whose mother was a Blackfoot, is dressed after the fashion of the downriver Mandans and Minnetarees. Glass beads and brass rings were obtained from the traders, as were the colorful blankets. Bear-claw necklaces and eagle-wing fans were produced by the Crows. Father and son departed Fort McKenzie with the ill-fated brigade headed for Kutenai territory that Maximilian describes on August 30 as "the expedition to the Kutenais."

As among the Indians in general, the lot of a Plains Indian woman was not an easy one. The men hunted, fought, and made their own weapons. The rest was left to the women. As Maximilian observed, "The women, who in general are well-treated among the Blackfeet [*that is, presumably, if one overlooks the custom of nose-chopping; see Maximilian's entry for August 15*], have to perform all the heavy work. They pitch the tents, chop sod, and lay it around the hem of the tents at the base. They cook, cut, gather and carry home the firewood, tan the hides, and care for the pieces of clothing. In short, they are rather busy." *Opposite:* a young Piegan Blackfoot woman whose husband allowed her to pose in return for a gift of vermilion and glass beads. *Above:* A snake Indian woman, wife of the *engagé* Marcereau. Maximilian attributed her dark complexion to a liver disorder.

Two chiefs of the Gros Ventres des Prairies who were first encountered on the upstream voyage at the Stone Walls on August 5 later showed up at Fort McKenzie, where Bodmer continued work on their portraits. *Above:* Niatohsa (the little French man) who received a warm reception at the fort on August 14. *Opposite:* Mexkemanastan (the iron that stirs) was known as a deceitful and dangerous man. He had been expelled from the fort the year before for threatening to shoot David Mitchell, but behaved well enough during the 1833 trading session. *Overleaf:* A view of the Rocky Mountains painted in September from the vicinity of Fort McKenzie, looking south across the Missouri. This is probably the Little Belt Range.

The medicine men of many of the Plains tribes wore their hair in a topknot bound with a leather thong, as shown in the portraits of these three Blackfeet. *Opposite page:* Pioch-Kiaiu (the distant bear), a Piegan notable whose portrait Bodmer took because of his remarkable physiognomy. After the battle with the Assiniboins on August 28, he told Bodmer with great satisfaction that no bullet had touched him, doubtless because of the strong medicine of the painting. Others among the Blackfeet were not so fortunate. But even the severely wounded recovered, according to Maximilian, although scarcely because of the ministrations of the medicine men. The prince noted in his field journal that "the medicine men of the Blackfeet are rather awkward. They spat water on the severely wounded, distributed whiskey in large quantities, shouted and pulled the wounded about from one spot to another. The Blackfeet have allegedly healed some serious wounds with good results, but from what I have seen, I have to attribute this success primarily to the strong constitutions of these primitive men."

*Opposite:* Mehkskehme-Sukahs (the iron shirt), a principal chief of the Piegan Blackfeet, dressed for the ceremonial opening of trade at Fort McKenzie on August 10. Earlier in the day, Maximilian had been a guest at a feast in his tepee. Iron Shirt's hairdress includes an ermine skin, grizzly-bear claw, and feathers from various birds of prey. His buckskin shirt had an otter collar and was ornamented with bright buttons and blue and white beadwork. The black face paint indicates an heroic deed of recent vintage. *Above:* A Piegan warrior posed for Bodmer in a nicely worked buffalo robe. His identity is unknown.

*Below:* Stomik-Sosak (the bull's hide), a **Blood** chief whose son had killed the young *engagé* Martin on August 12, touching off a bloody dispute with Ninoch-Kiaiu and his band of Piegans. Once the Piegans had finally departed, Stomik-Sosak was able to lead his small band of Bloods into the fort for trading on September 4. *Opposite:* An unidentified Piegan warrior who posed in his elaborately painted elkhide robe, wearing his rifle sheath as a headdress. Bows and guns indicate weapons captured, while enemies wounded or slain are symbolized by hourglass figures. The octopuslike black symbols on the lower skirt are scalps. At his shoulder, the triangular yellow and green figures probably represent horsewhips which always accompanied horses presented as gifts. Thus, this combination of whips and weapons most likely details this warrior's generosity. The numerous horse tracks indicate stolen horses.

*Above:* Natoie-Poochsen (the word of life), a Piegan elder and uncle of Ninoch-Kiaiu, in mourning for his grand-nephew, who was killed by a Blood Indian on August 16. The mourning customs of the Blackfeet were similar to those of the other Plains Indians. The men cut their hair, donned their poorest clothes, and painted their faces white. Women chopped off a finger joint. *Opposite:* Ninoch-Kiaiu (the chief of the bears), a bellicose Piegan chief whom David Mitchell honored with the gift of an expensive uniform at the opening of trade on August 10. Formerly known as Spotted Elk, he had changed his name after leading a successful war party against the Flatheads three months earlier. The Bear Chief and 500 Piegan warriors had fallen upon a band of 45 Flatheads and two French-Canadians in the Rocky Mountains. All 47 were killed and their scalps taken, the Blackfeet losing six dead and a number wounded. Ninoch-Kiaiu's feud with the Bloods led to the murder of his nephew. When he appeared at the fort on August 16 vowing vengeance, he was dressed in mourning, although he had not cut his hair, explaining to Maximilian that the head of Ninoch-Kiaiu "was too great and strong to do this."

*Above:* Pachkaab-Sachkoma-Poh (the wretched boy), a young Piegan, posed with his feather fan and trade blanket. The demand for large bird feathers among the Blackfeet was such that the Company had begun shipping turkey tails up to Fort McKenzie from the Lower Missouri. Young men of fashion favored the trade blanket made into a cloak far above the traditional leather shirts. *Opposite:* Ihkas-Kinne (the low horn), a Siksika Blackfoot chief in his war dress: otter skins ornamented with pieces of mother of pearl. He delivered a speech at the fort on August 30 complaining that the whites were not liberal enough with alcohol and other gifts to the chiefs. *Overleaf:* Detail from a watercolor painted in September, just before the expedition's departure for Fort Union, showing the Missouri with the Bear Paw Mountains in the distance.

In the autumn rutting season, vast herds of buffalo gathered along the Missouri and were ardently pursued by hunting parties.

## PART V

# Fort McKenzie to Fort Clark

## September 14-November 8, 1833

Accepting the advice of David Mitchell and Tatsiki-Stomik against attempting to winter in the Rockies, Maximilian turned his face downstream. His new plan was to ship down the Missouri past Fort Union to Fort Clark and there emulate Lewis and Clark by spending the winter among the Mandans and Minnetarees. That he would be traveling the same stretch of river up which he had so recently voyaged dismayed the prince not at all. He was more than ready for another glimpse of the natural wonders of the Upper Missouri. But if the whites had felt it necessary to exercise caution in passing through Indian country on their way upstream, the need would be even greater on the way down. The Assiniboins, through whose territory they would be passing, would be unlikely to forgive the whites for the role they played in support of the Blackfeet during the recent battle. Moreover, in place of the keelboat and its complement of fifty hardened Company men with whom Maximilian journeyed upstream, the downstream voyage would be made in a small Mackinaw boat manned by a crew of seven: Maximilian, Bodmer, Dreidoppel, the helmsman Henry Morrin, and three young Canadian *engagés* who did not even possess their own rifles. The small party would offer an irresistible temptation to any band of marauding Indians.

SEPTEMBER 14, 1833

The morning was fine and bright, and promised us a pleasant voyage. By noon all our effects were put on board the new boat, and it became more and more evident that we had not sufficient room in this vessel. The great cages, with the live bears, were placed upon the cargo in the centre, preventing us from passing from one end of the boat to the other; besides this, there was not room for us to sleep on board; this was a most unfavourable circumstance, because it obliged us always to lie to for the night. At one o'clock in the afternoon, we took leave of our kind host, Mr. Mitchell, and his companion, Mr. Culbertson; all the inhabitants of the fort accompanied us to the river, where a cannon was placed to

"Our hunters killed a very large buffalo. Mr. Bodmer made a drawing of the head of the magnificent animal whose thick, coal-black frontal hair was eighteen inches long."

salute us. We had lived so long together in the wilderness, that we naturally took a lively interest in the fate of those who remained behind to pass the winter in a place where they would be exposed to so many dangers and privations, and wished them courage and perseverance to encounter them. Our boat glided rapidly along, and we soon took a last look at the fort and its inhabitants, to whom we waved our hands to bid them at last farewell. In half an hour we reached the place where we had passed the night before we arrived at the fort in the keel-boat, and the steersman now chose the northern channel, which led, about half-past two o'clock, by the ruins of the old fort.

Towards four o'clock a thunder-storm came on, and the sky became entirely covered with thick clouds. As we had reason to be on our guard against the Indians, we regretted that my two bears were unusually dissatisfied with their confinement, and manifested their feelings by moaning and growling, which might very easily have attracted some hostile visitors. We lay to, before twilight, at a prairie on the right, where we had an extensive view, kindled a fire, and dressed our meat, part of which was put on board, and we continued our voyage. When night was fully set in, we were on the steep high bank of the south side of the Missouri, and, as it was too dark to proceed, we fastened the boat to some trunks of trees, and passed a very uncomfortable night, lying in our boat, while a heavy cold rain prevented us from sleeping.

SEPTEMBER 15, 1833

In the morning we were in a lamentable plight. We were all of us, more or less, wet and benumbed, as the boat had no deck, and we found, to our great dismay, that this new vessel was very leaky, so that the greater part of our luggage was wet through. The rain had ceased, and a bleak wind chilled our wet limbs; as soon, therefore, as we had bailed out the greater part of the water, we hastened to proceed on our voyage. When we approached the Gate of the Stone Walls, the sun was just rising behind that interesting opening. Some numerous herds of antelopes and bighorns looked down from the singular sand-stone walls on the early disturbers of their respose. We would gladly have gone in pursuit of these animals, in order to obtain some game; but it was high time to ascertain the damage done by the water. When the sun had risen a little higher, we landed on the south bank, and made

a large fire, for which we took the wood of an old Indian hunting-hut, in a wood of tall poplars. Our drenched buffalo robes and blankets were brought on shore to dry, and I discovered, to my great regret, that the pretty striped squirrel, which I had hoped to bring alive to Europe, was drowned in its cage.

After stopping about an hour, during which time we had warmed and refreshed ourselves with coffee and meat, we proceeded, and at half-past nine reached the commencement of the Stone Walls. At any other time I should have been again highly interested by the remarkable features of this spot; but now I was extremely impatient to know the extent of our loss.

Numbers of wild sheep were everywhere seen; but the still more numerous colonies of swallows had retired at the coming of autumn, and, instead of these, we saw flocks of magpies on the mountains. We gave chase in vain to a couple of very large elks. At half-past eleven we passed the mouth of Stonewall Creek, and lay to on the north bank. As the sun now shone with considerable power, we hastened completely to unload the boat, to open and unpack all the chests and trunks, one by one. How grieved were we to find all our clothes, books, collections, some mathematical instruments, in a word, all our effects, entirely wet and soaked. The chests were, for the most part, open in all the joints, and quite useless; but what afflicted me the most, was my fine botanical collection of the Upper Missouri, made with labour and expense of time, which I could not now put into dry paper, and which therefore, was, for the most, lost, as well as the Indian leather dresses, which became mouldy. We had now no resource but to remain where we were till most of our things were dried; a most disagreeable necessity. A large spot of the prairie was covered with our scattered effects, and a wind arising caused some disorder among our goods, and we were obliged to take care that nothing might be lost. My extensive herbarium had to be laid, on account of the wind, under the shelter of the eminences of a small lateral ravine, which took me the whole day, and yet all the plants became black and mouldy.

At this place, Morrin killed, for the use of our kitchen, a deer (*Cervus macrotis*), which had already assumed its grey under coat. This kind of deer is distinguished and well known by its long ears, which are especially remarkable in the female. When the flesh was cooked, we all wrapped ourselves in our blankets, and lay down to sleep on the high bank of the river, while two persons constantly kept guard, and were relieved every two hours. I had to keep watch with Thiebaut from nine to eleven o'clock, which was not an unpleasant time, as the night was warm and still, and rather moonlit. A deer crossed the river pretty near us, as it began to dawn, but nobody fired, in order not to make any unnecessary noise.

### SEPTEMBER 16, 1833

We remained at this place till nearly evening. Happily for us the sun was again very warm, and, combined with the wind, saved a part of our effects. After our cooking was finished, and all the chests put on board again, we continued our voyage, passed the Citadel Rock, to which we bid adieu for ever, not without regret; saw wolves, wild sheep, and a multitude of bats, the latter of which flew rapidly over the bright mirror of the river, and halted for the night at a sandy flat below a high bank, where I had the first watch. While the remainder of the company lay on the ground, wrapped in their blankets, and sunk in deep sleep, I amused myself with contemplating the grotesque ghost-like formation of the white sand-stone of the Stone Walls, amidst the howling of the wolves, and the melancholy note of the owl.

### SEPTEMBER 17, 1833

We passed rapidly through the Gate of the Stone Walls, where the wonders described earlier passed us as in a dream. They would, perhaps, have left but an indistinct and gradually fading impression, had not the skilful hand of the draughtsman rescued them from oblivion. Only trappers and the *engagés* of the fur company sometimes look with indifference on these interesting scenes of nature, the value of which few of them can appreciate; the greater number esteem a few dollars above all the wonders of the Rocky Mountains. Towards eight o'clock we prepared our breakfast in a prairie on the northern bank, and warmed our benumbed limbs, while herds of buffaloes were grazing on the hills. On the beach we saw the track of a large bear, and of many stags, elks, and buffaloes. Eagles, ravens, crows, and magpies flew above the river. At ten o'clock we reached the place where, on our journey up the river, we had met the Gros Ventres des Prairies; now we did not see a living creature—a most striking contrast!

### SEPTEMBER 18, 1833

This day led us through the remarkable valley of the Mauvaises Terres. Unfortunately we had a bleak cold wind on our backs, which frightened away the numerous bighorns, elks, and many herds of buffaloes that were grazing on both sides of the river, in the little prairies covered with artemisia, at the foot of the steep, bare eminences. The wind enabled them to scent our approach at a considerable distance, as soon as our boat got into a bend of the river, and we often landed in vain to add to our stock of provisions. On this occasion we had many amusing scenes. A herd of twelve elks passed the river before us; the last was a large stag with colossal horns, this being the rutting season of these animals. The herds of buffaloes were sometimes thrown into the greatest confusion and consternation when we came too near them: they galloped along the bank, and when they were tired of this, they turned into a lateral ravine, where we saw these heavy animals ascend the high steep mountains. It often appeared inconceivable how these colossal masses could make their way up the steep naked walls. Sometimes, however, they were obliged to turn back, and we intercepted the only way to the river. They were then frequently compelled to gallop along the narrow beach near to our boat, which, being carried rapidly down the stream, gave us frequent opportunities of overtaking them, and we might easily have killed several of them, but, as they were almost all bulls, we let them escape unmolested. (Among these animals there are some that are very large and fat, with longer horns than the others; these are such as have been castrated by the Indians when calves. They are said to become extremely fat and heavy.)

About ten o'clock we lay to, on the north bank, at a wild prairie, benumbed by the cold wind, and warmed ourselves. Among the Canadian pines the note of the little tree frog was still very loud in this cold weather. At two in the afternoon we reached the mouth of Winchers Creek, near which a large herd of buffaloes was grazing; in fact, we had seen, on this day, many thousands of these animals in Mauvaises Terres, where, as we went up the river, all was still and dead. This was a sign that there were no Indians in these parts; they had, doubtless, been hunting in the prairies, and driven these animals away. We saw everywhere buffaloes in herds, or in small parties, which gave much variety to our voyage. As we were rapidly carried down by the current, in a turn of the river, we suddenly saw a herd of at least 150 buffaloes, quite near to us, standing on a sand bank in the river. The bulls, bellowing, drove the cows along; many were in motion, and some standing and drinking. It was a most interesting scene. My people laid aside their oars, and let the boat glide noiselessly along within a short rifle-shot of the herd, which took no notice of us, doubtless taking our boat for a mass of drifting timber. Scarcely sixty paces further down, there was, on a sand bank, a troop of six elks, with a large stag, which covered one of the animals three times in our presence. We saw him lay his horns on his back when he uttered his singular whistling cry. [*For Bodmer's watercolor of this scene, see pages 162–163.*]

We reached Lewis and Clark's Tea Island, to which we had given the name of Elk Island, and where, on our voyage up, we had found plenty of game. I landed Morrin and Dreidoppel on the upper end, to go in quest of game; the rest of us proceeded down towards the lower end, where we stopped to cook. Buffaloes and elks had crossed the river before us, and we heard the noise they made in the water at a considerable distance. The island was covered with lofty trees, and, in many places, with tall plants, especially artemisia, but had many grassy and open spots, and we found on it five buffaloes, and several troops of elks and Virginian deer. A white wolf looked at us from the opposite bank, and the great cranes flew slowly and heavily before us. Our fire soon blazed in the forest, and Morrin brought in some game, which afforded us a good supper. While it was getting ready, we rambled about the island, and heard in all directions the bellowing of the buffalo bulls, and the whistling of the elks. I found the rutting places of the latter in the high grass, but soon returned to the fire, as the cry of the owl warned us of the approach of night.

On consideration we judged this place to be ill suited for our night's quarters, as we might easily have been surprised by the Indians; we, therefore, went on board again, as soon as the meat was dressed, and continued our voyage, in the bright moonlight, till near nine o'clock. The evening was warm and pleasant. We often heard the noise made by the buffaloes crossing the river. The forests on the bank to the right and left resounded with the whistling of the elks, alternating with the howling of the wolves; and the shrill cry of the owl completed the nocturnal chorus of the wilderness. Our blankets and buffalo robes, which were still wet, froze during the night, as we had lain down on the strand by the

Wolves feeding on the carcass of a buffalo along the Missouri.

Coyotes, or prairie wolves as Maximilian called them, serenaded the travelers nightly on the downstream voyage.

river side, where we had a cold, uncomfortable couch. The manner in which we passed these nights was not calculated to afford any very refreshing sleep; for, to be ready, in case of alarm, we could never venture to undress, but lay down in a buffalo skin and a blanket, and the same to cover us, with our loaded guns under the blanket to keep them dry. We were pretty safe from a surprise, two persons always keeping watch, relieved every two hours.

SEPTEMBER 19, 1833

We set out early. A fog rose from the river, and we sat wrapped up in our cloaks, quite benumbed with cold, while the whistling cry of the elks was heard all around us. Five females of this species, followed by a proud stag, swam through the river before us; we fired too soon, on which the stag turned round; the animals came near us, and thereby afforded an opportunity to fire with effect; one of the animals was wounded, but proceeded on its way, and we did not get possession of it. At the moment, when the other animals sought to reach the bank, another noble stag appeared, which stopped at the distance of fifty paces, and uttered a loud cry. I quickly threw off my cloak, and took my rifle; but at that moment my pilot, Morrin, fired his long piece, and the stag fell. We immediately lay to, ascended the steep bank, and were astonished at finding a most magnificent stag of twenty points stretched on the ground. I immediately took the measure of the gigantic animal, and found the horns, from the head to the point of the uppermost antler, in a straight line, four feet one inch; the weight of both horns, sawn off at the head, was twenty-six pounds. The colour of the stag in this autumnal season was very beautiful: the whole body of a pale yellowish-brown; the head, neck, the under side of the belly and extremities, a dark blackish-brown, which looked very handsome, especially at a distance. We soon had an excellent fire in the thick forest, which revived our chilled limbs. Breakfast was quickly got ready, and the enjoyment of it was much enhanced by our success. The stag was cut up, and the beautiful skin prepared entire for the zoological collection, which gave us full employment till dinner-time. Meantime our beds and other baggage, which had been wetted by the rain, were dried in the sun.

When our work was finished, the boat was again loaded, and we put off from the bank. After the shot we had fired, the cry or whistle of the elks had ceased; but we saw several of those animals, and also buffaloes, flying in different directions. When evening came, bats flew about over the river, and eagles and falcons appeared on the bank. As soon as twilight commenced, we proceeded softly and cautiously down the river. Our boat glided noiselessly along, while profound silence, which was seldom interrupted, reigned in the extensive wilderness that surrounded us, and in the dark forests on the banks. Man naturally seeks and takes pleasure in the sight of his fellows; but we were very glad that there were no human beings here besides ourselves. We continued our voyage for a long time by moonlight; but the dark shadows of the banks were dangerous, for the water dashed and foamed against the visible and invisible snags, which it required the greatest care to avoid. It was fortunate for us that Morrin was a very good pilot, who was well acquainted with the Missouri. We passed the night on the flat sandy beach, where we might have been betrayed by the disagreeable roaring of our bears. Those who kept watch had the pleasure of seeing a fine aurora borealis, which continued for half an hour in all its splendour.

SEPTEMBER 20, 1833

Very early we saw a large bear, which was pursued without success. A large herd of buffaloes being found in a favourable situation, Morrin and Dreidoppel landed to approach them behind the willow thickets, and they succeeded in killing two fat cows, which furnished us with an ample supply of excellent meat. The immense horns of an elk, fixed at the head of the boat, the antlers of which were all hung with joints of meat, had a singular appearance. These provisions sometimes procured us a visit from the forward magpies, which, without the least shyness, perched on the stem of the boat, and uttered their note, which is quite different from that of the European magpie. This magpie is a droll bird, much more so than those of Europe, and often diverted us by its impertinence. We saw some numerous flocks of small birds setting out on their autumnal migration, and I observed, among others, a flock of the beautiful bluefinch, which flew across the river. At noon we lay to at an old poplar grove to prepare our dinner. Buffaloes and elks were very numerous at this place, and we might have shot several of them had we not thought it prudent to avoid all unnecessary noise.

Porcupine, whose quills were important to the Indians for their handicrafts, were still relatively plentiful in 1833.

Having reached Musselshell River early in the morning, provisions were soon obtained from a numerous herd of buffaloes standing on the bank: a shot from our boat killed a calf. We immediately lay to, and, following the bloody trace, found the animal dead in the grove of poplars. It was of a dark brown colour, the nose and muzzle rather lighter; its horns were just sprouting. Our firing, and the smell of the meat while breakfast was preparing, immediately attracted the wolves. We soon heard them howling in the vicinity, and, in a short time, saw them assembling on a sand bank on the other side of the river. Twelve of them, of different colours and sizes, had galloped up on hearing the shot, stopped a moment and looked at us, then turned back for a short distance, lay down or seated themselves, and entertained us with a concert of their sweet voices. Some of them were quite white, others rather grey on the back, many very old and corpulent, others small, young, and slender.

We left this place about nine o'clock, and, with the help of my skilful pilot, passed, without accident, some parts of the river which were full of snags. The foliage of the poplar woods was now quite yellow, especially that of the young trees. A few swallows were still to be seen; the red-tailed woodpecker and the magpie were frequent in these parts. We saw some very large male elks, many Virginian deer, and buffaloes; some of the latter were rolling on their backs in the parched prairie, making the dust fly in clouds. Numbers of wolves were seen the whole day, doubtless attracted by the scent of the pieces of meat that were hung up about the boat. Herds of buffaloes were likewise met with, which we often overtook as they were swimming in the river, but did not fire at them; there were also large troops of elks, among which were some stags of extraordinary size. This great abundance of wild animals was a very satisfactory proof to us that the Indians were at a distance from this part of the river. The weather had been, on the whole, very favourable; on this day it had been very warm, but the evening was rather cool. The people laid aside their oars, and suffered the boat to drift down the stream. A solemn silence prevailed in the vast solitary wilderness, where Nature, in all her savage grandeur, reigned supreme. Not a breath of air was stirring; buffaloes were quietly grazing on the sides of the hills, and even my bears lay still, after a fresh bed of poplar branches had been made for them. Nobody spoke a

After months of searching, Maximilian finally obtained a gopher for Bodmer's sketch pad, near Fort Union.

word; it seemed as if we were involuntarily led by the impressions made by the scene, at the solemn evening hour, to give way to serious contemplation, for which there was ample matter. It was our constant caution to let our boat glide silently along in the evening, because it was necessary, at that time, to be more on our guard against the Indians, who are said, generally, to return to their tents in the evening. We passed today, after dark, the White Castles, which have been mentioned before, and much regretted not having once more seen these extraordinary formations, below which we lay to.

### SEPTEMBER 22, 1833

Our voyage, early in the morning, was very pleasant and interesting. A herd of buffaloes raised a great cloud of dust in their flight, and it seemed that they must be pursued by the Indians. Kingfishers, which we had not seen in our progress up the river, were now pretty numerous on all these banks; and when we lay to at eight o'clock to get our breakfast ready, the note of the little tree frog, with which I did not become acquainted, was heard among the wormwood bushes. We often passed what are called Indian forts, and our people generally looked very anxiously to see if they were occupied, which, luckily for us, was nowhere the case. My Canadians were so timid that they did not venture to speak loud, and, if we stopped for a moment, they testified, by their restless gestures, their apprehensions and their impatience. At half-past eleven o'clock, between Musselshell and Milk Rivers, we passed the Half-way Pyramid, which lay to the south of us. During the whole day we saw many buffaloes and elks, and a skunk on the bank, which escaped us, and a small flock of the whooping crane, one of the finest birds of North America, which was on its flight to warmer regions. The moon shone with extraordinary splendour when we lay to for the night, while the howling of the wolves and the whistle of the elks were heard all around.

### SEPTEMBER 23, 1833

The morning was fine and pleasant; but so violent a wind soon arose, that we were compelled to lie to at the prairie near a poplar wood. We took this opportunity of drying our damp baggage in the wind, setting a watch in the prairie, that we might not be surprised by the Indians. During this time a great bear came out of the willow bushes, and swam directly towards us, across the river; we had already posted ourselves behind some trees to receive him with a volley at his coming on shore, when, perhaps, he perceived the smell of our boat, lying near the bank, and, to our no small chagrin, quietly turned back. It was not till five o'clock that the wind abated so as to allow us to proceed. We were entertained by the loud whistle of the elks, many of which were lying in the river to cool themselves. Morrin wounded a young deer at a great distance, and we immediately saw a wolf go after it, which, doubtless, soon put an end to the poor animal.

### SEPTEMBER 24, 1833

Autumn had already tinged the foliage with various colours. We did not indeed see here the scarlet stag's-horn sumach, but a couple of other species of that genus were, in some degree, substitutes for that colour. At half-past two in the afternoon, we passed near the mouth of Milk River, where we remarked great numbers of bears, elks, deer, and wolves on the bank, and some wild geese and sandpipers on the strand. At the place where we killed the three bears, on our voyage up the river, we now found numerous elks; magpies, blackbirds, and the great prairie larks abounded. We saw today several beaver dens, and counted twenty-seven in all from Fort Mc Kenzie to Fort Union.

### SEPTEMBER 25, 1833

Towards three o'clock such a violent storm arose, that we hastened to secure our heavily-laden boat on the bank, behind a snag: this was 400 or 500 paces from the spot where the keel-boat was wrecked the year before. The bank was very steep, and on the summit there was a wood of poplars. The storm increased in violence to such a degree that it seemed as if it would throw down the trees on our heads; and it brought clouds of dust from the opposite sand banks into our forest, so that the air was darkened. Sparrow-hawks, ravens, crows, and blackbirds, took refuge in the recesses of the forest; a herd of antelopes had also sought protection at the skirts of the wood, and we observed the buck pursue and drive back any of the females that attempted to leave the herd. We built ourselves a fort in the Indian fashion, of trunks of trees and branches, where we took up our lodging for the night, when we could scarcely hear the cry of the elks or the growling of a bear for the roaring of the storm.

### SEPTEMBER 26, 1833

The storm abated, and allowed us to proceed on our voyage, so that by day-break we reached Mr. Mitchell's petit fort, of which the prairie hens had taken possession. Swans and ducks animated the river, and flocks of the little finch were flying about on the bank. In the evening we had a heavy rain, and our bivouac was very uncomfortable; after mounting guard for a couple of hours, we had to lie down under our buffalo skins and blankets, which were wet through.

### SEPTEMBER 27, 1833

About eleven in the morning we reached the Prairie à la Corne de Cerf. The sky was overcast, the weather very cool, and about noon it began to rain so heavily, that we lay to at a lofty wood to seek for shelter, but were soon wet through while we were erecting a slight wooden covering against the torrents of rain, which we covered with our skins and blankets. Of half a dozen deer which we met with in the neighbourhood we killed one, the flesh of which refreshed us. The unfavourable weather continued till midnight.

### SEPTEMBER 28, 1833

Our thoroughly soaked effects were brought on board about nine o'clock, and we continued our voyage. The wind blew bleak and unpleasant the whole day. We soon came to the rude, apparently desolate chain of hills that extends to Fort Union, proceeded till one o'clock in the morning, and then, cold and benumbed, lay at a sand bank, when those whose turn it was to keep watch had no very enviable lot.

### SEPTEMBER 29, 1833

Cranes awoke at the same time as we did, and rose with loud cries in the misty air. We were stiff with cold, till the sun, as he rose higher in the heavens, warmed us a little. About nine o'clock we lay to at the sandy coast before the forest, on the south bank, kindled a fire, and prepared breakfast—a blessing which only those can appreciate, who, like us, have been long exposed to bad weather, cold, wet, storms, and privations of every kind. It was high time for us to reach Fort Union, for our most necessary provisions were exhausted, and, in another day, we should have been deprived of the comfort of coffee, which we should have felt more than all the rest. A large deer but lately had his lair very near us, and, perhaps, we had disturbed him; we, however, had no time at present to go in pursuit of him, for it was necessary to arrange our dress, which was completely disordered, and make ourselves a little decent, before we could show ourselves in society. The business of the toilet took us no little time; so that it was twelve o'clock before we could set out for Fort Union, where we arrived safe at one o'clock, after an absence of about three months.

Maximilian found Fort Union and its surroundings much changed since his visit in July. The large Indian encampments had disappeared and a solitary tepee, inhabited by a half-breed Blackfoot, was all that remained. The prairie was dry and the vegetation withered. Mornings and evenings were chilly; the nights cold. Kenneth McKenzie was not in residence, having taken a company of twenty men downstream to the Little Missouri, and was not expected back for two months. During his absence the fort was under the command of his English adjutant, James A. Hamilton, assisted by three clerks: Brazeau, Moncrevier, and Francis A. Chardon, who was to have a long and somewhat controversial career with the Company. Many of the fort's fifty *engagés* were at work rebuilding the wooden palisades, and Maximilian noted with approval that a new powder magazine, constructed of hewn stone, had been completed. (The year before, the old wooden powder magazine, containing 2,000 pounds of gunpowder, had very nearly been set afire by a wind-whipped blaze that did a great deal of damage to the fort. The suave Hamilton received the prince and his party with great cordiality and assigned the three Europeans a pleasant apartment. Maximilian spread his collections out to dry in the loft of the commandant's quarters and settled in for a stay of four weeks. One of the first things he wanted to do was take part in a buffalo hunt:

Drawing of a magnificent elk with a rack of twenty points that was killed by an expertly placed shot from the Mackinaw boat on September 19, by Henry Morrin, the helmsman.

### OCTOBER 11, 1833

As the hunters of the fort generally went out twice in a week to replenish our stock of meat, I resolved to accompany them, and join in the chase of the buffalo on horseback. After breakfasting earlier than usual, the horses were sent, in a large boat, across the Missouri. The weather was pleasant; at half-past seven the thermometer was at 40°, and in the afternoon at 65½°. We landed in a lofty forest of poplar, ash, negundo, and elm, with a thick undergrowth of snowberries, roses covered with beautiful red blossom, and buffalo berries, which had then ripe red fruit. Here we collected the horses and mules, of which we had eighteen, loaded them, and warmed ourselves a little while at a fire. Our party consisted of Mr. Bodmer, Chardon, and myself, and the half-breed Cree Dechamp, Marcellais, Joseph Basile, and Antoine Fleming, the Negro slave of Mr. Mc Kenzie. In addition, there were three or four more men who led the horses that were to carry the meat. We soon proceeded on our expedition; and, as we rode along, were amused by the cheerful and enterprising Chardon, who had lived long among the Osages, and was able to give the most authentic information respecting that people, and the Indians in general. Listening to his animated descriptions, his communications relative to the Indian languages, alternating with Indian songs and the war-whoop, we passed through the forest, then across a meadow, where a few isolated bushes grew, and where we raised a covey of prairie hens; and then over a chain of hills, where we followed a beaten path. Skeletons of buffaloes, nearly entire, and numbers of skulls, which might have furnished many an osteological cabinet, lay scattered around.

We proceeded in quick trot and gallop across the prairie, where the larks flew up before us, and ravens and crows appeared in great numbers. A few buffaloes that we saw at a distance did not induce us to stop, for we had twenty miles to ride before we could think of the chase. Towards noon we came to a little creek, called the Rivière aux Tortues, meandering through a meadow, a hill on the north side of which protected us from the wind. Here we halted a little, the baggage was taken off the horses, and they were left to graze, while a fire of buffalo dung was kindled, and a duck

roasted, which had been shot by a half-breed, who had hastened on before us. After resting for some time, we proceeded over gentle hills till about five in the afternoon, when we came to a pretty considerable hill, beyond which herds of buffaloes are usually met with. Before we reached the summit, we crossed a small ravine, where we found a spring of cool clear water, which refreshed us greatly.

When we reached the top of the hill, we examined with the telescope the extensive plain, and perceived some small groups of buffaloes, four, five, or six together, the most numerous of which we resolved to attack. The pack-horses followed slowly, and the hunters proceeded, in quick trot, to a hollow between two hills, where we saw the animals at no great distance on our left hand. With our pieces ready to fire, we made a regular cavalry charge on the heavy animals, which, however, galloped away at a pretty brisk rate. The horsemen divided, and pursued the bulls, which were partly shot by the practised marksmen, and partly wounded by the others; these were pursued, and did not fall till many shot had been fired at them. I had followed a wounded bull into the ravine, and three of us repeatedly fired at him. He often put himself in a threatening attitude, and even pursued us for ten or twenty paces, but, in such cases, it is easy to avoid him, and the frightened animal immediately took to flight again as soon as we halted. At length, after twenty shot, perhaps, had been fired at him, his strength failed, and he sank down.

The half-breeds and the Indians are so skilful in this kind of hunting on horseback, that they seldom have to fire several times at a buffalo. They do not put the gun to their shoulder, but extend both arms, and fire in this unusual manner as soon as they are within ten or fifteen paces of the animal. They are incredibly quick in loading; for they put no wadding to the charge, but let the ball (of which they generally have several in their mouth) run down to the powder, where it sticks, and is immediately discharged. With this rapid mode of firing these hunters of the prairie soon make a terrible slaughter in a herd of buffaloes. In the present case, the whole of the little herd of buffaloes was killed; nine bulls lay on the field, and our hunters had dispersed in such a manner that we had not a little trouble to collect our whole party. I had separated from the rest, rode for some miles over low eminences, and, at length, when it was getting dusk, met with Marcellais, who had killed a buffalo.

Here, too, I found Mr. Bodmer, who took a sketch of the animal that was killed. [*For the completed painting, see pages 164–165.*] We rode back to the ravine, and endeavoured to kindle a fire of buffalo dung in this place of general rendezvous; the wind was bleak, and we could not make our fire burn bright. There was no wood at all; but we threw fat and marrow-bones into the fire, by way of fuel. Some meat was roasted as well as the circumstances permitted; and when we were going to lie down to rest, it appeared that my portable bed, of buffalo skins and blankets, had been forgotten. This was no very pleasant discovery, for the wind was raw, the fire bad, and the rain falling; however, the hunters, who were quite used to such bivouacs, gave me a part of their blankets, and we slept very comfortably.

OCTOBER 12, 1833

We breakfasted on roast meat and buffalo marrow; the horses were collected and saddled, and the flesh of the buffaloes fastened to the pack-saddles. Eighteen years before I had had my mules collected in the same manner in the Campos of Brazil, when I wanted to continue my journey; but in that beautiful and warm country, where Nature is so grand and so rich, the bivouacs in the forest are more cheerful and pleasant, and form a striking contrast to the melancholy life in the prairies, where you have to suffer so many privations. We rode rapidly forward, and halted at noon, in the bed of a dried-up stream, in order to rest, and take some refreshment. About four miles from Fort Union, our half-breed Indians found the fresh traces of an Indian war party, who had, probably, observed us in the prairie, and might have cut off our retreat in the only path among the hills and ravines to the banks; we therefore put spurs to our horses, and rode the whole way at full gallop, so that we were much out of breath when we arrived at the bank opposite the fort. We hastened to cross the river, and the pack-horses, with the meat, arrived soon after. A bleak, disagreeable wind had prevailed the whole day, the temperature, at noon, being only 61°. We, therefore, enjoyed the evening in conversation with Mr. Hamilton, by the fire-side, over a glass of punch, which beverage was our daily refreshment during our four weeks' stay at Fort Union. I obtained from Mr. Hamilton much information relative to the country in which we now were; and he read to us an interesting manuscript which

An Assiniboin hunter, dressed for the oncoming winter weather, visited Fort Union on October 21 during Maximilian's layover there. His name was Pasesick-Kaskutau (nothing but gunpowder).

he had composed, respecting the life of Glass, the beaver hunter, written down from his own words a short time before he was shot, with two of his companions, by the Arikaras. A man of the name of Gardner, who afterwards happened to meet with these Indians, killed two of them with his own hand, and I received the scalp of one of them, as a present, during my stay in the fort.

The weather turned colder as the month wore on. Bodmer worked on his watercolors at the fort while Maximilian roamed the countryside, making frequent visits to Fort William, a new trading post being completed a few miles downstream by an Opposition outfit, Sublette and Campbell. Robert Campbell, the resident partner, regaled him with stories of the early days of the fur trade in the Rocky Mountains, and the prince plied him with questions about the mountain tribes. Occasionally an interesting Indian or two would turn up at Fort Union:

OCTOBER 16–20, 1833

A number of Cree Indians arrived at Fort Union, among whom was the celebrated medicine man, or conjuror, Mahsette-Kuinab (*le sonnant*), whose portrait Mr. Bodmer took with great difficulty, because he could not get him to sit still. He was suffering severely from an affection of the eyes; complained of his poverty, and wanted to borrow a horse, promising to pay for it at a future time. This man is highly respected among his countrymen, because his incantations are said to be very efficacious; and even the *engagés* of the Company firmly believe in such mummeries. They relate wonderful anecdotes of this Indian. "Often," they say, "he has caused a small tent to be covered with skins and blankets, and closely shut, he himself having his arms and hands bound, and being fastened to a stake, his whole body closely muffled up. Some time afterwards, sounds of drums, and the schischikué, were heard; the whole tent began to tremble and shake; the voices of bears, buffaloes, and other animals, were heard; and the Indians believed that the evil spirit had come down. When the tent was afterwards opened, the conjuror was found fastened and bound as before, and he related what

he had learnt from the spirit whom he had interrogated." The Canadians and Indians affirm, that his predictions invariably come to pass; and it would have been in vain to attempt to convince these superstitious people of the contrary. On one occasion it was said, that Le Sonnant was at Fort Clark, where all persons present witnessed his performances. He told them, beforehand, that a horseman would arrive upon a grey horse, and be killed; and not long afterwards some Cheyenne Indians arrived, of whom one, riding a grey horse, was taken and killed. This circumstance is still quoted as a proof that Le Sonnant has intercourse with supernatural powers.

OCTOBER 21, 1833

Several Assiniboins, whom we had not seen before, arrived successively and General Jackson [*an Assiniboin chief whom Maximilian had met at Fort Union on his way upstream*] with twenty-three of his warriors made his entry in due form to the fort. They advanced in a line, and were conducted to the Indian apartment, where they smoked their pipes. Among them was a man wearing his winter dress, having on his head a badger's skin, by way of cap, and gloves, which are very rare among the Indians. His name was Pasesick-Kaskutau (nothing but gunpowder), and Mr. Bodmer took an admirable full-length portrait of him. Many women arrived with their loaded dogs, and I never saw such miserable, starved animals. Their backs were quite bent, and they could hardly walk, yet they were cruelly beaten. One of them was lame, and could not go on, and at every blow the poor animal howled most lamentably; another, quite starved, fell down dead near the tent. The Indians themselves frequently suffer hunger, and their dogs, of course, suffer still more; so that the poultry in the fort was in constant danger.

OCTOBER 24, 1833

Several beaver hunters arrived today, among whom was the Cree Indian Piah-Sukah-Ketutt (the speaking thunder), who is engaged as a hunter in the service of the Company. He brought me a part of the skin of the head of an original [*French-Canadian term for a moose*] which he had killed on the Milk River, and affirmed that he had there found the entire skeleton of a colossal serpent. A part of a tooth which he brought proved that these bones belonged to a fossil mastodon, which, unluckily, was at too great a distance for me to be able to go and examine it. He said that he had broken the head to pieces, in order to obtain the piece of the tooth. Mr. Bodmer drew a very good portrait of this Cree in his Indian dress. [*For this painting, see page 68.*]

The routine of preparing the fort for winter continued. Indians stole Maximilian's thermometer, and a reward of ten dollars had to be paid in order to get it back. One of the Company clerks purchased an Indian bride amid much ceremony only to have her run off with a renegade *engagé* after less than a week of wedded bliss. Maximilian at last obtained an Indian skull for his collections by robbing a corpse lashed to one of the Assiniboin burial scaffolds in the prairie. On October 27 the first snowstorm of the season served notice that it was time to quit the comforts of Mr. Hamilton's hearth and his evening grog ration for the final leg of the trip down to Fort Clark. Hamilton provided a somewhat larger boat than the one the voyagers had used on the trip from Fort McKenzie, and on October 30 the party took its leave. Morrin was again at the tiller. Four other Company employees rounded out the crew. The journey required ten days, with many layovers for hunting excursions, for, as Maximilian remarked, "If the Canadians are not always well fed, there is no depending upon their perseverance." The two bears also proved troublesome if not fed regularly. No buffalo were to be seen; elk, deer, and prairie hens saw the party through. Ice floes from the tributaries sometimes littered the smooth surface of the river, and frozen riverbanks collapsed with a sound like muffled cannon fire, but the weather continued favorable. On the afternoon of November 8 Morrin steered the heavily laden boat around a bend where the Mandan village Mih-Tutta-Hang-Kush occupied the promontory, and the travelers disembarked at Fort Clark. They were greeted by the fort's director, James Kipp, whom they had last seen in June.

Mahsette-Kuinab, a Cree medicine man, whose art is described by Maximilian in the entry following that of October 12.

Maximilian's voyage down the Missouri from Fort McKenzie to Fort Union took only fifteen days, less than half the time it had taken him to cover the same 650 miles in the cumbersome keelboat *Flora* during the upstream voyage in July and August. Carried by the current, the small party floated easily in their Mackinaw boat through a naturalist's paradise. September was the rutting season for elk and buffalo, and vast numbers of these animals had gathered along the river. The bellowing of the bulls and whistling of the stags were heard day and night. There were bighorn sheep, pronghorn antelope, deer, and grizzlies in impressive numbers. Flocks of migrating fowl flew high overhead: geese and swans, ducks, cranes, and hawks. In the entire two weeks the party sighted not another human being. The beauty of the passing scene through the warm days and moonlit nights moved Maximilian to unaccustomed eloquence: "A solemn silence prevailed in the vast solitary wilderness, where Nature, in all her savage grandeur, reigned supreme."

*Opposite:* After breaking the voyage with a month's stay at Fort Union, Maximilian and his companions headed downstream once again, bound for their winter quarters at Fort Clark. Early in November, several days short of their destination, Bodmer made this sketch of the evening bivouac as the Europeans lighted up their meerschaums while waiting for the game to cook. The cages containing Maximilian's tame bears can be seen in the stern of the moored boat. *First overleaf:* Steering downstream on September 18, the party swept silently past a herd of buffalo and a troop of elk, neither of which paid them the slightest notice. *Second overleaf:* During his stay at Fort Union, Maximilian and Bodmer participated in a mounted buffalo hunt on the prairie, a day's journey from the fort. Bodmer's painting of a mortally wounded bull was made on October 11.

Animal studies made on the trip downriver. *Opposite top:* A female bighorn sheep which Maximilian compared, for agility, to the European chamois. *Below:* A male pronghorn antelope, known as "cabri" to the French-Canadians. *Above:* A muskrat, whose numbers, like those of the beaver, were in serious decline, because of indiscriminate trapping.

Rattlesnakes were in plentiful supply along the Missouri in 1833, as was the now-threatened whooping crane. Vultures (*opposite*) vied with wolves and coyotes for the carrion of the prairie. *Overleaf:* Bodmer sketched this herd of buffalo on September 19 in the Mauvaises Terres.

19 Septembre 1833.

K. B. Ime...

Bison dance of the Mandan Indians, performed by the Berock-Ochateh bull band before the medicine lodge at Mih-Tutta-Hang-Kush.

# PART VI

# Sojourn at Fort Clark

## November 8, 1833 – April 18, 1834

Fort Clark, situated on the west bank of the Missouri forty-five miles north of present-day Bismarck, North Dakota, was built in the spring of 1831 by the American Fur Company. Lewis and Clark had spent the winter of 1804–05 here in the vicinity of the Mandan villages, and from the earliest days of the fur trade there had been a post of some sort in the neighborhood. It was a strategic location. The Mandans and their upstream neighbors, the Minnetarees, as semi-agriculturists were the only tribes on the Upper Missouri to dwell in fixed villages that could offer year-round support for a small trading post. The area was also a crossroads for migratory bands of Sioux, Assiniboins, and Crows.

The fort itself was built on the same plan as the other forts of the Company, but was much smaller than Fort Pierre or Fort Union. (Maximilian described the stockade as being about forty-five paces square.) Three hundred yards up-stream was the main Mandan village, Mih-Tutta-Hang-Kush, consisting of about sixty-five large timber and sod huts, enclosed within a rather ramshackle wall of wooden pickets, for defense. The village occupied a high promontory on the west bank of the river. Ruhptare, the second Mandan village, was located three miles farther upstream on the same bank. It consisted of thirty-eight huts. Fifteen miles farther along were the three villages of the Minnetarees, all located on the Knife River near its junction with the Missouri. Both the Mandans and Minnetarees maintained winter villages that were built in sheltered groves of cottonwood and willow, where the inhabitants took refuge during the worst months of the winter. The winter village of Mih-Tutta-Hang-Kush, which Maximilian often refers to as the "lower village," was located somewhat downstream from the summer village on the West bank of the river.

At Fort Clark the Opposition to the fur company were traders employed by Sublette and Campbell who lived among the Indians in the various villages. Principal among them was Joseph Dougherty (brother of Major John Dougherty, Indian agent at Bellevue) whose hospitality Maximilian was to enjoy at one of the Minnetaree winter villages. There, too, Maximilian would renew acquaintances with crafty old Toussaint Charbonneau, who had temporarily deserted the Company to work for the Opposition among the Minnetarees. For its part, the Company also maintained agents in some of the villages, among them Honoré Picotte, who wintered with a large band of Yanktonan Sioux on the eastern side of the Missouri several days' journey downstream from Fort Clark. As the Yanktonans were camped nearer to the winter buffalo range than the Mandans, parties were sent from the hungry garrison at Fort Clark to Picotte several times during the winter in quest of meat.

Beavers were trapped in the fall, winter (weather permitting), and early spring when their fur was at its best. Stiff competition between the Company and Opposition had elevated the price of good beaver pelt to as much as twelve dollars at Fort Clark during the time of Maximilian's visit. This same pelt brought only half that in St. Louis. The Company could stand this sort of arithmetic; the Opposition couldn't. Sublette and Campbell sold out to the Company in 1834.

All told, Maximilian and his two companions were to spend nearly five and a half months at Fort Clark, living through an unusually brutal winter under primitive conditions. Over the months the white population fluctuated at about a dozen, sometimes less, which was just as well since the fort was frequently on starvation rations, and, as a result, Maximilian contracted scurvy. Despite the bitter cold, food shortages, and his illness, however, the prince worked away through the winter with his usual diligence. He interviewed Mandan and Minnetaree chieftains until late into the night. He interrogated Kipp and Charbonneau to the limits of their patience. He tramped the prairie and visited neighboring villages to witness the festivals and ceremonies that the Indians celebrated to pass the severe winter months. He sent Dreidoppel out to shoot specimens in fair weather and foul and goaded

Bodmer on and on. All winter long a procession of Indians trooped through the Europeans' drafty quarters. Entertained by Bodmer's music box and rewarded by gifts of tobacco and trinkets, Mandans, Minnetarees, and an occasional Arikara or Sioux posed for hours on end as the artist worked away on their portraits while trying to keep his pots of paint from freezing solid. It was a rigorous existence, but somehow they survived it, and it was during these five months that Maximilian and Bodmer made their supreme contribution to American ethnology. Maximilian's narrative picks up again shortly after his arrival at Fort Clark on November 8:

Mih-Tutta-Hang-Kush, the principal Mandan village, seen from the eastern bank of the Missouri, looking downstream.

NOVEMBER 9–12, 1833

No important change had taken place at Fort Clark during our absence. We found there, besides Mr. Kipp the director, and his family, two interpreters, Belhumeur for the Mandan language, and Ortubize for the Sioux; the former was a half-breed Chippewa, and did not speak the Mandan language as well as Mr. Kipp. Besides these men and their families there were in the fort only six white *engagés,* one of whom was a smith. Some of them were married to Indian women. We unfortunately missed Mr. Mc Kenzie, who had left only four days before to return to Fort Union. We had received, through him, a very welcome packet of letters from Germany, which I found here. As I had written to Mr. Mc Kenzie, requesting him to provide us with a winter residence at Fort

Clark, in order more closely to study the Indian tribes in the neighbourhood, instead of accepting his invitation to pass that season with him at Fort Union, where we should have been accommodated in a far more comfortable and agreeable manner, he had had the kindness to give orders for completing a new building at Fort Clark, in which we were to reside.

This order unfortunately came too late, and it was necessary to finish the work in a hurry in the month of November, when the frost was very severe, particularly during the nights, so that our dwelling, being very slightly built, afforded us but little protection from the cold. The large crevices in the wood which formed the walls, were plastered up with clay, but the frost soon cracked it, so that the bleak wind penetrated on all sides. Our new house, which was one story high, consisted of two light, spacious apartments, with large glass windows; we inhabited one of these rooms, while the other served for a workshop for the carpenter and the joiner. Each room had a brick chimney, in which we burnt large blocks of green poplar, because, for want of hands, no stock of dry wood had been laid in for the winter. The consequence was, that we were obliged to send men every morning, with small carts or sledges, for some miles into the forest, to fetch wood for the daily consumption, which in the intense cold was a truly laborious task. An *engagé* who

was employed in our service brought the wood covered with ice and snow into our room, which considerably increased the cold which we already experienced.

As our lodging was not habitable for some time after our arrival, and there was no other room in the fort, Mr. Kipp received us in the small apartment which he himself inhabited with his family, and, though our beds were removed in the morning, yet our presence made it more difficult and troublesome to find accommodation for the numerous Indian visitors who came every day. The stores of the fort were at this time well filled; there were goods to the value of 15,000 dollars, and, in the loft, from 600 to 800 bushels of maize, which a great number of Norway rats assiduously laboured to reduce.

Some changes had taken place among the Indians in the vicinity of the fort. At the time of my first visit, in the summer of 1833, the Yanktonans had expressed a wish to make peace with the Mandans and the Minnetarees, in which they did not succeed at that time, but accomplished it in September. Two hundred tents of those Sioux had then been pitched in the prairie behind the village; they remained there three or four days, and some traces of their camp still remained. There had been feasting and dances, and Fort Clark was crowded the whole day with Indians of the three tribes. At this time the prairie in the neighbourhood of the fort was

Mandan bull boats were made by covering a frame of willow branches with the thick hide of a mature bull buffalo, the tail serving as a handy tow rope. The boats were light and durable and were used primarily by the women in their endless task of conveying firewood and other necessities across the Missouri.

desolate and deserted; part of the Indians had already gone to their winter villages in the forest; many, however, remained in the summer villages, and we had plenty of Indian visitors during the whole winter.

Unpleasant news was received from the United States. The cholera had again broken out at St. Louis, and carried off a great number of persons. It had been brought, by the steamboats, to the trading-posts on the lower Missouri; at Bellevue, Major Dougherty's post, seven of the ten white inhabitants had died in a few days. The major himself had been very ill, but had happily recovered. Several persons were likewise carried off at the post of Major Pilcher, formerly that of Mr. Cabanné. This dangerous disease had not penetrated to that part of the country where we were; but, as there was too much reason to apprehend that it might extend so far, Mr. Mc Kenzie had taken a physician with him to Fort Union.

Our first employment was to go on hunting excursions into the prairies round the fort, which afforded us an opportunity of collecting the seeds of the dried plants of the prairie. On one of these excursions, when Mr. Bodmer and Mr. Kipp had gone out together, they happened to separate, when a couple of Indians approached the former with their bows bent, and uttering the war-whoop; he cocked his double-barrelled gun and prepared to defend himself, when Mr. Kipp came up, and relieved him from these unwelcome visitors, the Indians taking flight as soon as they perceived him. Fresh scaffoldings for the dead were erected in the vicinity of Mih-Tutta-Hang-Kush, several Indians having died of the whooping-cough, which was very prevalent. Every day we saw inhabitants of the summer villages removing, with much baggage, laden horses and dogs, to the winter villages. Among other things they carried the strange dresses belonging to the several bands, such as the buffalo heads of the band, Berock-Ochateh, and a live owl, which they keep as a fortune-teller. Other Indians dragged dead dogs by a strap, probably as a bait to catch wolves or foxes. We heard, in the village, loud lamentations, and saw the women working at the erection of a scaffold for a woman who had just died.

## NOVEMBER 13, 1833

Early in the morning, several Indians arrived, who related, with much gravity, that in the preceding night they had observed an extraordinary number of falling stars, all moving in a westerly direction, which they said was a sign of war, or of a great mortality, and asked Mr. Kipp what he thought of it. Many other Indians visited us, of whom several were in mourning, that is, rubbed over with white clay, and all of them spoke of the ominous phenomenon. They were much pleased with Mr. Bodmer's Indian drawings, and asked us many questions about their enemies, the Blackfeet. Among our most constant visitors were the distinguished chief, Mato-Topé (the four bears), and Sih-Chida (the yellow feather). The former came with his wife and a pretty little boy, to whom he had given the name of Mato-Berocka (the male bear). He brought his medicine drum, painted red and black, which he hung up in our room, and so afforded Mr. Bodmer an opportunity of making a drawing of it. Sih-Chida, a tall, stout young man, the son of a celebrated chief now dead, was an Indian who might be depended on, who became one of our best friends, and visited us almost daily. He was very polished in his manners, and possessed more delicacy of feeling than most of his countrymen. He never importuned us by asking for anything; as soon as dinner was served he withdrew, though he was not rich, and did not even possess a horse. He came almost every evening, when his favourite employment was drawing, for which he had some talent, though his figures were no better than those drawn by our little children. [*See pages 224–225 for Bodmer's portrait of Sih-Chida and an example of this Indian's skill at drawing.*]

## NOVEMBER 14, 1833

Ortubize, the interpreter, had moved, with his family, to the post of Picotte, a trader among the Yanktonans, where he was to pass the winter. The people who had been sent thither returned with the information that the Sioux were dispersed in the prairie, and that they had made capital bargains with them for beavers' skins. At our post we had to encounter the mercantile opposition of Messrs. Sublette and Campbell, whereby the price of the buffalo skins was very much raised. As our armed men now consisted of seventeen *engagés*, Mr. Kipp went to work and had my Mackinaw boat drawn to land, and secured from the ice.

## NOVEMBER 15, 1833

Today was the first day we saw ice in the Missouri; the sand banks were covered with a wide, thick sheet of ice, but the river was still open.

## November 16, 1833

Mr. Kipp sent the men who had come down with me back, on foot, to Fort Union. They took with them two dogs, which drew well-laden *travois* (sledges), and hoped to arrive there in about nine days. Sih-Sa (the red feather), the young Mandan Indian who, during the day, takes charge of the horses belonging to the fort in the prairie, came back to-day, having painted his whole body with spots of white clay. I asked him why he had done this? to which he replied, that he was thereby enabled to run faster.

Every evening brought me a visit from Dipauch [*a Mandan notable*], who came to tell me all the legends and traditions, as well as the religious views of his people—conversations which interested me much, and which frequently lasted till late at night. Among his auditors were several young people, who sat listening with the most riveted attention to the disjointed sentences of our narrator; while Mr. Kipp, with great patience, performed the office of interpreter.

## November 22, 1833

We took possession of our new apartment, which was now completed, except that the white-washed walls were still damp, and the constant wind generally filled it with smoke. We were, however, thankful to have space to carry on our labours, to which we now applied with great assiduity, to make up for the time we had lost. The large windows afforded a good light for drawing, and we had a couple of small tables and some benches of poplar wood, and three shelves against the walls, on which we spread our blankets and buffaloes' skins, and reposed during the night. The room was floored; the door was furnished with bolts on the inside, and the firewood, covered with frozen snow, was piled up close to the chimney. We all felt indisposed soon after we took up our abode in this lodging, and were obliged to have recourse to medicine, but this was, probably, to be ascribed principally to the way of living and the state of the weather; for Sih-Sa and other Indians had bowel complaints, catarrh, and violent coughs, for which Mr. Kipp gave them medicines. I examined all the medical stock of the fort, and found neither pepper-

mint nor other herbs, which would have been serviceable at this time; only a handful of elder flowers, and rather more of American camomile, which has a different taste to the European. There were some common remedies, but unfortunately we were without a medical man.

## November 23, 1833

Snow-storms, with a high west wind, had set in, and the country was covered with snow, and the Missouri froze for the first time, below the village of Mih-Tutta-Hang-Kush. It is remarkable that it was frozen on the very same day in the preceding year. We saw the Indian women, as soon as the river was covered with ice, break holes in it, to wash their heads and the upper part of their bodies. The Indians had brought many beaver skins for sale, of which Mr. Kipp purchased eleven large ones, in exchange for a horse and some red cloth; the remainder, for which they demanded another horse, they took back with them.

Mato-Topé had passed the evening with us, and, when we went to bed, laid himself down before the fire, where he soon fell asleep. On the following morning he rose early, washed himself, but left his two buffalo skins lying carelessly on the floor, for us to gather them up, these Indians taking every opportunity to be waited on by the Whites. As we were molested during the night by numerous rats, we put my little tame prairie fox into the loft above us, where some maize was kept, and here he did excellent service. This pretty little fox afforded us much amusement during the long winter evenings. He was nearly a year old, but still liked to be caressed and played all kinds of antics to attract notice.

## November 24, 1833       [Field Journal]

I gave Mato-Topé a bear-claw necklace which he will complete for me. For this purpose I purchased an otter skin and blue glass beads at the Company store. In addition he received paint and paper from Mr. Bodmer in order to make a picture of one of his exploits for me. [*Mato-Topé's painting of his combat with a Cheyenne chief may be found on page 221.*] Some Minnetarees had brought in a great many beaver pelts from their hunt and came to inquire about prices. Mr. Kipp intends to buy, on the morrow, between 100 and 150 beaver pelts, which would have a value here of a couple of thousand dollars. The old Addih-Hiddish (he who makes the path) sat with us the entire evening and smoked. His appearance was odd. He wore an old round hat, and his hair was wildly dishevelled. On his torso he wore an old vest. His arms were naked. This man is said to be a very good Indian. [*For a portrait of Addih-Hiddish, see page 209.*]

### NOVEMBER 25, 1833

In the evening we were alarmed by information that some hostile Indians were near the fort. Dipauch and Berock-Itainu, who were called the soldiers of the fort, immediately took their arms, cautiously opened the gate, and discovered a Minnetaree, who was concealed near one of the block-houses, from which he was soon driven rather roughly. At this time, Charbonneau came to invite us to a great medicine feast among the Minnetarees, an invitation which I gladly accepted.

### NOVEMBER 26, 1833

We had fine weather and a clear sky, very favourable for our expedition. At nine o'clock, Bodmer, Charbonneau, and myself set out, on foot, with our double-barrelled guns and the requisite ammunition, accompanied by a young Minnetaree warrior. We proceeded up the Missouri in a direction parallel with the river, leaving Mih-Tutta-Hang-Kush on our right hand, and taking the way to Ruhptare which runs along the edge of the high plateau, below which there is a valley extending to the Missouri, covered with the maize plantations of the Mandans. We proceeded for several hours through the desolate plain, which was covered with yellow, withered grass, now and then broken by gentle eminences, where bleached buffaloes' bones, especially skulls, are scattered about. We met with a couple of Indians, heavily laden with skins, resting themselves, who immediately asked us for tobacco. We had here an opportunity of seeing the wolf pits, in which the Indians fix sharp stakes, and the whole is so covered with brushwood, hay, and dry grass, that it cannot be perceived. As our feet began to be very painful, we sat down to rest near a stream, now almost dry, bordered with high grass, which at this time was lying on the ground. As I was no longer accustomed to such long journeys on foot, I had asked Mr. Kipp for horses for this journey, but there

An old Minnetaree named Birohka (the robe with the beautiful hair) had his portrait taken on March 1.

were none in the fort at that time. Our European boots and shoes had wounded our feet, and it was with much pain that we ascended the rather steep hills which now again came nearer to the river. I obtained from Charbonneau a pair of Indian shoes, in which I found it easier to walk, but the thorns of the cactus, which grew on the hills, pierced through them, and caused me pain in another way.

Towards evening, when we descended from the hills to the river, we again came to an extensive wood on the banks, in which one of the winter villages of the Minnetarees is situated. We had, however, to walk several miles along a very winding path before we reached it. Being extremely tired, and our feet sore and wounded, it cost us some exertion to get over fallen trunks of trees, sharp stones, &c., in the way. The scenes which are inseparable from the dwellings of the Indians soon appeared; slender young men, galloping without saddle, who were driving their horses home from the pasture; women cutting or carrying wood, and the like. A young Indian joined us, who immediately offered, out of civility, to carry my gun, which I did not accept. He was an Arikara, who had been captured, when a child, by the Minnetarees— a good-tempered, well-behaved young man. He was tall and slender, with a pleasing countenance, long, narrow eyes, and a slightly curved nose.

It was nearly nightfall when we reached the Minnetaree village, the large huts of which were built so close to each other that it was sometimes difficult to pass between them. We heard loud lamentations as we approached, and learnt that a child had just died, and that a corpse had been deposited, a few days before, on poles placed in the boughs of a tree. At the farther end of the village was the residence of Mr. [*Joseph*] Dougherty, a long, low, log-house, divided into three apartments, of which that in the centre was used for a store-house, the northern apartment being assigned to the family, and the southern to the *engagés*. We were received with much kindness, and, being thoroughly tired by a fatiguing journey, we were truly glad to rest our weary limbs before a blazing fire. A number of Minnetaree Indians were assembled, who, however, gradually retired whilst we took some refreshment, not having tasted anything since we breakfasted at Fort Clark.

It being reported that herds of buffaloes were at no great distance, a party of Indians resolved to give them chase on the following day, and to implore the blessing of heaven upon their undertaking by a great medicine feast. Notwithstanding the pain I suffered in walking, the prospect of witnessing so novel a scene was so exciting that I immediately set out about seven o'clock in the evening, accompanied by Dougherty and Charbonneau, to see the Indian ceremony, which was instituted by the women.

Between the huts, in the centre of the village, an elliptical space, forty paces or more in length, was enclosed in a fence, ten or twelve feet high, consisting of reeds and willow twigs inclining inwards. The spectators, especially the women, were seated: the men walked about, some of them handsomely dressed, others quite simply; children were seated around the fires, which they kept alive by throwing twigs of willow trees into them. Soon after Charbonneau had introduced us to this company, six elderly men advanced in a row from the opposite hut, and stopped for a moment at the entrance of the great medicine lodge. They had been chosen, by the young men, to represent buffalo bulls, for which they afterwards received presents. Each of them carried a long stick, at the top of which three or four black feathers were fastened; then, at regular intervals, the whole length of the stick was ornamented with small bunches of the hoofs of buffalo calves, and at the lower end of the stick were some bells. In their left hand they carried a battle-axe, or war club, and two of them had a stuffed skin which they called a badger, and used as a drum. They stood at the entrance, rattled their sticks incessantly, sang alternately, and imitated, with great perfection, the hoarse voice of the buffalo bull. They were followed by a tall man, who wore a cap, trimmed with fur, because he had been formerly scalped in a battle. He represented the director of the ceremony and the leader of the old bulls, behind whom he made his appearance. The bulls now entered the medicine lodge and took their seats near the fence, behind one of the fires.

Several young men were now employed in carrying round dishes of boiled maize and beans, which they placed before the guests. These dishes were handed to each person successively, who passed them on after tasting a small quantity. Empty wooden dishes were frequently brought and placed at our feet, the reason of which I could not, at first, comprehend, but soon learned from my neighbour, the Yellow Bear [*one of the principal chiefs of the Minnetarees*]. As soon as the provision bearer—a tall, handsome, very robust, and broad-shouldered man, wearing only his breech-cloth, ornamented at the back with long tufts of hair—came to take away one of these empty dishes, the old chief held his hands before his face, sang, and made a long speech, which seemed to me to be a prayer uttered in a low tone of voice, and then gave him the dish. These speeches contained good wishes for success in hunting the buffalo, and in war. They invoke the heavenly powers to favour the hunters and the warriors. In this manner two dishes were sometimes placed before us, and we also exerted ourselves in uttering good wishes in the English and German languages, which the Indians guessed from our motions, though they could not understand our words. If the speech was lengthy, they were specially gratified; the provision bearer stopped, listening very attentively, nodded his satisfaction, and passed his hand over our right arm from the shoulder to the wrist, and sometimes over both arms, and then again spoke a few words expressive of his thanks.

In this manner the ceremony of the repast lasted above an hour; every person present partook of it, and offered up their good wishes for a successful buffalo chase. Meantime, the young men, in the centre of the space, prepared the tobacco pipes, which they brought first to the old men and the visitors; they presented the mouth-piece of the pipe to us in succession, going from right to left: we each took a few whiffs, uttered, as before, a wish or prayer, and passed the pipe to our next neighbours. Among those who carried the dishes and pipes, there was another young man who had been scalped, and who also wore a cap; he had received many wounds in the attack made by the Sioux on the Minnetaree villages, and had been left on the field as dead. The pipe bearers often turned their pipes towards the cardinal points, and performed various superstitious manœuvres with them. The six buffalo bulls, meantime, sitting behind the fire, sang, and rattled the medicine sticks, while one of them constantly beat the badger skin. After a while they all stood up, bent forward, and danced; that is, they leaped as high as they could with both their feet together, continuing to sing and rattle their sticks, one of them beating time on the badger. Their song was invariably the same, consisting of loud, broken notes and exclamations. When they had danced for some time, they resumed their seats.

The whole was extremely interesting. The great number of red men, in a variety of costumes, the singing, dancing, beating the drum, &c., while the lofty trees of the forest,

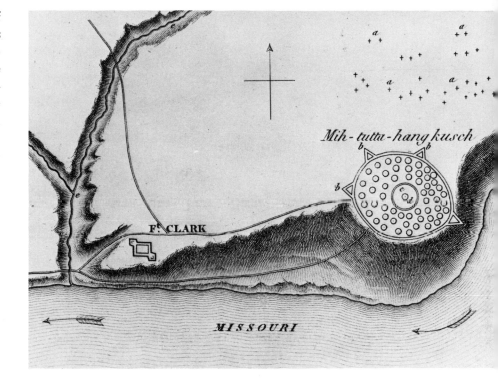

A plan of Mih-Tutta-Hang-Kush shows its relationship to Fort Clark and gives an idea of its construction. Some sixty-five circular huts were tightly grouped around a central space where the ark of the first man was kept. The village was enclosed within a wall of wooden pickets from which projected several wickerwork strong-points. These fortifications, which had been originally built under the supervision of the whites, were in a state of general disrepair by the time of Maximilian's visit. Crosses on the prairie north of the village indicate burial stages. The good-sized tributary entering the Missouri downstream from Fort Clark was known as the Stream Where the Dishes Are Washed.

The ark of the first man, a wooden cylinder about five feet high, stood at the center of Mih-Tutta-Hang-Kush and served as an altar around which important ceremonies were performed. The effigy figure atop the pole, draped in animal skins, is Ochkih-Hadda, the spirit of evil. It is set directly in front of the medicine lodge. Scaffolds located before the huts were used to dry meat and corn.

illumined by the fires, spread their branches against the dark sky, formed a *tout ensemble* so striking and original, that I much regretted the impracticability of taking a sketch of it on the spot.

When the ceremony had continued a couple of hours, the women began to act their part. A woman approached her husband, gave him her girdle and under garment, so that she had nothing on under her robe; she then went up to one of the most distinguished men, passed her hand over his arm, from the shoulder downwards, and then withdrew slowly from the lodge. The person so summoned follows her to a solitary place in the forest; he may then buy himself off by presents, which, however, few Indians do. This honour was offered to us, but we returned to the lodge, after having made a present, on which pipes were again handed to us. The fires already burnt dim, many Indians had retired, and we asked the old chief, whether we might be permitted to do the same? At first he refused, but then gave us leave.

In the morning some very handsome men appeared, very strong muscular figures with expressive faces, often nicely painted and adorned. In general, the Minnetarees are taller than the Mandans. All have scars, thick welts on the breast and arms. These have their origin from a feast of penance that is celebrated in the spring. They cut their bodies in order to produce loops of flesh and skin to which they attach heavy objects such as buffalo heads that they then drag about. Young people were playing a game on a long, straight track in the village that is generally called "billiards" by the Whites. Two players run along next to each other and attempt to hit a rolling leather hoop with long spears. Many children were playing on the river, which was completely frozen. Women played a game with a large leather ball. They toss it on the foot and then keep it in the air by kicking it. [*See page 233 for an example of this ball.*]

### November 28, 1833

On the second day of our sojourn at the Minnetaree winter village, I paid a visit, accompanied by Charbonneau, to the Yellow Bear. Mr. Dougherty had formerly resided in the hut which he now inhabited, and for which he had to pay 80 or 100 dollars. The beds, consisting of square leathern cases, were placed along the sides of this spacious hut, and the inmates sat around the fire variously occupied. The Yellow Bear, wearing only his breech-cloth, sat upon a bench made of willow boughs, covered with skin, and was painting a new buffalo robe with figures in vermilion and black, having his colours standing by him, ready mixed, in old potsherds. In lieu of a pencil he was using the more inartificial substitute of a sharp pointed piece of wood. The robe was ornamented with the symbols of valuable presents which he had made, and which had gained the Yellow Bear much reputation, and made him a man of distinction.

About twenty Minnetarees had gone to hunt buffaloes, and as we had no meat, we waited with no small degree of impatience for their return. Our fast was of longer duration than we liked, for it was late before a few of our hunters arrived, and the scalped man brought us some meat, so that we did not get our meal till evening. At nightfall, a handsome young man came to us, accompanied by two girls, it being the custom of the Indian youths to stroll about in this

manner. They had not been long in our room, when somebody knocked at the door, on which the two girls crept into Charbonneau's bed to hide themselves, as they suspected it was some of their friends come to look after them; but it proved to be only a messenger from Charbonneau, who, wishing to produce us a pleasant diversion for the evening, let us know that the women in a certain hut were about to perform a medicine dance; and, availing ourselves of the intimation, we hastened to the spot without loss of time.

On the left hand of the wooden screen at the door of the hut a fire was burning, and before it were spread out skins upon some hay, on which five or six men were seated in a row, one of whom beat the drum, and the other rattled the schischikué. They were more than usually vehement in the performance of this music; the drummer especially exerted himself to the utmost, and all the rest accompanied him with singing. Some elderly women were seated near the wall; a tall, robust woman, however, especially attracted our attention; she was standing in the centre of the hut; her dress consisted of a long yellow leather robe, trimmed with a quantity of fringes, and ornamented with pieces of red and blue cloth. We took our places to the right of the musicians, just in front of a number of spectators, consisting of women and children, who were prevented from pressing forward by a young man, who made use of the official dignity of a stick, with which he was invested for the occasion.

The woman standing in the centre pretended that she had a head of maize in her stomach, which she would conjure up, and again cause to disappear. We had come rather too late, for the ear of maize had already disappeared; but Charbonneau spoke to the people, to whom we gave ten carrots of tobacco, and the trick was repeated. Our tobacco was thrown on a heap of roasted buffalo ribs, which were piled up on willow boughs, and there it remained till the end of the ceremony, the object of which was to procure a good crop of maize in the succeeding year. The din of the music now recommenced with renewed vehemence, and four women began to move. They waddled like ducks, making short steps, with their feet turned inwards, and keeping time to the quick beat of the drum; while their arms hung down motionless by their sides. The medicine woman danced alone near the fire, to which she sometimes put her hands, and then laid them upon her face. At length she began to totter, to move her arms backwards and forwards, and to use convulsive motions, which became more and more violent. Now, as she threw her head backwards, we saw the top of a white head of maize fill her mouth, and gradually came more forward, while her contortions greatly increased. When the head of maize was half out of her mouth, the dancer seemed ready to sink down, when another woman advanced, laid hold of her and seated her on the ground. Here, supported by her companion, she fell into convulsions, and the music became overpoweringly violent. Other women brushed the arm and breast of the performers with bunches of wormwood, and the head of maize gradually disappeared; on which the juggleress rose, danced twice round the hut, and was succeded by another female. After this second woman had danced in the same manner, a stream of blood suddenly rushed from her mouth over her chin, which, however, she extracted from a piece of leather that she held in her mouth. She, too, was cured of her convulsions as she lay on the ground, and then danced around the fire. Other women came forward and danced behind one another, which concluded the ceremony.

Almost all these people pretended that they had some animal in their stomach; some a buffalo calf, others a deer, &c. The scalped man told us that he had a buffalo calf in his left shoulder, and often felt it kick. Another, who pretended that he had three live lizards in his inside, complained to Charbonneau that these animals gave him pain, on which Charbonneau gave him a cup of coffee, but as this remedy did not relieve him, a cup of tea was given him, and this produced the desired effect. Notions of this kind are so common among the Indians, and they are said to have so firm a hold on the faith of the people, that it would be labour lost to attempt to convince them of their folly.

NOVEMBER 29, 1833                    [FIELD JOURNAL]

During the entire preceding night there was a great deal of noise, shrieking and singing in the Minnetaree village and the surrounding woods. Others lamented for their dead. The female sex was everywhere being called upon by the young men and put into action. This type of pastime is the main entertainment of the Indians, as almost all are lewd. Today Mr. Bodmer painted a rooster and a horse on the buffalo robes of two Indians. Through this they hope to become bullet proof. In the evening Mr. Dougherty and Mr. Bodmer went to the buffalo medicine feast, which was being repeated.

Tonight, however, the women did not make them any invitations. After they returned home we discussed this change of behaviour, speculating that perhaps the Indians had felt insulted. But nobody could offer a well-founded conjecture, not even Charbonneau, who knew these Indians so well. In the dark, the door of our hut was pushed open twice. The Minnetarees are coarser than the Mandans. Mr. Dougherty, who does not have a fort and lives in the village, has much to endure from their obtrusiveness and rudeness. He concedes them everything in order to avoid more considerable annoyances. Should he refuse them something or send them away, they would revenge themselves and he could find himself in a dangerous position. One may never trust the Indians. Intercourse with them is always risky and dangerous.

NOVEMBER 30, 1833

We had not been able to borrow horses to return to Fort Clark; but today Mr. Dougherty succeeded in obtaining one, and Durand, a clerk of Messrs. Sublette and Campbell, who had arrived on horseback, returned with us and allowed Mr. Bodmer to ride with him.

DECEMBER 3, 1833

The Mandan village near the fort was now entirely forsaken by the inhabitants. The entrances to the huts were blocked with bundles of thorns; a couple of families only still remained, one of which was that of Dipauch, whom Mr. Bodmer visited every day, in order to make a drawing of the interior of the hut. [*For this painting, see pages 230–231.*]

Having been invited by the Mandans to their winter village, to be present at a great medicine feast, we proceeded thither in the afternoon. Mr. Kipp took his family with him, and Mato-Topé and several other Indians accompanied us. We were all well armed, because it was asserted that a band of hostile Indians had been seen among the prairie hills on the preceding day. Our beds, blankets, and buffalo skins were laid on a horse, on which Mr. Kipp's wife, a Mandan Indian, rode. Thus we passed, at a rapid pace, through the prairie, along the Missouri, then below the hills; and I cannot deny that, in the valleys and ravines, our whole company looked anxiously to the right and left to see whether any enemies would issue from their ambush. We had to pass a narrow

gorge behind a thick copse, where many Indians had been killed by their enemies. After proceeding about an hour and a half we reached the village in the wood, which is the winter residence of the inhabitants of Mih-Tutta-Hang-Kush. We stopped at the hut of Mr. Kipp's father-in-law, Mandeek-Suck-Choppenik (the medicine bird), who accommodated us with a night's lodging. We had still a little time before the commencement of the medicine feast, which consisted of the dance of the half-shorn head, which the band of the soldiers sold to the raven band. This feast was to last forty nights, and the son-in-law of our host was among the sellers.

We sat around the fire and smoked, while the drum was beat in the village to call the two parties together. After seven o'clock we repaired to the medicine lodge; it was entirely cleared, except that some women sat along the walls; the fire burned in the centre, before which we took our seats, near

the partition, with several distinguished men of the band of the soldiers. At our left hand, the other soldiers, about twenty-five in number, were seated in a row; some of them were handsomely dressed, though the majority were in plain clothes. They had their arms in their hands, and in the centre were three men, who beat the drum. On the right side of the fire stood the young men of the raven band, who were the purchasers; they were obliged to satisfy the soldiers, who were the sellers, by making them valuable presents, such as horses, guns, powder and ball, blankets of different colours, kettles, &c.; to continue the feast forty nights; to regale them, for that time, with provisions and tobacco, and offer their wives to them. The soldiers had consented to these terms, and the festival took place every evening.

We had all taken our seats before the band of the sellers arrived; but we soon heard them singing, accompanied by

Mandan lodges were sturdy enough to serve as grandstands for spectators during ceremonial dances and feasts in the village.

the drum, and they entered with their insignia; these consisted of four poles, or lances, seven or eight feet long, the iron points of which resembled sword blades, and were held downwards; the rest of the instrument was wrapped round with broad bands of otter skin and decorated at the point and other places with strips of skin. Two of these poles were curved at the top. The others were a club with an iron point, painted red and ornamented with feathers; then three lances, decorated alternately with black and white feathers; and, lastly, a very beautifully ornamented bow and quiver. [*Similar ceremonial lances are to be seen in Mato-Topé's painting on page 238.*]

These nine insignia were brought in, the soldiers, however, stopping, at first, near the door behind the cross wall. When they had remained for some time in this position, singing and beating the drum with great violence, they entered, placed the lances against the wall, and fixed the club in the ground near one of the pillars that supported the hut; after which they all took their seats near the wall. While the singing and dancing were continued alternately for some time, the purchasers filled their pipes and presented them to all of us in succession. We took one or two whiffs; they did the same, and carried the pipe round to the left hand, but offered it only to the visitors and to the sellers.

In about half an hour two of the soldiers rose and danced opposite each other. One of them was a tall, powerful man, with a weak, effeminate voice. He wore nothing but his robe and leggins, but without any ornaments; he took the club and held it firmly in his left hand; his right hand hung straight down; he bent his body forwards and danced, keeping time with the music. The head and legs of the other dancer were very handsomely ornamented, but the breast and shoulders were bare. He took one of the first four lances, which he held in both hands, and the two men then danced, or leaped, opposite each other. In a few minutes the first dancer put the lance aside and sat down, while all the other members of this band uttered the war-whoop, accompanied by the quick beating of the drum, now and then shouting aloud. Silence then ensued; the man with the club addressed the purchasers, called them his sons, and enumerated some of his exploits; after which he presented to them the war club. One of the purchasers called him his father, passed his hand along his arm, took the weapon from his hand, and put it in its place again. The other dancer again came forward, did the same,

Maximilian made a floor plan of a Mandan hut (*below*) after spending the night in one at a Mandan winter village on December 3. The entrance at the front of the hut could be closed by a door made of a piece of leather stretched on a frame and positioned directly behind the entrance. Behind this obstacle was a long, high, transverse wall made of woven willow rods and draped with hides as a protection against drafts. A lower wall, only three feet high, partitioned off the right portion of the hut as a stable for horses. The central fire pit was surrounded by the four main posts of the hut and four oblong benches made of basketry and covered with skins. Against the back wall was positioned a bed (*above*) which Maximilian described as "consisting of a large square case made of parchment or skins, with a square entrance. They are large enough to hold several persons who lie very comfortably and warm on skins and blankets." [*For Bodmer's watercolor of the interior of a similar hut, see page 231.*]

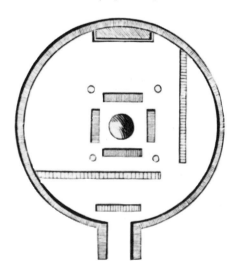

spoke of his exploits, and presented the lance to a man or son of the other band, who received it with the same ceremony, and put it also in its place again. There were singing and dancing in the intervals, but no schischikué was heard. Two other soldiers then rose, related their deeds, how they had stolen horses, taken a medicine from the enemy, and the like, and presented two of the insignia to the purchasers.

When this had been done four or five times, the women of the raven band rose; four of them threw aside their robes, snatched up the lances, carried them successively out of the hut, and some time after, brought them in again. They hastened to pass by us, and some of them appeared to feel ashamed. This ceremony was repeated twice: these women then came, passed their hands down the arms of the strangers and of the fathers, took up their robes and went out, in the same manner as has been related in the medicine feast of the Minnetarees. When they returned the second time, Mr. Kipp rose to go away, and I followed him. Some of the women were fat and corpulent, others very young, and one but little past childhood.

### DECEMBER 4, 1833

Early in the morning, we left the winter village to return to Fort Clark. We did not keep along the hills, but took another path through the thickets, which led in some places over frozen marshes, which were partly covered with reeds. The wood, which was spangled with hoar frost, is very much cleared, and contains but few large trees. A high, cold southeast wind blew in the prairie, and afterwards became violent. At eight o'clock we reached the fort, where we much enjoyed a hot breakfast. Several Mandans came to see us, among whom was the strongest man of this nation, named Beracha-Iruckcha (the broken pot), whom no one had yet been able to overcome in wrestling, though he had been matched with white men, Negroes, and Indians, remarkable for their strength. Sih-Chida and Mahchsi-Karehde (the flying eagle), also visited us; the latter was the tallest man among the Mandans, and belonged to the band of soldiers. [*For his portrait, see page 237.*] Snow had already set in, yet still the buffaloes did not come nearer, and we were in want of fresh meat, and of tallow to make candles; and all the meat we could get was obtained from individual Indians returning from the chase.

### DECEMBER 5, 1833 [FIELD JOURNAL]

In the fort this morning was one of those who are called bardaches by the French. They dress like women and do women's work. They tan skins, paint robes, and make articles of clothing. In a word, they are complete women. It is even said that young men lie in wait for them and make declarations of love to them. Mr. Kipp alleges that these men take a kind of vow, as in religious orders where a vow of poverty is taken, and claims to see nothing wrong with the bardaches' way of life. Others take a different point of view.

Both the mute Mandans came back from hunting today. They brought sufficient meat so that we in the fort got some of it. Our stock of meat had been completely consumed, and the men received corn cooked in water without any fat. My bears have not had anything other than corn for a long time. They eat about a bushel a week, which costs two dollars.

### DECEMBER 6, 1833 [FIELD JOURNAL]

We had talked with Charbonneau last night about the unpredictability of the Indians, and we all agreed that in this region, the Mandans were the most reliable. Nevertheless, they have shot men even here inside the fort. The site of Fort Clark is particularly dangerous because there are permanent Indian villages here and enemies like to attack them. Several white men have been shot because of this. A far greater number of Whites are shot each year by the Blackfeet in the Rocky Mountains.

### DECEMBER 10, 1833

Charbonneau returned to the service of the American Fur Company [*after a falling out with Joseph Dougherty*] and took up his quarters in the fort, which gave me an opportunity to have much conversation with him respecting the Minnetarees with whom he was well acquainted.

### DECEMBER 15, 1833

On the preceding evening, we had a heavy fall of snow, which ceased when the wind veered a little to the north. At eight o'clock the mercury in Fahrenheit's thermometer was at 14°. The appearance of the prairie at this time was very remarkable, resembling the sea agitated by a terrible storm. The extensive surface of the snow was carried by the wind in a cloud; it was scarcely possible for the eye to bear the cold blast which drove the snow before it, and enveloped us in a dense cloud, above which the sky was clear, and the tops of the prairie hills were visible. We were, therefore, the more sensible of the enjoyment of our bright fire, seated about which we passed our time agreeably in various occupations. About this time the enemy had stolen six horses from the Minnetarees. We had been for some time without meat, when the Indians, hunting at a considerable distance, killed fifty-five buffaloes. On this occasion, Mr. Kipp's horse was lost, which, bridled and saddled as it was, had joined a herd of buffaloes; and two foals had perished in the cold.

### December 20, 1833

Some of Mr. Sublette's people arrived from St. Louis, which they had left on the 14th of October, and confirmed the accounts which we had already received of the cessation of the cholera. They told us that, in October, the snow was fifteen inches deep on the banks of the Kansas River, and that the party escorting the caravan from Santa Fe had been so closely hemmed in by the Indians (probably Arikaras), that they had been compelled, by want of provisions, to slaughter fourteen of their horses.

### December 23, 1833

On this day, at noon, we heard the drums of the Indians, and a crowd of their people filled the fort. At their head were fourteen men of the band of the bulls, from Ruhptare, distinguished by their strange costume. The whole head was covered with a wig, consisting of long plaits of hair, which hung down on every side, so that even the face was completely concealed. The appearance of these men was very singular in the cold weather, for their breath issued from between the plaits of hair like a dense vapour. They wore in their heads feathers of owls, ravens, and birds of prey, each of which had at the tip a large white down feather. One of them had a very handsome fan of white feathers on his head, doubtless the entire tail of a swan, each of the feathers having at the tip a tuft of dyed horse-hair. They were closely enveloped in their robes, and had bow-lances ornamented with feathers, coloured cloth, beads, &c., and most of them

had foxes' tails at their heels. Some of these men beat the drum, while they all formed a circle, and imitated the bellowing of the buffalo bulls. After they had danced awhile, some tobacco was thrown to them, and they proceeded to the village in the forest further down the river, taking off their wigs. The frozen Missouri was covered with Indians on this occasion, and presented an interesting scene. At this time the Sioux stole from the prairie thirty-seven horses belonging to the Mandans.

Our cook, a Negro, had a violent dispute with an Indian from Ruhptare, who had taken a piece of meat out of his pot, and the affair might have led to unpleasant consequences. The Indians of that village are the worst of the Mandans. Several articles had been stolen, which was nothing uncommon among our worthy neighbours, for even the wife of Mato-Topé had pilfered something in our room.

### December 25, 1833

At midnight the *engagés* of the fort fired a volley to welcome Christmas day, which was repeated in the morning. The 25th of December was a day of bustle in the fort. Mr. Kipp had given the *engagés* an allowance of better provisions, and they were extremely noisy in their Canadian jargon. The poor fellows had had no meat for some time, and had lived on maize, boiled in water, without any fat. Pehriska-Ruhpa, a robust Minnetaree, who had long lived among the Mandans, visited us, and soon afterwards Mato-Topé, but they took no notice of each other, as they were not on good terms, and the former immediately withdrew. He promised to have his portrait taken in his handsome dress. [*For this painting, see page 222.*]

At noon there was a concourse of Indians in the fort: the woman's band of the white buffalo cow came to perform their dance. The company consisted of seventeen, mostly old women, and two men, with the drum and schischikué; the first of these two men carried a gun in his hand. A stout elderly woman went first; she was wrapped in the hide of a white buffalo cow, and held, in her right arm, a bundle of twigs in the form of a cornucopia, with down feathers at the top, and at the lower end an eagle's wing, and a tin drinking vessel. Another woman carried a similar bundle. All these women wore round their heads a piece of buffalo's skin in the form of a hussar's cap, with a plume of owl's or raven's feathers in front, some of which were dyed red; only two of

them wore the skin of a polecat; all the men were bare-headed. The women were uniformly painted; the left cheek and eye were vermilion, and they had two blue spots on the temple near the right eye. All except the first wore painted robes, and two of them only had the hairy side outwards. When they had formed a circle the music began in quick time; the men sang, and the women who were dancing responded in a loud shrill voice. In their dances they rock from side to side, always remaining on the same spot. [*A sketch of two women of this band is on page 214.*]

## DECEMBER 28, 1833

As we had now no meat, our breakfast consisted of coffee and maize bread, and our dinner of maize bread and bean soup. Our people caught an Indian dog in the fort, intending to put him in a sledge, but he was so wild and unruly, bit and howled so furiously, that it was long before they could obtain the mastery. An *engagé* then knelt upon him to put on the harness, but when this was done he discovered that he had killed the poor dog. These dogs, if they are not broken in, are quite unfit for the sledge; when, however, they are accustomed to the work, they draw a sledge over the snow more easily than the best horse. If the snow is frozen, they run over it, where the horse sinks in, and they can hold out much longer. They can perform a journey of thirty miles in one day; and if they have rested an hour on the snow, and had some food, they are ready to set out again. A horse must have sufficient food, frequent rest, and a good watering place, and when it is once tired it cannot be induced to proceed. I have been assured by some persons that they had made long journeys, for eight successive days, with dogs, during which time the animals did not taste any food. In the winter when the Indians go to hunt the buffalo, they drive, in light sledges, over the frozen snow, into the midst of the herd; the Indian, with his bow and arrows, sits or kneels down in the sledge; and the dogs that have been trained, cannot be held back when they perceive the buffalo herd. In the north three good dogs are seldom to be purchased for less than 100 dollars. A single dog, when it is very good and strong, costs sixty or seventy dollars; on the Missouri, however, they are by no means so dear.

About noon, we again heard the Indian drums: several soldiers announced the band which had lately purchased the

Sih-Sa (the red feather), a handsome young Mandan who was in charge of the horses at Fort Clark, posed in his finest attire.

dance of the half-shorn head. The whole company, very gaily and handsomely dressed, soon afterwards entered the fort, followed by a crowd of spectators. About twenty vigorous young men, with the upper part of the body naked (having thrown off their robes which they wore at their entrance), painted and ornamented in the most gaudy manner, formed a circle in the court-yard of the fort.

As soon as the drum was beat, the dancers bent their bodies forward, leaped up with both feet together, holding their guns in their hands, and the finger on the trigger, as if going to fire. In this manner they danced for about a minute in a circle, then gave a loud shout, and, having rested a little, began the dance again, and so on alternately. Some tobacco was thrown on the ground before them, after which they soon broke up, took up their robes, and went to Ruhptare, where they danced and passed the night, and then exhibited their performances among the Minnetarees.

Maximilian deciphered this "letter" from a Mandan to a fur trader thusly: "The cross signifies, 'I will barter or trade.' Three animals are drawn to the right of the cross: one is a buffalo (probably a white buffalo); the two others, a weasel and an otter. The writer offers in exchange for the skins of these animals the articles that he has drawn on the left side of the cross: a beaver and a gun. To the left of the beaver are thirty strokes, each ten separated by a longer line. This means, 'I will give 30 beaver skins and a gun for the skins of the three animals on the right side of the cross.'"

Mr. Kipp had received orders from Mr. Mc Kenzie to go to Fort Union, and he accordingly made the necessary preparations for this winter's journey. He purchased, from the Indians, eighteen dogs; and the getting of sledges in readiness caused some bustle in the fort.

### December 29, 1833

The thermometer, at eight o'clock in the morning, was at 19° Fahrenheit, and the high north-west wind was so cutting that we could not hold out long in the prairie. Notwithstanding this, the dogs were collected, and harnessed with considerable difficulty, as they made much resistance. Mr. Kipp travelled with five Indian sledges, with a sufficient number of well-armed *engagés*. Charbonneau accompanied him on what is called a cariole (a convenient wooden sledge, drawn by one horse), in order to purchase meat for us of the Indians. The appearance of the caravan was very amusing, for many of the dogs, not trained to this service, jumped from one side to the other and could not be brought into order but by the use of the whip.

About noon the snow-storm increased, and it was so cold in our apartment that, notwithstanding a good fire, we were unable to work. The high wind drove the snow through the crevices in the walls and the doors, and the whole place was filled with smoke. The thermometer at noon was 14° Fahrenheit. The night, too, was stormy.

### December 30, 1833

The continuing hurricane from the west roared exactly as at sea; a great deal of snow lay in our room, and the water was frozen. In the prairie we could not keep our eyes open on account of the excessive glare: exposure to the weather was painful both to man and beast. It was hoped, however, that it would soon cause the herds of buffaloes to come nearer to us; but this expectation was not realized, though it was said that there were many at the post of the Yanktonans. Our horses were obliged, during this dreadful weather, to walk about the whole night in the court-yard of the fort, with a mass of ice and snow on their backs. As Gautier, an old *engagé*, was bringing wood into the room, and the door remained open a short time, Mr. Bodmer's colours and pencils froze, so that he could not use them without hot water. Writing, too, was very difficult, because our ink was congealed; and, while the side of our bodies which was turned to the fire was half roasted, the other was quite benumbed, and we were often forced to rise in order to warm ourselves. The cook had his ears frost-bitten in going to fetch water.

To add to our chapter of misfortunes, news was received that the Yanktonans had stolen some horses from the Mandans, and killed several. This was the fourth time that these Indians had broken the peace concluded in the preceding September, and the Mandans were so incensed at their treachery that they were disposed to recommence the war.

## December 31, 1833

The last day of the year was clear and cold: at eight o'clock in the morning the mercury was at 2° below zero: a vapour rose from the river. Towards noon the wind again blew high, the frozen snow crackled, and no animals, not even wolves or ravens, were to be seen. Before this weather set in, the Indians had ridden fifteen miles into the prairie, where many of them were almost frozen to death, but were recovered by being wrapped up in blankets, and laid before the fire.

## January 1–5, 1834

January set in with increasing cold, which at eight o'clock in the morning was 9° below zero Fahrenheit, and on the 2nd at the same hour, 24° below zero. On the 3rd the mercury sank into the ball, and was frozen; it remained there on the 4th, but on the 5th it rose, and at eight in the morning was 9° below zero. During these cold days, some of our wood-cutters had their noses and cheeks frost-bitten. The horizon was hazy; the river smoked; neither man nor animal was to be seen; yet a party of Mandans, with their wives, were in the prairie hunting buffaloes, of which they killed forty. At night the cold was so intense, that we could not venture to put our hands from our bodies, lest they should be frozen. In the morning we could scarcely endure the severity of the weather, till we had a blazing fire, for the bleak north-west wind penetrated through all the seams of the building. We received information that Mr. Kipp had remained with the Minnetarees till the 2nd of January, and had not proceeded on his journey till the cold had somewhat abated. Almost all his people had some part of their body frost-bitten, and eight of his dogs had

run away. Some Indians who visited us presented rather a novel appearance, having their hair, and even their eyelashes, covered with hoar frost and icicles. In our own room, the boots and shoes were frozen so hard in the morning, that we could scarcely put them on; ink, colours, and pencils were perfectly useless. During this cold we were visited by a deaf and dumb Mandan, who had no covering on the upper part of his body under his robe.

On the 3rd of January, at noon, when the sunbeams, shining on the frozen snow, were extremely dazzling, the thermometer being at 24° below zero, I saw no living creatures in the neighbourhood of the Indian village, except flocks of the snow-bunting, and a few ravens, two species of birds which are capable of enduring the severest cold. The Yanktonans, and the people whom we had sent to Picotte, returned, on the 4th of January, with dried meat, as well as tallow for candles: they said that, during the two coldest days, they had halted in the forest, but that, in the night, the wolves had carried off part of their meat.

It was scarcely possible to obtain water from the river, and the water-casks in our room were frozen to the bottom. Unfortunately, too, our wood-cutters brought us only driftwood, which had lain so long in the water that it would not burn.

## January 7, 1834        [Field Journal]

In the afternoon snow fell and it was less cold. Belhumeur called for me and I had to help him to weigh out several buckets of metal, as he could neither read nor write nor differentiate between the numbers on the weights. Among all the men who are at the fort there is not a single one who can read or write. I have to write down everything whenever something must be recorded. And when they receive letters, I have to read their secrets to them. Sih-Chida slept again in our room. After he undressed, he lay down on his back on his robe and made a speech, something like a prayer, to the lord of life, from which we understood a few things. He said, among other things, may the lord of life send them buffaloes, in order to save them from hunger. He spoke in a swift, low voice and without gesticulation.

## January 8, 1834

At noon, when I went to look at the thermometer, I found that it had been stolen by the Indians. Our friend Sih-Chida immediately ran out, and discovered the instrument concealed by a woman under her robe, and, to my great joy, brought it back to me. Bidda-Chohki (generally called *la chevelure levée,* the scalped man), visited us, and gave me some words of Minnetaree language, but he was not in a very good humour, because he could not get any brandy.

### January 9, 1834

The next day this man dressed himself very handsomely in order to have his portrait taken, but the mercury was again 20° below zero, and it was too cold in our room to paint, for colours and pencils were frozen, though standing close to the fire, and had to be thawed in hot water. We calculated that we should burn in our chimney at least six cords of wood in a month if this cold continued. Mato-Topé had become reconciled to Pehriska-Ruhpa, and purchased a green blanket, which he showed to us, as a present for him. We heard that a wolf had attacked three Indian women in the forest, who had been obliged to defend themselves with their hatchets.

### January 14, 1834

The cold was only 8° below zero, but there was such a high, piercing wind, that our wood-cutters complained more than when the cold was more severe. In these prairies it is, for the most part, the wind which makes the cold intolerable; and though persons who ventured out wore woollen caps which left only the eyes exposed, yet their faces were frost-bitten. Our provisions were very bad, for Picotte had sent us only tough, hard, stale meat, besides which we had nothing but maize and beans, and the water of the river.

### January 15, 1834         [Field Journal]

Towards noon, Mato-Topé came with many Indians. They were going to Ruhptare, where a medicine son was to be adopted. Mato-Topé was handsomely-attired. He had marked all his wounds in his hair with small sticks. Four of these were yellow, one blue, and one red. In addition, he wore on the right side of his head a knife made of wood and painted red, signifying that he had killed a Cheyenne chief with a knife. On the top of each wooden stick, there was the head of a

yellow nail that had been driven in. He was wearing at the back of his head a large tuft of owl feathers [*dyed yellow*] as a sign of the dog band. Eagle feathers projected like rays from his hair. One of his eyes was painted yellow, the other red, and his forehead and jaw were red as well. His body and arms were painted with reddish-brown streaks and his coups were indicated by yellow horizontal stripes on his arm. On his chest, a yellow hand showed that he had taken prisoners. [*Two days later, Bodmer persuaded Mato-Topé to don his war paint once again for the portrait that appears on page 218. Maximilian noted elsewhere that the six wooden sticks with brass nail heads denoted bullet wounds, while the split turkey feather in the center of his headdress signified an arrow wound.*]

### January 16, 1834

In the night the wind blew with such violence, that it scattered the heap of ashes from the fire-place all over the room, so that our beds, benches, and clothes were completely covered with them. Mato-Topé returned on this day from Ruhptare, and told us, with great satisfaction and self-complacency, that he had enumerated all his exploits, and that no one had been able to surpass him. Old Garreau, who was constantly with our *engagés* in the fort, complained to me, that, for a long time, he had lived on nothing but maize boiled in water; and this was really the case with many persons at this place, as game became more and more scarce. When Garreau first came to these parts, game abounded, and beavers were heard in all the streams, striking with their tails; now, however, even the Indians are often reduced to want.

### January 23, 1834

Information was brought that a herd of buffaloes was only six miles from the fort; accordingly, three *engagés,* with an Arikara, who was staying in the fort, were sent in pursuit of them, and returned at night with two cows and a young bull, two of which were given to the fort. The Mandans had killed about fifty of this herd. Our hunters had almost all their fingers frozen, but they knew well how to restore circulation by rubbing the limbs with snow. The Indians did not visit us so frequently at this time, because they were well supplied with meat: the Arikara, however, came to us to attend a feast in Belhumeur's apartment, where we were to be regaled with buffalo flesh.

JANUARY 29, 1834

Women of the band of the white buffalo cow, from Ruhptare, came to the fort to perform their dance, on which occasion they were dressed in the same manner as the women from Mih-Tutta-Hang-Kush, only they had not the bundles of brushwood. The musicians were three men, who wore caps of white buffalo skin. Knives, tobacco, and glass beads were laid on the ground as presents for them, after which they proceeded to the lower Mandan village.

JANUARY 30, 1834

Mr. Kipp arrived today from Fort Union, with three or four dog sledges, and six men. They were completely covered with ice, their noses and cheeks were livid, and they appeared quite frost-bitten. Besides staying four days with the Minnetarees, Mr. Kipp and his party had been twelve days on their journey to Fort Union. At the beginning they had nothing to eat; and the poor dogs had been so completely starved for nine days, that they could scarcely crawl along, so that no burden could be laid upon them, and the party were obliged to travel the greater part of the way on foot, in deep snow. They encountered a war party of nine Assiniboins, some of whom ran away, but the others were sent by Mr. Kipp to hunt, by which means he procured meat, and the *engagés,* too, succeeded in killing a few elks and deer. It was affirmed that the mercury of Fahrenheit's thermometer had been for a whole fortnight at 45° below zero (77° below freezing point), at Fort Union. No buffaloes had appeared in the vicinity, nor any Indians, who remained further down the river. The hunters of Fort Union had been absent nearly a month, in which time they killed only two bulls, two cows, and a calf.

Except in some few places, provisions were extremely scarce this winter on the whole of the Missouri, from Fort Clark upwards. No accounts had been received from Fort Mc Kenzie. I had wished to receive several articles from Fort Union; but Mr. Hamilton was not able to send them, the sledge being too heavily laden; he, however, promised to forward them without fail, in the spring, with the people who were to be sent to conduct us down the Missouri to Fort

Psichdja-Sahpa, a Yanktonan Dakota who had wandered upstream from his tribe's winter encampment on the Missouri, came often to Maximilian's quarters to roast ears of corn in the fireplace during the bitterly cold weather of January.

Pierre. Mr. Kipp had been eleven days on his journey back, and had again been obliged to perform a considerable part of it on foot. The dogs had had nothing to eat for three days, and now the poor beasts were fed with hides cut in pieces, for we had no meat. Numbers of fowls in the forest perished in the intense cold.

## January 31, 1834

On the last day of January there was a change in the weather; at eight in the morning, with a west wind, the mercury was at 22° Fahrenheit, and we could scarcely bear the warmth of the fire in our apartment. Towards noon a complete thaw set in, and the mild weather immediately brought us a number of Indian visitors.

## February 1, 1834

Mr. Kipp sent three *engagés,* with two dog sledges, down the river, to the post among the Yanktonans, which was under the superintendence of Picotte, to procure meat, for we subsisted entirely on maize broth and maize bread, and were without tallow for candles; the dogs that were sent with the *engagés* howled most piteously when they were harnessed, their feet being still sore and bleeding from the effects of their late journey. On this day news was received from Mih-Tutta-Hang-Kush, that three hostile Indians (Assiniboins), had been in the village during the night, for the purpose of shooting somebody, for in the morning the place where they had concealed themselves was discovered, from one of the party having left his knee-band behind. They had not been able to fire through the wall of the hut, and had retired at daybreak without attaining their object; traces were also found of some hostile Indians, who had come over the river.

## February 2, 1834

One of the sledges sent to Picotte came back, having been broken on the way. The man who came with it fell in with the Mandans, who were going to hunt buffaloes, and detained him, lest he should frighten the animals away. In the preceding night, the Assiniboins had stolen three horses from the Minnetarees, 150 of whom immediately mounted their horses to pursue and kill them.

## February 3, 1834

At eight o'clock in the morning, the thermometer stood at 39°; the face of the country had assumed quite a different aspect; large tracts of land were wholly free from the snow, which was fast melting away, and only the hills were partially covered; yet, with this rapid thaw, the ground had not become wet, for it was immediately dried by the continual wind; but there was a considerable quantity of water on the ice which covered the river. The ravens and magpies again flew about in the prairie in quest of food.

In the afternoon news was received that the Minnetarees, who had gone in pursuit of the Assiniboins, had overtaken a small party, and killed a young man, whom they had found asleep, cruelly awakened with whips, and then murdered in cold blood. These Assiniboins are very daring, and often approach the villages of the Mandans and Minnetarees, either singly or in small parties, and sometimes surprise individuals and shoot them.

Thus, some time ago, an Assiniboin suddenly fired at a number of young people who were standing near the palisades of the village, and killed one of them. The others raised an alarm, while the murderer took the scalp of the youth he had killed, fled down the steep bank of the river, where many persons were bathing, and made his escape through the very midst of all these people. Other Assiniboins stole eleven horses from a Minnetaree hut, and were not ever perceived till they were in the act of leading off the last of the animals. They stole four horses from a hut in which Charbonneau was sleeping, and made their escape with their booty, without being seen by any one. Today arrows were found sticking in the huts and posts of the Mandan village, which intruders had discharged at random during the night in the hope of killing one of their foes.

## February 4, 1834                                    [Field Journal]

Early in the day a young Indian came, carrying fastened to a stick with a string the severed hand of the Assiniboin who had been killed yesterday. A group of children surrounded him. Sih-Sa took this trophy of barbarism from him and carried it about with satisfaction. Belhumeur went hunting buffalo today with three men and eight horses. Charbonneau was absent again. This seventy-five-year-old man is always running after women.

A tall, eminent Mandan warrior named Up-Sich-Te (the great blackness) was painted holding his eagle-wing fan and looking-glass, a trade item avidly sought after from the whites.

## FEBRUARY 5–9, 1834

On the 4th and 5th, the weather was mild; the horses were again sent out to graze in the prairie, our waggons went to fetch grass, and, towards noon, the day was really quite warm. We were still without meat, none of the parties whom we sent out having been able to procure any. Our stock of tallow, too, was exhausted, and we were obliged to content ourselves with the light of the fire. For several succeeding days, the weather being still mild, we were much interested in watching the activity of the Indians on the river; among them a number of women brought heavy burdens, especially of wood, from the lower forest village, to Mih-Tutta-Hang-Kush. They had to pass, opposite the fort, a channel formed through the midst of the frozen river, which was covered with a thin coat of ice; this they broke very deliberately with their long poles, and then waded through. Some carried their small leathern boats to the channel, in this they deposited the wood, and then pushed it along. The manner in which they took up the heavy burdens was remarkable. A woman lay down on her back, upon the bundle of wood, while another raised her with the burden till she was able to bend forward, and then stand upright with her load. A great many women were thus occupied, for the Indians were desirous of going to their summer village, because they were now too much scattered to be safe while the enemy was so near at hand.

On the 9th of February the inhabitants of Ruhptare had all removed from their winter to their summer quarters; they were evidently afraid that the ice would break up early, and the water of the Missouri rise considerably.

## FEBRUARY 10, 1834

Two of our people came from Picotte, with a sledge drawn by two dogs, and informed us that there were many buffaloes in the neighbourhood, consequently our fear of want of provisions was dispelled. At Fort Pierre the cold had been more intense than had been known for many years, the mercury having remained for a considerable time between 30° and 40° below zero. Three of Mr. Laidlaw's people, who were travelling at the time, had suffered so severely from the frost, that their lives were despaired of. The ice of the Missouri had, for a few days, been very unfavourable for travelling, as it was covered to some depth with water, and our people, consequently, had suffered much. In the afternoon of that day, the Minnetaree chief, Lachpitzi-Sihrish (the yellow bear), arrived, bringing on his horse a small supply of meat, and an unborn buffalo calf, which he presented to us, this disgusting little black animal being reckoned a great dainty by them. His robe was painted with suns, and on his back he carried his bow, with a beautifully ornamented quiver of panther's skin.

## FEBRUARY 11, 1834

The fort was crowded with Minnetarees who wished to perform before us the scalp dance, in commemoration of having slain an enemy on the preceding day. A number of tall, handsomely-dressed men, having their faces blackened, soon filled every apartment. Itsichaika (the monkey-face), and the other chiefs, had arrived, and these Indians, who are not nearly so well behaved as the Mandans, very deliberately took possession of all our seats and fire-places. We bolted the door of our own apartment, where we quietly remained, permitting only a very few of the Indians to enter.

At two o'clock the Minnetaree women arrived in procession, accompanied by many children and some Mandans. Eighteen women, marching two and two in a close column, entered the court-yard of the fort, with a short-measured, slow pace. Seven men of the band of the dogs, having their faces painted black, or black striped with red, acted as musicians, three of them having drums, and four the schischikué. They were wrapped in their buffalo robes, and their heads were uncovered, and ornamented with the feathers of owls and other birds. The faces of some of the women were painted black, others red, while some were striped black and red. They wore buffalo dresses, or blankets, and the two principal were enveloped in the white buffalo robe. The greater part of them had the feather of a war eagle standing upright, and one only wore the large handsome feather cap.

In their arms they carried battle-axes or guns, ornamented with red cloth and short black feathers, which, during the dance, they placed with the butt-end on the ground; in short, while performing this dance, the women are accoutred in the military dress and weapons of the warriors. The right wing was headed by the wife of the chief, Itsichaika, who carried in her hand a long elastic rod, from the point of which was suspended the scalp of the young man slain on the preceding day, surmounted by a stuffed magpie with outspread wings;

lower down on the same rod hung a second scalp, a lynx skin, and a bunch of feathers. Another woman bore a third scalp on a similar rod.

The women filed off in a semicircle; the musicians, taking their stand on the left wing, now commenced a heterogeneous noise, beating the drum, rattling the schischikué, and yelling with all their might. The women began to dance, waddling in short steps, like ducks; the two wings, or horns of the crescent, advanced towards each other, and then receded, at the same time singing in a shrill tone of voice. It was a complete caterwaul concert. After awhile they rested, and then recommenced, and continued dancing about twenty minutes. The director of the fort now caused tobacco, lookingglasses, and knives, from the Company's stores, to be thrown on the ground in the middle of the circle. Hereupon the women once more danced in quick time, the musicians forming themselves into a close body, and holding their instruments towards the centre. This concluded the festivity, and the whole band retired to the Mandan forest village. [*Bodmer's sketches of these dancers are on pages 214–215.*]

## FEBRUARY 12, 1834

There was a heavy fall of snow during the night, and the morning again presented the landscape clothed with its white covering. Mr. Bodmer had taken an excellent portrait of Mahchsi-Nika, the deaf and dumb Mandan, in his war dress. He came to our residence today with angry gestures, and evidently greatly enraged against us, so that I was afraid that this half-witted, uncivilized man would attack the artist. Mr. Kipp was requested to clear up the matter, and it appeared that his anger had been caused by a malignant insinuation of the perfidious old Garreau, who had pointed out to him that Bodmer had drawn him only in a mean dress, while all the other Indians were represented in their handsomest robes. This ill-natured insinuation completely exasperated the poor man, and we in vain endeavoured to pacify him, by assuring him that we intended to make him known to the world in a truly warlike costume. Mr. Bodmer then thought of an expedient: he quickly and secretly made a copy of his drawing, which he brought in, tore in half, and threw into the fire, in the presence of the Indian. This had the desired effect, and he went away perfectly satisfied. [*For this portrait, see page 239.*]

In the afternoon the Minnetarees returned from the Mandan village, and again took deliberate possession of the various apartments of the fort. The Monkey-face, a cunning, perfidious Indian, who wore a new red felt hat, is the chief who now takes the lead among the Minnetarees. Accordingly, as soon as he took leave, all the Indians followed him. One of the chiefs, with his family, sat a long time in our room, and were much interested with Mr. Bodmer's drawings, and astonished and delighted with our musical box. A Mandan who was present thought that a little white man, who was making this pretty music, must be concealed in it. All of them asked for presents, and they would certainly have pilfered many things if we had not kept close watch over them. At length our door was opened, and a tall, heavy man, with a blackened

## FEBRUARY 20, 1834

The Mandans told us, that they had gone, some days before, to hunt buffaloes, and had driven a herd of them towards the mountains, where there is a good opportunity to use the bow and arrows; they had, therefore, pursued the animals rapidly, but, on reaching them, they found but a very few buffaloes, the others, as they affirmed, having sunk into the ground. (They had, doubtless, taken refuge in the nearest ravines.) They assigned, as the cause of this sudden disappearance of the buffaloes, that their party was headed by a man who, in the preceding year, had caused five Assiniboins, who had come to them as messengers of peace, to be killed, and that, on account of this unjust act, he was now always unsuccessful in hunting.

face, entered, and, like all the rest assembled there, demanded something to eat. We, however, gave him to understand that we had nothing to give them, as we were supplied by Mr. Kipp, and with this answer they were obliged to be satisfied. Towards evening our provision store was replenished by three sledges, laden with meat, sent by Picotte, which arrived in the fort.

## FEBRUARY 13, 1834

A very high, cold wind arose today, which blew the snow off from the ice that covered the river, and the Indian women, carrying their burdens, frequently fell down on the slippery surface. The Mandans had found a dead buffalo cow in the prairie, and, although it was in part decayed, they greedily devoured it.

Pipe of the Mandan notable Dipauch. Bowl of clay, stem of wood.

## FEBRUARY 24, 1834

At daybreak, the mercury was at 26°, Fahrenheit, below zero, or 59° below freezing point; and at 8 o'clock, when the sun shine brightly, at 11° below zero, with a west wind. During the night, the horses had broken a window in Mr. Kipp's room, so that we had a very cold breakfast there. In our apartments everything fluid was frozen, and the quilts on the beds were covered with hoar frost. We had now some fresh meat, but our stock of sugar was at an end, and we had to sweeten our coffee with molasses. We were visited by the three deaf and dumb Mandans, whose fourth brother, Berock-Itainu, whom we have before mentioned, is not so afflicted: there is, likewise, a deaf and dumb child in the village. Kiasax, the Blackfoot, who had accompanied us to Fort Union, visited us today for the first time, and we showed him the portraits of his countrymen, with which he was much pleased. The Indians were busy in conveying many things to the summer village, though the prairies were covered with snow; and numerous horses were seeking a scanty subsistence by scraping it away with their hoofs to get at the dry grass.

## FEBRUARY 27, 1834

Mr. Kipp had pieces of ice hewn on the river to fill his ice cellar. A high west wind increased the cold, but the snow melted away because the thermometer was at 38° at noon. We saw the Indian boys pursue and catch the snow-buntings, of which there were large flocks in the neighbourhood of the villages; and the prairie wolves now prowled about in couples. In the evening there was a heavy fall of snow. The Indians removed to their village. All their horses, even the foals, were loaded; they likewise cut blocks of ice from the river, which the women carried home on their backs, in leather baskets, in order to melt them to obtain water. The Indian children amused themselves with ascending the heaps of snow, and gliding down on a board, or a piece of the back-bone of a buffalo, with some of the ribs attached to it.

## FEBRUARY 28, 1834

Mato-Topé paid us a visit in a very strange costume; his head-dress was much more suitable for an old woman than for a warrior. His head was bound round with a strip of wolf's skin, the long hairs of which stood on end, and which hung down behind. Some feathers, standing upright, were placed among the hair, which, except at the tip, were stripped, and painted red. This chief, indeed, had on a different dress almost every time he came to see us. Sometimes he wore a blue uniform, with red facings, which he had obtained from the merchants. Mr. Bodmer took the portrait of a handsome Minnetaree partisan today. [*For the portrait of this warrior, see page 235.*] He was not pleased that we intended to keep his portrait, as he was going on a military expedition, and said that Mr. Bodmer ought, at least, to give him a copy of the drawing. This being refused, he drew a portrait of the artist, and his performance showed that he possessed some talent.

## MARCH 1, 1834

Mr. Bodmer drew the portrait of an old Minnetaree, whose proper name was Birohka (the robe with the beautiful hair), but the Mandans called him "Long Nose," on account of the prominence of that feature. He wore a cap of white buffalo skin, and an ample brown robe painted with wreaths of feathers. Before he would suffer his portrait to be taken, he demanded a black silk neckerchief as a recompense, which was given him. As all the Indians had now removed to their summer village, Mr. Kipp took the usual complement of soldiers into the fort, four of whom served as a guard against the importunities of the women and children; they were Mato-Topé, Dipauch, Berock-Itainu, and another whose name I do not know.

## MARCH 6, 1834

Mato-Topé introduced to us a tall, robust Arikara, named Pachtuwa-Chta, who lived peaceably among the Mandans. He was a handsome man, but not to be depended upon, and was said to have killed many white men. [*For his portrait, see page 234.*] Another tall man of the same nation frequently visited us, generally observing that he was not like Pachtuwa, as he had never killed a white man. Mato-Topé, after repeated solicitations, prevailed on Mr. Bodmer to paint for him a white-headed eagle, holding in his claws a bloody scalp, to which he, doubtless, attached some superstitious notion, but I could not see exactly what it might be. Mato-Topé gave me very accurate information respecting his own language, and that of the neighbouring Indian nations, and took great pleasure in communicating to me some words of the Mandan and Arikara languages, the latter of which he spoke fluently.

## MARCH 7, 1834

The band of the Meniss-Ochata (dog band), from Ruhptare, danced in the medicine lodge at Mih-Tutta-Hang-Kush. Mr. Bodmer went to see the dance, and met Mato-Topé, who, however, puffed up by his high dignity as a dog, would not notice him. Sih-Chida, who also belonged to this band, went into the lodge, where he discharged his gun. In the afternoon the band approached the fort, and we heard the sound of their war whistles at the gates. A crowd of spectators accompanied the seven or eight and twenty dogs, who were all dressed in their handsomest clothes. Some of them wore beautiful robes,

or shirts of bighorn leather; others had shirts of red cloth; and some blue and red uniforms. Others, again, had the upper part of their body naked, with their martial deeds painted on the skin with reddish-brown colour. The four principal dogs wore an immense cap hanging down upon the shoulders, composed of raven's or magpie's feathers, finished at the tips with small white down feathers. In the middle of this mass of feathers, the outspread tail of a wild turkey, or of a war eagle, was fixed. These four principal dogs wore round their neck a long slip of red cloth, which hung down over the shoulders, and, reaching the calf of the leg, was tied in a knot in the middle of the back. These are the true dogs, who, when

Bodmer's pencil was seldom idle, even in the coldest weather.

a piece of meat is thrown into the fire, are bound immediately to snatch it out and devour it raw.

Two other men wore similar colossal caps of yellow owl's feathers, with dark transverse stripes, and the rest had on their heads a thick tuft of raven's, magpie's, or owl's feathers, which is the badge of the band. All of them had the long war whistle suspended from their necks. In their left hand they carried their weapons—a gun, bow and arrows, or war club; and in their right hand the schischikué peculiar to their band. It is a stick adorned with blue and white glass beads, with buffalo or other hoofs suspended to it, the point ornamented with an eagle's feather, and the handle with slips of leather embroidered with beads. [*For a portrait of the Minnetaree warrior Pehriska-Ruhpa as a member of the dog band, see page 223.*]

The warriors formed a circle round a large drum, which was beaten by five ill-dressed men, who were seated on the ground. Besides these, there were two men, each beating a small drum like a tambourine. The dogs accompanied the rapid and violent beat of the drum by the whistle of their war whistles, in short, monotonous notes, and then suddenly began to dance. They dropped their robes on the ground, some dancing within the circle, with their bodies bent forward and leaping up and down with both feet placed together. The other Indians danced without any order, with their faces turned to the outer circle, generally crowded together; while the war whistle, drum, and schischikué made a frightful din.

MARCH 10, 1834

On the 10th of March, two *engagés*, sent by Picotte, arrived, with letters and a sledge laden with dried meat. One of these men was blinded by the snow, a circumstance very usual in this month, from the dazzling reflection of the sun from an expansive surface of snow. He was obliged to get his companion to lead him by taking hold of a stick.

MARCH 11, 1834

I felt the first symptoms of an indisposition, which daily increased, and soon obliged me to take to my bed. It began with a swelling in one knee, and soon extended to the whole leg, which assumed the colour of dark, extravasated blood. A violent fever succeeded, with great weakness, and, having neither medical advice nor suitable remedies, my situation became daily more helpless and distressing, as there was nobody who had any knowledge of this disorder. The other inhabitants of the fort were likewise indisposed, and our provisions were very bad and scanty. To economize our stock of coffee we were forced to make it wretchedly weak, and, for want of sugar or molasses, to sweeten it with honey, of which we had about twenty pounds. Our beverage was, generally speaking, the water from the river; and, as our supply of beans was very low, our diet consisted almost exclusively of maize boiled in water, which greatly weakened our digestion.

[*This was the absolute low point of Maximilian's journey. All of the company were half-starved and suffering from physical complaints of one sort or another. The winter seemed interminable and spirits were very low. In the entry for this day in his field journal Maximilian permitted himself an uncharacteristically harsh comment on his hosts:*]

We are tired of life in this dirty fort to the highest degree. Our daily routine is conducted in such a filthy manner that it nauseates one. Since our Negro cook Alfred suffers from a severe rheumatic disease, we now have a filthy attendant and cook named Boileau who wears a fur cap, sits down among us and handles the cups and plates with his disgusting fists after cleaning his nose according to the manner of our peasants. This is also exactly the manner of the clerk of the fort, Kipp, who along with his wife and child scatters these items about and then cleans his fingers on the first object that comes to hand. The little boy has a gap in his trousers, both in front and in back, so that he may relieve himself quickly and without formality on the floor of the room, which happened

Young men of the Mandan and Minnetaree tribes played various games with hoops and spears. In one, the player would attempt to spear the center of a leather-laced hoop that was either thrown in the air or rolled swiftly on the ground.

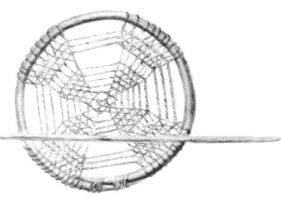

frequently during meals. The indolence and indifference of [*Mr. Kipp*] this otherwise commendable man goes so far that he eases himself near the fort in full sight of passersby, having neglected to build an outhouse for this purpose. In short, our sojourn here was a hard test.]

MARCH 13, 1834

The first wild ducks were seen on this day, flying up the Missouri, and Mr. Kipp immediately set about making shot, to go in pursuit of these birds, which we had been most anxiously expecting.

MARCH 14, 1834

Pehriska-Ruhpa spent several days with us, in order to have his portrait taken in his dress of one of the chiefs of the dog band. When the sitting was over, he always took off his ponderous feather cap, and rubbed it twice on each side of his head, a charm or precaution which he never neglected. [*See page 223 for this portrait.*] He then seated himself with his friend, Mato-Topé, by the fire-side, when both took their pipes, the latter, however, always turning round first, and making everybody in the room sit down. During the tedium of my confinement to bed, I was enlivened by the frequent visits of the Indians, and I never neglected to continue my journal, which, from fever and consequent weakness, was often very fatiguing. Mr. Kipp kindly sent me some new-laid eggs every day, as well as rice, which he had reserved for me, and from which I derived great benefit. The inmates of the fort had nothing to eat but doughy maize bread and maize boiled in water; but Mr. Kipp, who did not like the latter, was obliged to fast.

MARCH 16–25, 1834

The first wild swans were seen flying towards the northwest today. Ducks were in the pools of water in the maize plantations of the Mandans; and Dreidoppel had observed a finch as a harbinger of spring. Violent storms from the northwest had prevailed for some days; the Missouri was much swollen, but the breaking-up of the ice could not yet be expected, and we had repeated falls of snow. Mato-Topé and Pehriska-Ruhpa, who had gone out to hunt, succeeded in killing five buffaloes, and from them we obtained some meat; for, to show their liberality, they gave away a great deal of it, together with several coloured blankets. The first white-headed eagle was seen today; and I received the first prairie dog, which was also a sign of the approach of spring, as these animals leave their burrows at this season.

MARCH 27, 1834

The band of the mad dogs danced in the fort; and, towards evening, an Indian from Ruhptare, who had had a dispute with Mr. Kipp about a beaver skin, revenged himself by breaking a pane of glass in our room. Our people pursued, but could not overtake him. As it was feared that he might commit greater acts of violence, the soldiers of the fort were sent to Ruhptare to protect a fur trader who resided there.

APRIL 2, 1834

The women at Mih-Tutta-Hang-Kush celebrated the spring corn feast, of which Mr. Bodmer made a sketch. This feast is always observed on the return of the wild geese, which are the messengers of the old woman who never dies. The Indians had already killed some of these birds. The festival was over at eleven o'clock in the forenoon, but some of the women remained the whole day, reclining near the offerings hung up in the prairie. Great numbers of young men were running races, and all was animation about the village.

APRIL 3, 1834

The band of the [*ravens*], eighteen in number, danced in the fort, led by Mato-Topé, on horseback, in full dress, wearing his splendid feather cap. The ice broke up so rapidly in the river, that it was necessary to set a watch over our boats during the night, lest the water should carry them away.

APRIL 5, 1834

The weather being stormy in the morning, and the temperature 59½° Fahrenheit, the river had risen about a foot, and towards noon it suddenly rose between three and four feet more, so that, at twelve o'clock, the ice on the surface began to move, the temperature being 68°. But in the night the river again fell a foot, and there was a slight frost. At nine in

the evening the temperature was 55°, and we had a storm of thunder and lightning.

### April 8, 1834

Today the Minnetarees danced the scalp dance in the fort, and the Indians amused themselves in the prairie with races and various games. At one o'clock in the afternoon, the ice in the Upper Missouri suddenly broke up, and brought down many trunks of trees, which endangered our boats. The Indians immediately availed themselves of this opportunity to land a good deal of the wood; they also brought ashore a drowned elk, which, though already in a state of decomposition, they actually ate.

### April 9, 1834

Towards evening, nine men of the band of the buffalo bulls came to the fort to perform their dance, discharging their guns immediately on entering. Only one of them wore the entire buffalo head; the others had pieces of the skin of the forehead, a couple of fillets of red cloth, their shields deco-

rated with the same material, and an appendage of feathers, intended to represent the bull's tail, hanging down their backs. They likewise carried long, elegantly ornamented banners in their hands. [*See pages 212–213 for sketches of these dancers.*] After dancing for a short time before us, they demanded presents. Besides the strange figures of this dance, Mr. Bodmer painted the chief, Mato-Topé, at full length, in his grandest dress. The vanity which is characteristic of the Indians induced this chief to stand stock-still for several days, so that his portrait succeeded admirably. [*This portrait is on page 219.*] He wore on this occasion a handsome new shirt of bighorn leather, the large feather cap, and, in his hand, a long lance with scalps and feathers. He has been so often mentioned in my narrative, that I must here subjoin a few words respecting this eminent man, for he was fully entitled to this appellation, being not only a distinguished warrior, but possessing many fine and noble traits of character. In war he had always maintained a distinguished reputation; and on one occasion, with great personal danger, he conducted to Fort Clark a numerous deputation of the Assiniboins, who had come to Mih-Tutta-Hang-Kush to conclude peace, while his countrymen, disregarding the proposals, kept firing upon

the deputies. Mato-Topé, after having in vain exerted himself to the utmost to prevent these hostilities, led his enemies, with slow steps, amidst the whistling balls and the arrows of his counrymen, while he endeavoured to find excuses for their culpable conduct. He had killed many enemies, among whom were five chiefs. He gave me a fac-simile of a representation of one of his exploits, painted by himself, of which he frequently gave me an account. He was, on that occasion, on foot, on a military expedition, with a few Mandans, when they encountered four Cheyennes, their most virulent foes, on horseback. The chief of the latter, seeing that their enemies were on foot, and that the combat would thereby be unequal, dismounted, and the two parties attacked each other. The two chiefs fired, missed, threw away their guns, and seized their naked weapons; the Cheyenne, a tall, powerful man, drew his knife, while Mato-Topé, who was lighter and more agile, took his battle-axe. The former attempted to stab Mato-Topé, who laid hold of the blade of the knife, by which he, indeed, wounded his hand, but wrested the weapon from his enemy, and stabbed him with it, on which the Cheyennes took to flight. Mato-Topé's drawing of the scene in the above-named plate, shows the guns which they had dis-

charged and thrown aside, the blood flowing from the wounded hand of the Mandan chief, the footsteps of the two warriors, and the wolf's tail at their heels—the Cheyenne being distinguished by the fillet of otter skin on his forehead. The buffalo robe, painted by Mato-Topé himself, and which I have fortunately brought to Europe, represents several exploits of this chief, and, among others, in the lower figure on the left hand, the above-mentioned adventure with the Cheyenne chief. [*Bodmer's watercolor rendering of Mato-Topé's buffalo role is on page 220. For Mato-Topé's painting of his fight with the Cheyenne chief, see page 221.*]

## April 11, 1834

Several of our Indian friends, among whom was Sih-Chida, had taken leave, intending to assist a large party of Minnetarees and Mandans in a military expedition. They set out on their march about this time, and we afterwards learnt that a war party of the Minnetarees had completely plundered a couple of beaver hunters, white men; and that their partisan, whose name was Pierce Iron, had acted the principal part on this occasion. On the other hand, the Assiniboins had stolen

---

In early February the Mandans began returning to their summer village. Bodmer sketched women and dogs carrying goods across the ice of the Missouri. Later on in the spring, when the ice had broken up, the women launched their bull boats.

thirty-four horses from the Minnetarees, who shot one of them.

## APRIL 14, 1834

The people whom Mr. Mc Kenzie had promised to send to accompany me down the river to St. Louis, at length arrived from Fort Union. There were, however, many others with them, and the whole party amounted to twenty men, among whom were Belhumeur and Mr. Chardon as leader. The violent storm on the preceding days had hindered them from travelling, and they were obliged to halt. They brought us letters from Fort Union, and news from Fort Mc Kenzie. As my people could now be spared, I looked daily for the arrival of Picotte, who, with many men, was to go up to Fort Union, as, without the help of his men, my Mackinaw boat could not be caulked. A main point now was my recovery, which was singularly rapid. At the beginning of April I was still in a hopeless condition, and so very ill, that the people who visited me did not think that my life would be prolonged beyond three or, at the most, four days. The cook of the fort, a Negro from St. Louis, one day expressed his opinion that my illness must be the scurvy, for he had once witnessed the great mortality among the garrison of the fort at Council Bluffs, when several hundred soldiers were carried off in a short time. He said that the symptoms were in both cases nearly similar; that, on that occasion, at the beginning of spring, they had gathered the green herbs in the prairie, especially the small white flowering *Allium reticulatum,* with which they had soon cured the sick. I was advised to make trial of this recipe, and the Indian children accordingly furnished me with an abundance of this plant and its bulbs: these were cut up small, like spinage, and I ate a quantity of them. On the fourth day

the swelling of my leg had considerably subsided, and I gained strength daily. The evident prospect of speedy recovery quite reanimated me, and we carried on with pleasure the preparations for our departure, though I was not yet able to leave my bed.

### APRIL 15–17, 1834

Picotte arrived with about twenty men, and had his boat laden with maize, which he was to carry to Fort Union. They immediately set about preparing the Mackinaw boat for our voyage down the river, and Picotte set out on the 16th, notwithstanding a heavy rain. Every preparation was completed on the following day; the boat was brought to the landing-place, furnished on the deck with a spacious Indian tent covering, and all was made ready for our voyage, Mr. Char-don resolving to accompany me all the way to Fort Pierre.

### APRIL 18, 1834

At noon, the boat was loaded; and, after we had partaken of our last frugal dinner at Fort Clark, we took a cordial farewell of Mr. Kipp, with whom we had passed so long a time in this remote place, and who had done everything for me that was possible in his circumscribed condition. Accompanied by the inhabitants of the fort, and many of our Indian friends, among whom was Mato-Topé and Pehriska-Ruhpa, all of whom shook hands at parting, we went on board our boat. The weather was favourable, though there was a strong wind from the south-west. Some cannon-shot were fired by the fort as a farewell salute, and we glided rapidly down the beautiful stream of the Missouri.

Mandan women's corn feast, which Bodmer sketched on April 2.

# Afterword

Maximilian's voyage down the Missouri to St. Louis was accomplished in the company of Bodmer, Dreidoppel, a crew of four Company *engagés,* the two caged bears that had somehow survived the winter, and occasional river passengers. The trip required less than six weeks and was singularly uneventful, despite the usual hazards of Missouri River navigation: snags, sudden storms, and the intermittent drunkenness of the crew. At Fort Pierre the prince was feted at a banquet of stewed dog, buffalo still being scarce. At Pilcher's trading post he found his acquaintance of the previous year guarding a store of 24,000 muskrat pelts for delivery to St. Louis. Early in May the travelers encountered the steamboat *Assiniboin* headed upstream with the year's supplies for the Company posts. Maximilian spent a day aboard her giving Indian agents Sanford and Bean the year's news from the Upper Missouri. (Later on, during the summer, the *Assiniboin* was wrecked and burned on her way downriver. She was loaded with hundreds of bales of furs and seven large cases containing a sizable part of Maximilian's arduously gathered collections. The furs were saved, but not the collections—a bitter loss to the naturalist.)

Maximilian's health, which had been so shattered that he had to be helped aboard the boat at Fort Clark, improved steadily as the party progressed downstream, doubtless because of the warming spring weather and improved diet. Game was plentiful, and the trading posts offered fresh milk and dried vegetables, good palliatives for scurvy.

Arriving at St. Louis on May 27, after an absence of thirteen months, Maximilian renewed his acquaintance with Pierre Chouteau before boarding a steamer that carried him and his companions up the Ohio in early June. Proceeding alternately by horse-drawn stage, steamer, and canal barge, the party reached the headwaters of the Hudson by late June. They paused to take the measure of Niagara Falls ("We were struck mute at the overwhelming sight of this abyss of waters") and then continued on to New York via the Erie Canal and the Hudson. In New York, Maximilian required only ten days to complete his arrangements to quit the New World for the Old. On July 16, with his two companions, his two bears, and what remained of his collections, Maximilian took ship for Europe, arriving in Le Havre on the morning of August 8, after an easy crossing. The great adventure was finally ended.

Maximilian's expedition was just in time. Three years after his departure from Fort Clark a deadly smallpox epidemic swept up the Missouri, decimating the Plains tribes. The disease was brought upstream by the Company's annual steamboat and broke out among the Mandans in July of 1837. The Minnetarees were next, then the Assiniboins, Arikaras, Sioux, and Blackfeet. All felt the scourge of the disease. The most reliable estimates placed the number of victims at 17,000, or about a quarter of the tribal populations. Whatever the true figure, the epidemic permanently altered the balance of the Missouri tribes and, combined with the other deadly imports of the whites—alcohol and gunpowder—effectively wrote *finis* to the great period of Plains Indian culture.

The Mandans suffered most heavily. In fact, they were wiped out. In June, 1837, the tribe was thought to number 1,600 men, women, and children. By autumn only 100 remained alive. As the chiefs and warriors watched their tribe waste horribly away, anger mounted against the whites. Had they not brought the plague? Few whites perished: thus did they not have a secret remedy that they withheld from the Indians? Attempts were made to kill Francis Chardon, by then director at Fort Clark. The fort itself was virtually under siege throughout the entire summer. Even Mato-Topé contracted the disease. Having seen his wives and children succumb, he too at last turned against the whites and attempted to raise a last war party to attack Fort Clark. It was no use; the tribe was too far gone, and Four Bears himself died on

July 30. His last exhortation to the dying warriors of his tribe comes down to us in Francis Chardon's erratically punctuated journal:

My Friends one and all, Listen to what I have to say—Ever since I can remember, I have loved the Whites. I have lived With them ever since I was a Boy, and to the best of my Knowledge, I have never Wronged a White Man, on the Contrary, I have always Protected them from the insults of Others, Which they cannot deny. The 4 Bears never saw a White Man hungry, but what he gave him to eat, Drink, and a Buffaloe skin to sleep on, in time of Need. I was always ready to die for them, Which they cannot deny. I have done every thing that a red Skin could do for them, and how have they repaid it! With ingratitude! I have Never Called a White Man a Dog, but to day, I do Pronounce them to be a set of Black harted Dogs, they have deceived Me, them that I always considered as Brothers, has turned Out to be My Worst enemies. I have been in Many Battles, and often Wounded, but the Wounds of My enemies I exhalt in, but to day I am Wounded, and by Whom, by those same White Dogs that I have always Considered, and treated as Brothers. I do not fear *Death* my friends. You Know it, but to *die* with my face rotten, that even the Wolves will shrink with horror at seeing Me, and say to themselves, that is the 4 Bears the Friend of the Whites—

Listen well what I have to say, as it will be the last time you will hear Me. I think of your Wives, Children, Brothers, Sisters, Friends, and in fact all that you hold dear, are all Dead, or Dying, with their faces all rotten, caused by those dogs the whites, think of all that My friends, and rise all together and Not leave one of them alive. The 4 Bears will act his Part—

Mato-Topé's ceremonial drum, painted by Bodmer in 1833, was stilled forever by the terrible smallpox epidemic of 1837.

Bodmer and Maximilian spent more than five months at Fort Clark in daily contact with the Indians of the Mandan and Minnetaree tribes. At the time of their visit the Mandans numbered some 1,500 souls. [*Maximilian's estimate of between 900 and 1,000 was probably too low.*] Once they had been more numerous, but the predations of the smallpox and their traditional enemies, the Sioux, had reduced their numbers. Their allies, the Minnetarees, were an offshoot of the Crow nation that had settled near the Mandans, adopting their sedentary, semiagricultural existence and many of their customs as well. The Mandans were accounted the most culturally advanced of all the Plains tribes. Their social and religious customs were highly developed, and their handicrafts and dress were second only to those of the Crows. Moreover, they were not particularly warlike and had been friendly toward the whites for many years. Thus the two tribes presented a rich subject for Maximilian's ethnological inquiries. Through the long winter months there was time in abundance for Maximilian's interviews with chiefs and other notables. There were ceremonial feasts and dances to be observed, excursions to the villages to be made, and time for Bodmer to paint his meticulously detailed series of portraits and studies that must surely rank as the finest paintings ever made of an aboriginal culture.

*Opposite:* Addih-Hiddish (he who makes the path), a Minnetaree chief who related the history of his tribe to Maximilian over a number of winter evenings, posed for his portrait after considerable persuasion in late March. Maximilian remarked that he had blue-black tattoos not only on his body and arms but on his legs as well. The red coloring is vermilion mixed with fat to form a grease. His tomahawk handle is ornamented with a scalp, stretched on a circular frame, as was the custom.

In the prairie near Mih-Tutta-Hang-Kush, Bodmer found a number of medicine sites to which the Mandans repaired to beseech their gods. He made this painting in early November. Maximilian was unable to learn the significance of the two knives stuck in the earth or the red stripes painted on the human skulls. Numerous other skulls were scattered nearby, and the prince resolved to return by night in order "to commit a few thefts" in the interests of the advance of science.

In the late afternoon of April 9 a number of Mandans, members of the band of the buffalo bulls (Berock-Ochateh) came into the fort to stage an impromptu buffalo dance for the Europeans. Bodmer made these hasty sketches, which were later used as research for the copperplate aquatint reproduced on page 172. Bodmer never witnessed the dance in the village of Mih-Tutta-Hang-Kush itself, but his aquatint squares with firsthand descriptions.

During the winter and early spring, groups of women came on several occasions to dance at the fort, and Bodmer made color sketches for later use in designing his copperplate engravings back in Paris. *Opposite and top:* Minnetaree women who performed the scalp dance that Maximilian describes at some length in his entry for February 11. The musicians are men. *Left:* Mandan women of the band of the white buffalo cow who danced at Fort Clark on December 25. *Overleaf, left:* In late fall Bodmer painted a Mandan warrior who spent several days and nights fasting and crying out in supplication to the Mandan deities symbolized by the effigies atop the poles: the sun and the moon, representing the lord of life and the old woman who never dies. *Overleaf, right:* A leader of the Mandan buffalo bull society. He appears as the central figure in the aquatint on page 172.

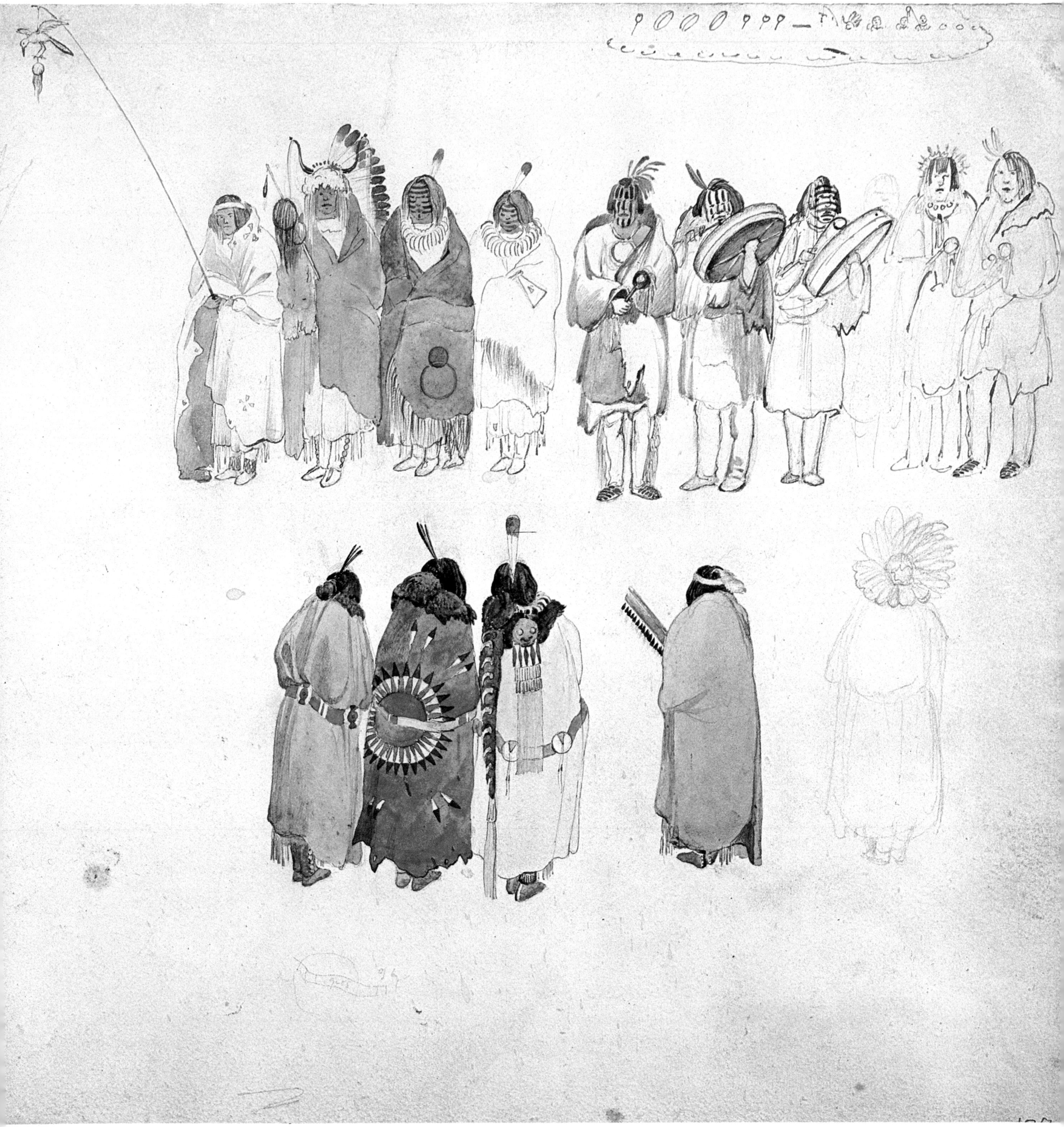

Mato-Topé (the four bears), second chief and hero of the Mandan nation. For an explanation of his war paint and headdress (*above*), see entry for January 15. For a brief biography and description of his ceremonial regalia (*opposite*) see April 9.

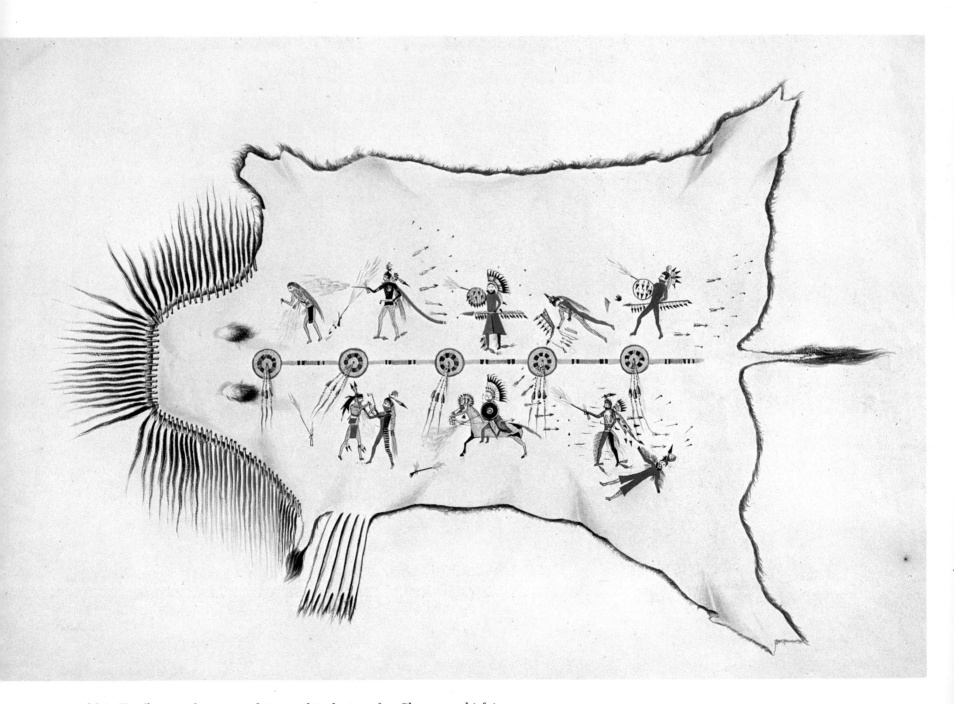

Mato-Topé's most famous exploit was his slaying of a Cheyenne chief in hand-to-hand combat, as described in Maximilian's entry for April 9. *Opposite:* In Mato-Topé's own drawing of this fight, made with materials given him by Bodmer, he is seen brandishing his tomahawk while receiving a wound on the hand from the Cheyenne. *Above:* Bodmer's copy of a buffalo robe that was also painted by Mato-Topé depicts some of his heroic deeds, including the fight with the Cheyenne, at lower left. The Mandan chief presented the robe to Maximilian. It is now in the collection of the Linden-Museum in Stuttgart.

*Overleaf:* Pehriska-Ruhpa (the two ravens), an eminent Minnetaree and close friend of Mato-Topé, paid many visits to Fort Clark during the winter. Bodmer painted him first in his ceremonial dress holding an enormous medicine pipe. Later (see entry for March 14), he portrayed him as a member of the dog band, a painting considered by many art historians to be the finest Indian portrait ever made. Although Pehriska-Ruhpa belonged to the dog band of the Minnetarees, his costume corresponds exactly to the ones described in the entry for March 7, on the occasion of a dance by the Mandan dogs.

Sih-Chida (the yellow feather), who became one of the Europeans' closest friends among the Mandans was in and out of their quarters all winter long (*see entry for November 13*). When he posed for his portrait (*opposite*), his attire included valuable strings of dentalium shells and an otter-skin shawl, although Maximilian noted that he was far from rich and did not even own a horse. Bodmer tutored him in drawing, and when he tried his own hand at a self-portrait (*below*), he dressed himself in a chief's long red military coat and his friend Mato-Topé's war bonnet. He is armed with a war shield, ceremonial lance, and rifle. *Overleaf:* Fort Clark and the Mandan village of Mih-Tutta-Hang-Kush as seen from the eastern bank of the Missouri. In winter the Indians used the frozen river as a thoroughfare to reach their firewood groves on the east bank and their winter village downstream.

The winter village of the Minnetarees was composed of a large number of small lodges sheltered in an extensive forest on the right bank of the Missouri. Like the Mandans, they retreated to their winter village with the onset of winter and stayed until late February or early March. Firewood was close at hand, and when storms kept their horses from the prairie, the beasts could survive by browsing on the bark of poplar trees. Maximilian and Bodmer trekked fifteen miles from Fort Clark to this village through the winter cold on November 26 in order to witness a buffalo medicine feast. During their three-day visit in late November, Bodmer made this rough watercolor sketch which he allowed to remain unfinished.

As sedentary tribes, the Mandans and Minnetarees enjoyed better living accommodations than the other Plains tribes. They used tepees while on hunting expeditions, but in the permanent villages they built good-sized lodges from heavy cottonwood timbers, wickerwork, and sod. Baskets, weapons, and parfleche bags filled with pemmican and corn were hung from the posts and scaffolding around the central fire pit. Specially prized horses were sometimes stabled in the lodge overnight as a precaution against theft. The entrance to the lodge is behind the wooden screen at rear. Both men and women participated in construction of the lodges. Each normally sheltered at least two families: a mature man, his eldest son or son-in-law, and their various dependents. Bodmer made this painting at the lodge of Dipauch, a leading warrior of Mih-Tutta-Hang-Kush. *Above:* A nicely-worked Mandan quiver of otter skin. The Mandans were accounted the best arrow-makers along the Missouri.

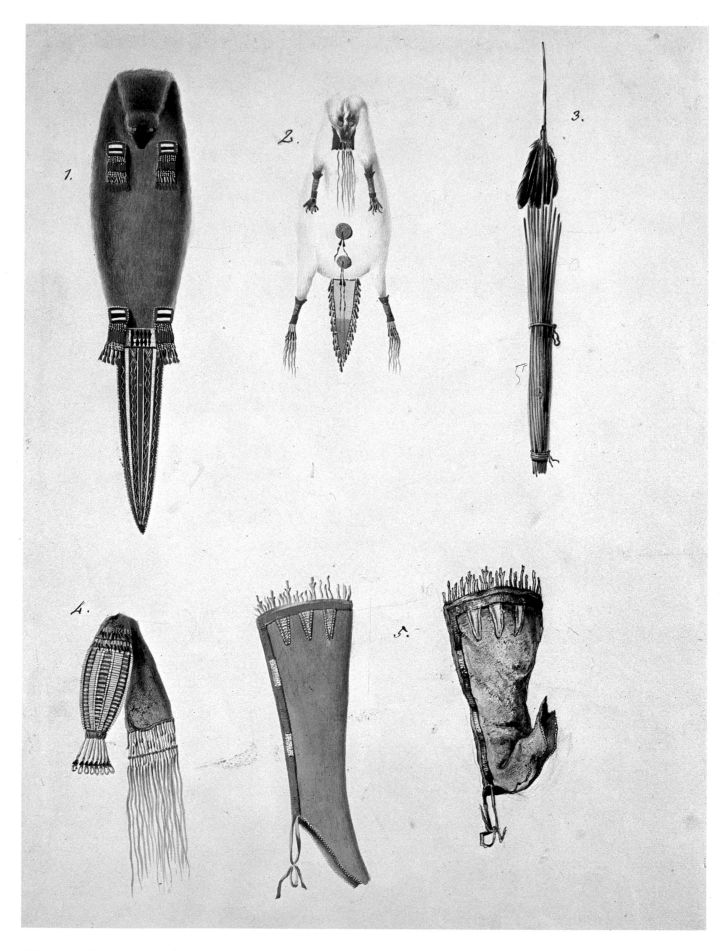

Watercolor drawings of artifacts collected by Maximilian on the expedition, most of which are now in the Linden-Museum, Stuttgart. The tribal origin of some of the items is either confused or unknown. 1: Otter-pelt medicine bundle. 2: White skunk tobacco pouch (Dakota). 3: Minnetaree conquest bundle for counting sexual exploits (see page 243). 4: Minnetaree pouch.

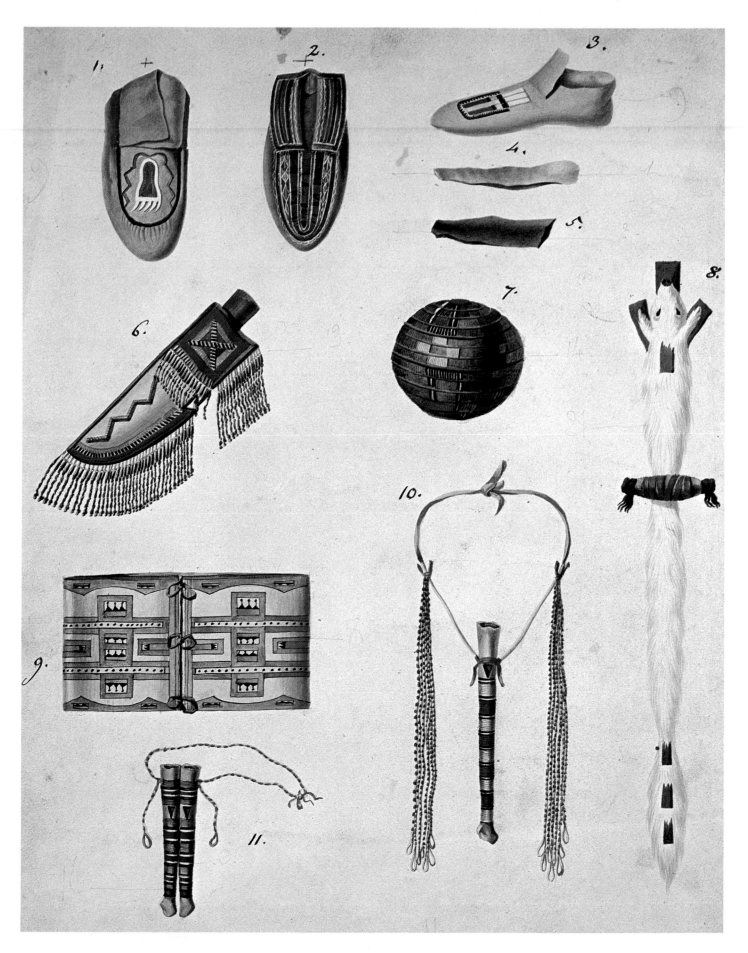

5: Winter legging, drawn diagrammatically and realistically. 1–3: (*this page*) Moccasins (probably Dakota). 4–5: Stone knife blades. 6: Mandan knife sheath. 7: Quilled leather ball used in Mandan women's game. 8: Ermine-pelt medicine bundle. 9: Painted parfleche for pemmican (Dakota). 10–11: Mandan war whistles made from the hollow wing bones of large birds.

Pachtuwa-Chta, an Arikara warrior who had taken up residence with the Mandans when his tribe abandoned their villages on the Missouri because of hostilities with the whites. He posed willingly enough for Bodmer, although he had a reputation for treachery (*see entry for March 6*). *Opposite:* Ahschupsa-Masihichsi (the chief of the pointed horn), a Minnetaree war leader whose portrait was taken on the eve of his departure with a war party (*see entry for February 28*). *Overleaf:* Two brothers of the Mandan tribe. *Left:* Mandeh-Pahchu (the beak of the bird of prey) holds the wooden flute on which he played a "tender" melody for Maximilian. *Right:* Mahchsi-Karehde (the flying eagle), the tallest warrior among the Mandans, whose bear-claw necklace, eagle-wing fan, and ornamented leggings and moccasins indicate a man of substance. The wolves tails attached to his heels signify that he killed two enemies in a single battle. Like many of his compatriots, he had a second name: Kuha-Handeh (I hear something coming)

Mato-Topé was not only the leading warrior chief of the Mandans but most certainly their leading artist as well. His painted buffalo robes are to be found in a number of museums today, and he made other paintings for Maximilian on paper supplied by Bodmer. In the painting below he depicts himself wearing his eagle-feather war bonnet flanked by ceremonial staffs. For an example of the oratory of this remarkable chieftain, on the bitter occasion of the destruction of his people by smallpox, see the Afterword. *Opposite:* Maximilian reported encountering a variety of congenital deformities among the Plains Indians: cripples, a dwarf, several harelips, and a hunchback. At Fort Clark he met a family of deaf-mutes: two brothers and a sister who conversed in sign language and led more or less normal lives, although one of the brothers was a berdache. Mahchsi-Nika (the young eagle), the nonhomosexual brother, posed for Bodmer with his face painted black, in honor of his part in the killing of an Assiniboin on February 3. A confrontation between Bodmer and the aggrieved mute over this unfinished portrait is described in the entry for February 12.

# Mandan Ethnology

Major portions of Maximilian's published text, as well as hundreds of pages in his field journal, are devoted to ethnologic studies of the various Indian tribes that he encountered. He had read widely in the existing literature, and, as he was a tenacious and meticulous researcher, his work is the most comprehensive and important to come down to us from this period. In editing his narrative text into the journal form employed in this book it was necessary to omit a considerable amount of this ethnographic material in order to produce a manageable text for the general reader. To balance these omissions, we here append an edited version of Maximilian's most comprehensive and interesting study—his treatise on the Mandans.

The Mandans were formerly a numerous people, who, according to the narrative of an aged man, lately deceased, inhabited thirteen, and perhaps more villages. They call themselves the Numangkake (*i.e.*, men), and if they wish to particularize their descent, they add the name of the village whence they came originally. The early history of the Mandans is involved in obscurity. They affirm that they descend originally from the more eastern nations, near the sea coast. When Charbonneau arrived here at the end of the last century, the two Mandan villages, which are still standing, were about six or eight miles further down the Missouri. The small pox and the assaults of their enemies have so reduced the people, that the whole number now reside in two villages, in the vicinity of Fort Clark. These two villages are Mih-Tutta-Hang-Kush (the southern village), about 300 paces above Fort Clark, and on the same side of the river, and Ruhptare, about three miles higher up, likewise on the same bank. The first had, at the time of our visit, sixty-five huts, and contained about 150 warriors; the other, thirty-eight huts and 83 warriors. According to this, the tribe had not more than 230 or 240 warriors; and, on the whole, scarcely 900

or 1,000 souls. [*Later estimates, at the time of the smallpox epidemic of 1837, placed the Mandan population at about 1,600, including children and infants.*]

The Mandans are a vigorous, well-made race of people, rather above the middling stature, and very few of the men could be called short. The women are pretty robust and sometimes tall, but, for the most part, they are short and broad shouldered. There are but few who can be called handsome as Indians, but there are many tolerable and some pretty faces among them. The children frequently have slender limbs, and very prominent bellies. Deformed persons are very rare among the Mandans. I, however, saw a very small dwarf with a long, narrow face, and one man who squinted. Persons who had lost the sight of one eye, or with a cataract, are by no means uncommon. There were several deaf and dumb, among whom two brothers and a sister were all born with this defect. Some goitres, or, rather, thick necks among the women, are, doubtless, caused by too great exertions in carrying burdens on their backs. Instances where joints of the fingers are wanting are frequent, but these come under the heading of voluntary mutilations.

## Daily Subsistence

The Mandans are hospitable and often invite their acquaintance to visit. They have a considerable variety of dishes. The Indians residing in permanent villages have the advantage of the roving hunting tribes, in that they not only hunt, but derive their chief subsistence from their plantations, which afford them a degree of security against distress. It is true, these Indians sometimes suffer hunger when the buffalo herds keep at a great distance, and their crops fail; but the distress can never be so great among the Missouri Indians, as in the tribes that live further northwards. The plants which they cultivate are maize, beans, French beans, gourds, sunflowers, and tobacco.

All kinds of animals serve the Mandans for food; the bear, when it is young and fat, the wolf, the fox, in short, everything except the horse; the ermine is not eaten by many; and of birds they dislike the turkey-buzzard, and the raven, because they feed on the dead bodies deposited on the stages. They have a great aversion from serpents, but eat the turtle; the buffalo is the chief object of their chase, as it supplies them with skins, meat, tallow, marrow-bones, sinews, and many other necessaries. Next to the buffalo the beaver is the most indispensable to them, since it not only furnishes them with valuable skins, but supplies them with delicate food, the fat tail, especially, being considered quite a dainty morsel by the Indians. Pemmican, which is so favourite a dish among the northern Indians, is not much in use among the Mandans. Their only drink is water, for they are unacquainted with the method of preparing fermented liquors. They did not obtain any spirits, either from the American Fur Company, or the agents of Messrs. Sublette and Campbell; hence an intoxicated person is scarcely ever seen. They are extremely fond of sugar, and likewise of salt, which they procure from their lakes, and, if the supply is insufficient, purchase from the Whites. They are likewise fond of coffee and tea, well sweetened. It has been affirmed, that several North American nations, especially those which speak the Algonquin language, are cannibals, and more particularly the Chippewas and Potawatomis; but I found no trace of this unnatural custom among the Missouri nations.

## Marriage and Family Life

Two, and sometimes three, families usually live together in an Indian hut, commonly the father, with his married sons or sons-in-law. Polygamy is everywhere practised, and the number of wives differs; however, they have very seldom more than four, and, in general, only one. If a young Indian desires to marry, and has obtained the consent of the girl, he endeavours to procure that of her father; when he is certain of this, he brings two, three, nay, even eight or ten horses, and fastens them to the hut of the young woman, who gives them to her father. The latter then takes other horses, and if he has them not himself, his relations assist him, and these horses are fastened, in return, to the hut of the intended son-in-law. In such a case an estimate is previously made of the number of horses possessed by the woman's relations, for all presents are returned in equal number. The bride next boils some maize, and daily carries a kettle or dish filled with it to the hut of the bridegroom. After some time has elapsed, the young man repairs to the hut of his bride, where he passes the night with her, and the marriage is considered as complete. The young couple often continue to reside in the hut of the father-in-law, but they more frequently build a new hut for themselves; sometimes, however, they afterwards separate. The father-in-law is, subsequently, the principal person in the hut; everything depends on him, and is done on his account, and for him; if game is killed, the flesh is first presented to him, &c. There are often many children in these Indian families; some had as many as ten; yet, on the whole, the Indians have not so many children as the Whites, doubtless because they keep them longer at the breast. They are extremely fond of them, but the children are often weak and sickly, in consequence, it is supposed, of the hard labour which the women have to perform. I was universally assured that the new-born children are of a reddish colour. The births are, in general, extremely easy, and the mother bathes in the river immediately afterwards, even if it is frozen; in ten days time the child is considered as safe, having got over the most dangerous period.

A person is paid to give it the name chosen by the parents and relations. The child is held up, then turned to all sides of the heavens, in the direction of the course of the sun, and its name proclaimed. They have cradles for their infants, consisting of a leather bag, which is suspended by a strap to a cross beam in the hut. These cradles of the Mandans are not so elegant and beautifully worked as those which we saw among the Sioux and Assiniboins. The children of these Indians are subject to no kind of discipline whatever; they may do and say whatever they please, and nobody finds fault with them. Everything is done to excite a spirit of independence and self-will in the boys; if the mother speaks to one of them, he will very likely slap her face, or kick her, nay, sometimes he will do the same to his father, who says, coolly, bowing his head, this boy will one day become a famous warrior. The men sometimes treat their wives very brutally; and it has not unfrequently happened, that a woman, after such treatment, has left the hut and hanged herself on a tree. This lately happened in the case of an aged woman, whose grown-up son had ill-treated her. She was missed, and was afterwards found suspended from a tree. The women have nothing to indemnify them for their incessant and laborious work, not even good clothing, for this right of the fair sex in Europe is claimed among the Indians by the men. It is singular that these women, who are condemned constantly to work like slaves, refuse to do any work whatever if they marry a white man, and, the Whites being entirely in the power of the Indians, and the relations of their wives, they are obliged to submit to this.

Sisters have great privileges among these Indians. All the horses which a young man steals, or captures in war, belong to them. If an Indian returns from an expedition on horseback, and meets his sister, he will immediately alight, and give her the horse; on the other hand, if he wishes to possess some object of value belonging to his sister, for instance, a dress, he goes and abruptly demands it, and immediately receives it; even should it be the very dress she is wearing, she will take it off at once, and give it up.

## Infidelity

Prudery is not a virtue of the Indian women; they have often two, three, or more lovers: infidelity is not often punished. There was only one woman among the Mandans, a piece of whose nose was cut off, a circumstance which is very common among the Black-feet. If an Indian elopes with a married woman, the husband whom she has abandoned avenges himself by seizing the seducer's property, his horses and other things of value, to which the latter must quietly submit. Such a woman is never taken back. If a man has the eldest daughter of a family for his wife, he has a right to all her sisters. A chief business of the young men among these Indian tribes is to try their fortune with the young maidens and the women, and this, together with their toilet, fills up the greater part of their time. They do not meet with many coy beauties. In the evening, and generally till late at night, they roam about the villages, or in the vicinity, or from one village to the other. They have a singular mode of displaying their achievements in this field, especially when they visit the women in their best dresses. On these occasions they endeavour to gain credit by the variety of their triumphs, and mark the number of conquered beauties by bundles of peeled osier twigs, painted red at the tips. These sticks are of two kinds. Most of them are from two to three feet in length, others five or six feet. The latter, being carried singly, are painted with white and red rings alternately, which indicates the number of conquests. The shorter sticks are only painted red at the tips, and every stick indicates an exploit, the number of which is often bound up into a pretty large bundle. Thick fasces of this kind are carried about by the dandies in their gallant excursions. Among the Mandans these sticks are generally quite plain; among the Minetarees, on the contrary, there is, usually, in the middle of the bundle, one larger stick, at the end of which there is a tuft of black feathers. These feathers indicate the favourite, and the dandies tell everybody that she is the person for whom this honour is intended. [*For a drawing of this "conquest bundle" see page 232.*] If these people have had familiar intercourse with a person who wore the white buffalo robe, a piece of skin of that colour is fastened to the stick; if she wore a red blanket, or buffalo robe, a piece of red cloth is fastened to the stick. This custom, which is well known among the Mandans and Minnetarees, has not, to my knowledge, been mentioned by any traveller.

They have distinct names for the several degrees of relationship. The father's brother is called father, and the mother's sister, mother; cousins are called brothers and sisters. The mother-in-law never speaks to her son-in-law; but if he comes home, and brings her the scalp of a slain enemy, and his gun, she is at liberty, from that moment, to converse with him. This custom is found among the Minnetarees, who have, doubtless, borrowed it from the Mandans, but not among the Crows and Arikaras. Among the Chippewas, and the Algonquins in general, the name must not be changed; and persons with the same name must not marry, but consider each other as brothers and sisters.

Among all the North American Indian nations there are men dressed and treated like women, called by the Canadians, bardaches, but there was only one such among the Mandans, and two or three among the Minnetarees.

## Moral Character and Intelligence

Some writers have spoken rather too unfavourably of the moral character of the aborigines of North America, and their domestic habits. According to them, distrust and hostile feeling prevail among them, for which reason they never leave their huts unarmed; but I can bear witness that they are frequently seen in their villages, as well as in the environs, without arms, and that it is only at greater distances, and when they appear in state, that they carry their weapons in their hands. I have never observed any disputes among them, but, on the contrary, much more unity and tranquillity than in civilized Europe. It has often been asserted that the Indians are inferior in intellectual capacity to the Whites; but this has been now sufficiently refuted. If man, in all his varieties, has not received from the Creator equally perfect faculties, I am, at least, convinced that, in this respect, the Americans are not inferior to the Whites.

Many of the Mandans manifest a great thirst for knowledge, and many desire to hear something of objects of a higher order; and if they were not so much attached to the prejudices inherited from their ancestors, many of them might be very easily instructed. The bad examples which they so often observe in the white men, who roam about their country in quest of gain, are not calculated to inspire them with much respect for our race, or to improve their morality. And if they have not been found inclined to the Christian religion, this is, certainly, in some measure, the consequence of the bad conduct of the Whites, who call themselves Christians, and are often worse, and more immoral, than the most uncivilized of the Indians. Many American and foreign works have taken notice of the striking good sense and wit, the correct judgment of the Indians, in all the occurrences of daily life, and it would be mere repetition here to quote examples. One is often at a loss to answer their questions, founded on correct and natural judgment. The inactive mode of life natural to the Indians, which disdains all laborious exertion, is a great obstacle to their adopting a different system. But they are not deficient in talent for drawing, music, &c., and this is quite manifest at first sight. Several Mandans not only took much pleasure in drawing, but had a decided talent for it.

Many of them dispute, with great earnestness, on more elevated subjects; thus, they inquired our ideas of the various heavenly bodies, and of the origin of the universe, as they, themselves, declare their own silly traditions to be insufficient. Some, indeed, thought our ideas on these subjects much more silly than their own. They laughed outright, when we affirmed that the earth was round, and revolved about the sun. Others, however, would not reject our views, and were of opinion that, as the Whites could do so much which was incomprehensible to them, it was possible they might be right on this point also.

The Mandans and Minnetarees are proud, and have a high sense of honour. If a person expresses a wish to possess some article belonging to them, he generally receives it as a present, but a present of equal, or greater value, is always looked for in return. They estimate all their effects at a very high rate, ascribing to them an imaginary and far too great value; and a trifling thing is often paid for with one or two horses. Among the articles of great value is the skin of a white buffalo cow. Fifteen florins are paid for a small ermine skin; whereas, a wolf's skin may be purchased for a small quantity of tobacco. One or two horses are frequently given for a feather cap; a horse for 100 or 150 elks' teeth, or for a handful of dentalium shells. The men are much given to indolence, when they cannot pursue their chief avocations, hunting and war. In general, the Mandans and Minnetarees are not dangerous, and, though there are many rude and savage men among them, they are, on the whole, well-disposed towards the Whites: the former, especially, manifest this, and have many good and trustworthy men among them. Some of them are addicted to thieving, especially the women and children; and it is said, that many of the Minnetarees, when they meet the Whites in the prairie, though they do not kill them, as they used to do, generally plunder them.

They have always free access to the forts of the trading companies; and, as at Fort Clark, there was no separate apartment for the Indians, we were molested by them, during the whole day, in every room; nay, they often took the place of the owners, which, during the severe cold in the winter time, was quite intolerable, as they stood in front of the fire, with their large buffalo robes, and kept the warmth from coming into the apartment. They require to be always regaled, which is generally done, and it was estimated that in one year they smoked 200 lbs. of tobacco at the expense of the Company. A few among them, indeed, manifested a much greater delicacy of feeling than the mass of them, and left the dining-room when the dinner-hour approached; but only a very small proportion possessed this correct sense of propriety, for the others generally came just at our dinner-time; it is true they had but little meat in the winter season, and fared but badly. Disputes and quarrels are very rare among them; but duels are frequent; and revenge for blood is still exercised.

Many of them are particularly cleanly in their persons, and bathe daily, both in winter and summer; their hands, however, are often smeared with colours and fat, nay, sometimes the whole body is bedaubed. The women are, in general, less cleanly, particularly their hands, which arises from their continual and severe labour. They generally let their nails grow long. These rude inhabitants of the prairies are extremely agile and hardy; they bathe, in the depth of winter, in the half-frozen rivers, and wear no covering on the upper part of their body under the buffalo robe; they are very expert swimmers, even when quite young. They often practise riding on horseback without a saddle, and very swift horse-racing. They are capital marksmen with the bow; all their senses are remarkably acute.

MEN'S CEREMONIAL BANDS

Among the Mandans, and all the nations of the Upper Missouri, as well as among most of the North American tribes, there are certain bands or unions or companies, which are distinguished from the others, and kept together by certain external badges and laws. They have three kinds of war or signal whistles, which are hung round the neck, and are among the badges of the unions, which divide the men into six classes, according to their age. The first band or union is composed of "the foolish dogs," or "the dogs whose name is not known." They are young people from ten to fifteen years of age, and wear a whistle made of the wing bone of the wild goose, which is but small. When they dance, three of them have a long broad piece of red cloth hanging from the back of the neck to the ground. Like every distinct class they have a particular song to accompany their dance. If a boy desires to enter the first band in order to become a man, he goes to a member of it, addresses him by the appella-

tion of father, and endeavours to purchase the rank, the dance, the song, and the war whistle belonging to it, for certain articles of value, such as blankets, cloth, horses, powder, ball, and the like, which the father pays for him. If this place is sold to him he has a right to all the distinctions and privileges of the band, and he who sold it thereby renounces all claim to it, and endeavours to purchase admission to a higher band. The dances of the several classes are in the main very similar, but there is a particular song belonging to each, and sometimes even a different step. The drum and schischikué must likewise be purchased at the same time. The latter, among this band, is spherical, with a handle, and is made of leather.

The second class or band is that of the crows or ravens; it consists of young men from twenty to twenty-five years of age. Frequently young people are in none of the bands for half a year or more. They then go to the band of the crows, and say, "Father, I am poor, but I wish to purchase from you." If the possessor agrees, they then receive the raven's feathers, which the band wear on their heads, a double war whistle, consisting of two wing bones of a goose joined together, a drum, schischikué, the song and the dance. Each of these bands has a leader, called, by the Whites, head-man, who decides on the sale of its rights and attributes. This head-man is chiefly applied to when any one wishes for admission; a festival than takes place in the medicine lodge, which is continued for forty successive nights. They dance, eat, and smoke there; the purchasers defray the expenses, and give up their wives every night to the sellers, till the fathers, as they are called, are satisfied, and transfer their rights to the purchasers, with which the festival concludes.

The third class or band is that of the soldiers, the most eminent and esteemed warriors. In their dances they paint the upper part of the face red, and the lower part black. Their war whistle is large, and made of the wing bone of a crane. Their badges are two long straight sticks bound with otter skin, to which owl's feathers are appended. When they go to war, they plant these sticks in the ground in front of the enemy, and, this done, they dare not leave them, not unlike the colours in a European army. They have a similar stick ornamented with raven's feathers. They likewise have a dance and song peculiar to their band, and must purchase their admission into higher classes. Their schischikué or rattle is made of iron plate, in the form of a small kettle, with a handle. They likewise possess two tobacco pipes, which are used for smoking on special occasions. Two men keep and carry with them these pipes. All the higher classes may, at the same time, belong to the band of the soldiers, who act as police officers; it is, however, understood that all the members must be satisfied with the purchase. If but one object to the sale, the bargain cannot be concluded. It often happens that some individuals do not immediately give their consent, in order to raise the price and sell to more advantage afterwards. These soldiers, as they are called, form a kind of committee, which decides all the principal affairs, particularly general undertakings, such as changes of their places of abode, buffalo hunting, and the like.

The fourth band, that of the dogs, wear in their dance a large cap of coloured cloth, to which a great number of raven's, magpie's, and owl's feathers is fastened, adorned with dyed horse-hair and strips of ermine; they have a large war whistle of the wing bone of a swan. Three of them have the same strips of red cloth hanging down the back, as have been mentioned, when speaking of the first band. The head is generally adorned with a thick tuft of owl's, magpie's, and raven's feathers hanging down behind, and often all the three kinds of feathers are mixed together. The three men before-mentioned, who wear the strips of red cloth (the true dogs), are obliged, if any one throws a piece of meat into the ashes, or on the ground, saying, "There, dog, eat," to fall upon it, and devour it raw, like dogs or beasts of prey. The schischikué of this band is a stick, a foot or a foot and a half long, to which a number of animals' hoofs are fastened. The costume of these three dogs is shown in the portrait of Pehriska-Ruhpa. [*For this portrait, see page 223.*]

The fifth band is that of the buffaloes. In their dance they wear the skin of the upper part of the head, the mane of the buffalo, with its horns, on their heads; but two select individuals, the bravest of all, who thenceforward never dare to fly from the enemy, wear a perfect imitation of the buffalo's head, with the horns, which they set on their heads, and in which there are holes left for the eyes, which are surrounded with an iron or tin ring. This band alone has a wooden war whistle, and in their union they have a woman, who, during the dance, goes round with a dish of water, to refresh the dancers, but she must give this water only to the bravest, who wear the whole buffalo's head. She is dressed, on these occasions, in a handsome new robe of bighorn leather, and colours her face with vermilion. The men have a piece of red cloth fastened behind, and a figure representing a buffalo's tail; they also carry their arms in their hands. The men with the buffaloes' heads always keep in the dance at the outside of the group, imitate all the motions and the voice of this animal, as it timidly and cautiously retreats, looking around in all directions. [*An aquatint of this dance is to be found on page 172.*]

The sixth band is that of the black-tailed deer. It consists of all the men above fifty years of age, who, however, likewise dance. Two women belong to the band, who wait on them at the dance, cook, carry water round to refresh them, and the like. All the men of this band wear a garland of the claws of the grizzly bear round their heads, and all insignia of their warlike exploits about their bodies, such as feathers on their heads, tufts of hair on their arms and legs, scalps, painting, &c.

All these bands, as well as the following dances, are bought and sold, and, as has been already observed, on these occasions, the buyer must give up his wife to the seller during the festivity. But if a young man is still unmarried, he will sometimes travel to a great distance to another village, to ask a friend or companion for his wife, who accordingly goes with him, and, on the evenings of the dance, gives up his wives for him. A man often brings three or four, and even more, wives, and gives them to his father, as he is called, as soon as the dancing, eating, smoking, and the relating of their exploits, are concluded. Thus one woman after the other comes, strikes, with her hand, the arm of the man whom she will favour, and goes to the entrance of the tent, where she waits till he follows her. The man so invited often keeps his seat, and bows down his head; the woman then goes home, brings articles of value, such as guns, robes, blankets, &c., which she lays, piece by piece, before him, till he is satisfied, stands up, and follows her.

There are other dances which are bought and sold, among which are a second dance of the third band, and the dance of the half-shorn heads, which the lower class may buy before they are old enough to belong to the third band. What is called the hot dance is now danced at Ruhptare, and by the Minnetarees, who bought it from the Arikaras. It is executed by the little dogs, whose name is not known. A large fire is kindled on the occasion, and a quantity of live coals is scattered on the ground, about which the young men dance, quite naked and barefooted. The hands, with the lower part of the arms, and the feet and ankles, are painted red. A kettle, with meat cut in small pieces, is hung over the fire; and when the meat is done they plunge their hands into the boiling water, take out the meat, and eat it, at the risk of scalding themselves. The last comers are the worst off, having to dip their hands the deepest into the boiling water. During the dance they have in their hands their weapons and the schischikué.

## WOMEN'S CEREMONIAL BANDS

The Mandan women are divided precisely in the same manner as the men, into four classes, according to their age. The youngest band is called the band of the gun. They wear in their hair some down feathers of the eagle, and have their peculiar dance.

The next class into which they obtain admission by purchase is the river class. When they dance they wear an eagle's feather, fastened to the fore part of the head with a piece of white ribbon, which projects on the left side, and is entwined round the quill with grass.

The third class consist of the women of the hay, who, when they dance, put on their best clothes, and sing the scalp song.

The fourth and last class is the band of the white buffalo cow. They paint one eye with some colour according to their taste, generally sky-blue. On the chin, this class, mostly consisting of aged women, tattoo themselves with black lines; round their heads they wear a broad piece of the skin of a white buffalo cow, something like a hussar's cap, with a tuft of feathers in it.

These unions, or bands, give occasion to many festivities, with singing, music, and dancing. But they have likewise other dances and diversions. One of these is the scalp dance, which may be more appropriately described among the usages of war. Their musical amusements are very simple. The mode of singing varies but little among all the American Indians; it consists of broken, deep exclamations, often intercepted by loud shouts, and is accompanied by a violent beating of time on the drum, and the rattling of the schischikué. Besides these two instruments, the Mandans have long wooden flutes, at the lower end of which there is generally an eagle's feather hanging by a string. Other flutes are thicker, about twenty inches long, and are perforated with holes; in this respect they differ from the war whistle. They are sometimes ornamented with pieces of skin, &c.

The Indians have also many games; the game called billiards, by the French Canadians, is played by two young men, with long poles, which are often bound with leather, and have various ornaments attached to them. On a long, straight, level course, or a level path in or near the village, they roll a hoop, three or four inches in diameter, covered with leather, and throw the pole at it; and the success of the game depends upon the pole passing through it. This game is also practised among the Minnetarees. The women are expert at playing with a large leathern ball, which they let fall alternately on their foot and knee, again throwing it up and catching it, and thus keeping it in motion for a length of time without letting it fall to the ground. Prizes are given, and they often play high. The ball is often very neat and curiously covered with dyed porcupine quills. [*For this artifact, see page 233.*]

SUPERSTITION AND RELIGION

The Mandans and Minnetarees are extremely superstitious, and all their important actions are guided by such motives. They have most strange ideas of surrounding nature, believe in a multitude of different beings in the heavenly bodies; offer sacrifices to them; invoke their assistance on every occasion; howl, lament, fast, inflict on themselves cruel acts of penance, to propitiate these spirits; and, above all, lay very great stress upon dreams. Some of their traditions have a resemblance to the revelations of the Bible; for instance, Noah's Ark and the Deluge, the history of Samson, &c. The question here arises whether these particulars have not been gradually introduced among them, from their intercourse with Christians, and this seems highly probable. If they have not yet embraced the Christian religion, it would, however, appear that they have adopted some portions which strike them as being either remarkable or interesting. In order to obtain correct information respecting all their traditions and ideas, we persuaded Dipauch to enliven our long winter evenings by his narratives, which he readily agreed to do. He spoke with much seriousness and gravity, and I had a most excellent interpreter in Mr. Kipp.

According to Dipauch, these Indians believe in several superior beings, of whom the lord of life, Ohmahank-Numakshi, is the first, the most exalted and the most powerful; who created the earth, man, and every existing object. They believe that he has a tail, and appears sometimes in the form of an aged man, and, at others, in that of a young man. The first man, Numank-Machana, holds the second rank; he was created by the lord of life, but is likewise of a divine nature. The lord of life gave him great power, and they, therefore, worship and offer sacrifices to him. Omahank-Chika, the evil one of the earth, is a malignant spirit, who has, likewise, much influence over men, but who is not as powerful as the lord of life and the first man. The fourth being is Rohanka-Tauihanka, who lives in the planet Venus, and it is he who protects mankind on the earth; for without his care the race would have been long since extinct. A fifth being, who, however, has no power, is something lilke the wandering Jew, ever in motion, and walking on the face of the earth in human form. They call him the lying prairie wolf. Besides these there is a sixth being, Ochkih-Hadda, whom it is difficult to class, and of whom they have a tradition, that whoever dreams of him is doomed soon to die. He appears to figure in their traditions as a kind of devil, is said to have once come to their villages, and taught them many things, but has not since appeared. They are afraid of him, offer sacrifices to him, and have in their villages a hideous figure representing him.

They worship the sun, because they believe it to be the residence of the lord of life. All their medicines or sacrifices are offered chiefly to the sun, or rather to the lord of life, as inhabiting it. In the moon, say they, lives the old woman who never dies, and who wears a white band from the front to the back of the head; sacrifices and offerings are likewise made to her. They do not know who she is, but her power is great. She has six children, three sons and three daughters, who all live in certain stars. The eldest son is the day (the first day of the creation), the second is the sun, in which the lord of life has his abode. The third son is the night. The eldest daughter is the star that rises in the east, the morning star; and they call her, "the woman who wears a plume." The second daughter, called "the striped gourd," is a high star which revolves around the polar star; and, lastly, the third daughter is the evening star which is near to the setting sun.

These Indians are full of prejudice and superstition, and connect all the natural phenomena with the before-mentioned silly creations of their own imaginations. They undertake nothing without first invoking their guardian spirit, or medicine, who mostly appears to them in a dream. When they wish to choose their medicine or guardian spirit, they fast for three or four days, and even longer, retire to a solitary spot, do penance, and even sacrifice joints of their fingers; howl and cry to the lord of life, or to the first man, beseeching him to point out their guardian spirit. They continue in this excited state till they dream, and the first animal or other object which appears to them is chosen for their guardian spirit or medicine. Every man has his guardian spirit. There is, in the prairie, a large hill where they remain motionless many days, lamenting and fasting; not far from this hill is a cave, into which they creep at night.

## MEDICINE OF THE WHITE BUFFALO COW

The skin of a white buffalo cow is an important article, and an eminent medicine in the opinion of the Mandans and Minnetarees. He who has never possessed one of them is not respected. Suppose two men to be disputing about their exploits, the one an old veteran warrior, who has slain many enemies, the other, a young lad without experience; the latter reproaches the other with never having possessed a white buffalo cow hide, on which the old man droops his head, and covers his face for shame. He who possesses such a hide generally offers it to the lord of life, to whom he dedicates it, or, which is equivalent, to the sun, or to the first man. He collects, perhaps, in the course of a whole twelvemonth, various articles of value, and then hangs them up all together on a high pole in the open prairie, generally in the neighbourhood of the burying-place, or in the village before his hut. Distinguished men and chiefs of eminence are for the most part poor, because, in order to gain reputation and influence, they give away everything of value which they possess. A large number of relatives is one of the chief means of acquiring riches, for a young man who wishes to distinguish himself, and to be liberal, does honour to the whole family, who assist him to the utmost of their power. When one of his relations has anything of value, the young man goes to the owner to demand it, and not unfrequently takes it away without ceremony. Sometimes he hangs his head in silence, and then something of value is given him, a handsome dress, a horse, &c. If he wishes to gain reputation and a claim to distinction, it is necessary that he should make presents.

All the people in the village notice very accurately what presents are made, and the donor has a right to display all such presents painted on his robes, and in this manner to hand down his reputation to posterity, as has been already related. This and military glory are, in the eyes of these men, the greatest virtues. They dare not draw a stroke too much on their robes for the horses, guns, &c., which they have given away, for the young men keep a most strict account against each other, and universal ridicule would be the immediate consequence of violating this rule. Among the distinctions of any man, the white buffalo hide is the greatest. He who has not been so fortunate as to kill a white buffalo himself, which is generally the case, as these animals are very rare, purchases a hide, often at a great distance from home, and other nations bring them hither, being well aware of the great value attached to them by the Mandans. The hide must be that of a young cow, not above two years old, and be taken off complete and tanned, with the horns, nose, hoofs, and tail. The value of ten to fifteen horses is given for it. A certain Mandan gave ten horses, a gun, some kettles, and other articles, for such a hide. The white hide of a bull or of an old cow is by no means so valuable. They do not wear it as a robe, like the Minnetarees, or, at the utmost, the wife, or one of the daughters of the family, wears it once at some great festival, but never a second time. The Mandans have particular ceremonies at the dedication of the hide. As soon as they have obtained it they engage an eminent medicine man, who must throw it over him; he then walks round the village in the apparent direction of the sun's course, and sings a medicine song. When the owner, after collecting articles of value for three or four years, desires to offer his treasure to the lord of life, or to the first man, he rolls it up, after adding some wormwood or a head of maize, and the skin then remains suspended on a high pole till it rots away. At the time of my visit there was such an offering at Mih-Tutta-Hang-Kush, near the stages for the dead without the village.

Besides the white buffalo skins which are offered in sacrifice and hung on poles, there are, in the vicinity of the villages of the Mandans and Minnetarees, other strange figures on high poles. These figures are composed of skin, grass, and twigs, which, it seems, represent the sun and moon, perhaps, also, the lord of life, and the first man. The Indians resort to them when they wish to petition for anything, and sometimes howl and lament for days and weeks together.

## THE OKIPPE CEREMONY

The Mandans have several medicine festivals, of which the Okippe, or the penitential ceremony of the ark, is by far the most remarkable. It is celebrated in the spring or summer, and I regret to say that I cannot describe it as an eye-witness. I am, however, enabled to give a circumstantial description of it, word for word, as it was communicated to me by men initiated in the mysteries of the nation. Numank-Machana, the first man, ordered the Numangkake to celebrate this medicine feast every year. When the village has fixed the time for this festivity, they choose a man of distinction, in whom confidence can be placed, who must put himself at the head, and direct the solemnities. In the year 1834 Mato-Topé was chosen. He is called Kani-Sachka. This man then causes the medicine lodge to be prepared and cleaned before the appointed time, and wood and other necessaries to be provided.

First day of the Okippe: At sunset the Kani-Sachka goes into the lodge, and begins the fast, which continues four days. With him are six men, who are to strike what is called the tortoise, a vessel or sack made of parchment, and filled with water. Three of the men must strike in the direction of the river downwards, and three in the direction upwards. They strike the tortoise during the whole night. Before sunrise a man representing the Numank-Machana, or the first man, arrives. He dresses himself in the medicine lodge in the following manner: round his body he fastens a wolf's skin, on his head, raven's feathers, in his arms he carries the medicine pipe, and in his robe a portion of pemmican. His face is painted red, and on the small of the back he binds a piece of wood, to which the tail of a buffalo cow is fastened. Dressed in this manner, he goes early in the morning of the first day of the festival, and sings on the open space in the centre. All kinds of valuable articles, such as guns, robes, blankets, &c., are thrown towards him, of which he afterwards takes possession, while on his part he distributes pemmican among the people. He then returns to the medicine lodge, but is not at that time permitted to speak.

The most eminent men of the nation now come to the lodge, address the first man as their uncle, and say, "Well, uncle, how did you fare in the villages? How did you find them? Were you well received?" To which he replies, "Very well, nephew. I have not once lowered my pipe to the ground." By which he means to say that he has received ample presents, and offerings of all kinds have been hung upon his pipe. He then says, "I have seen a great many buffaloes feeding in the prairie and drinking at the river; they are very abundant everywhere." These were the horses; but he means to intimate that, by the medicine of this day, the buffaloes will be attracted in great numbers. All those who intend to submit their bodies to a penance or certain tortures, in order to render themselves acceptable to the lord of life and the first man, come to the medicine lodge early in the morning. Their number is, of course, uncertain; sometimes many present themselves, at other times only a few. They are smeared all over with white clay, with no other covering besides their robes, with the hairy side outwards, and drawn over their heads, so that the face is covered, and they are quite wrapped up in them. In the medicine lodge they lay aside their robes. On the first day of the feast they go four times, wrapped up as before described, and dance around the ark, which stands in the centre of the open space. The Kani-Sachka remains during all this time moaning and leaning against the ark.

Second day of the Okippe: On the second day, early in the morning, eight men appear, who represent buffalo bulls. They are naked, wearing only an apron of blue and white striped woollen cloth. Their body is painted black in front, with two red perpendicular stripes like the facings of a military uniform, and with several white transverse stripes looking like lace or bands. The fore arm and ankles are alternately striped white and red. In their hands they carry a fan of green willow twigs, and on their back a buffalo robe, the head of which, with the long hair on the forehead, hangs over the face. To the middle of the robe a single buffalo horn is fastened, while at the head and loins green willow branches are appended. The eight buffalo bulls put on this fantastic dress in the lodge, and, when this is done, march out two abreast in an inclined posture, extending their robes with outspread hands, and holding the willow fans upright. In this manner they dance up to the ark, where they divide, four going to the left and four to the right round the space. They again join opposite the medicine lodge, and then return as before to the ark, where they continue to dance. When they are opposite to each other they stand upright and imitate the roaring of the buffalo. As soon as this dance begins, the

six tortoise strikers bring their instrument from the centre of the lodge, and place it near the ark in an easterly direction, striking it, and singing a certain song which is said to be a prayer. The Kani-Sachka stands, with his head bowed, leaning on the ark, directly opposite the tortoise, and moans without ceasing. He is quite naked except an apron of buffalo skin. His whole body is bedaubed with yellow, and on his forehead he has a wreath of bleached buffalo hair or wool hanging over the eyes. The eight buffalo bulls form a ring and dance round him, covering him with their robes; they dance in like manner to the tortoise, and next go to the door of the medicine lodge, where they make a kind of covered way with their robes, beneath which the tortoise is conveyed into the lodge. The whole ceremony is repeated eight times on this day, four times in the morning and four times in the afternoon.

Third day of the Okippe: The same masks as yesterday dance on this day twelve times, and are prohibited from either eating or drinking. A number of other masks join them. (1) Two men, dressed like women, who dance in this costume, keeping by the side of the eight buffalo bulls. They wear clothes of bighorn leather, women's leggins (mitasses), the robes having the hair outwards. Their cheeks are painted red, their chins tattooed, and their heads adorned with glass beads, as is the custom among the women. (2) Two other men represent a couple of swans; they are naked, carry a swan's tail in their hand, are painted all over white, only the nose, mouth (representing the bill), and the lower part of the legs and feet, black. (3) A couple of rattle-snakes; the back is painted with black transverse stripes, in imitation of those animals, the front of the body yellowish; a black line is drawn from each eye down the cheeks, and in each hand they carry a bunch of wormwood. (4) One man represents the evil spirit; he is conducted by two men of the village to the river, where he is dressed and painted; his entire body is painted black, and, as soon as this is done, he is not permitted to speak a word. They put on his head a cap, with a black cock's-comb; he likewise wears a mask, with white wooden rings left for the opening round the eyes. They then make for him large teeth of cotton yarn, paint the sun upon his stomach, the crescent upon his back, and on each joint of the arms and legs, a white circle; they then put on a buffalo's tail, and place a small stick in his hand, with a ball, made of skin, at the end, to which a scalp, painted red on the under side, is fastened. The ball represents the head of an enemy. When this monster is completed, they let him loose, and he runs, like one possessed, about the prairie, comes into the village, gets upon the huts, one after the other, and pries into every corner, while the inhabitants throw out to him all kinds of valuable articles as presents. As soon as he perceives this he turns towards the sun, and intimates to it, by signs, how well he is treated, and that it is foolish of it (the sun) to keep at so great a distance. He goes about and looks on the people's heads for vermin, and, if he finds any, he pretends to be very happy, and runs about with rapidity. The Indians are very much afraid of the devil, for which reason this part cannot be assigned to anybody; but he who wishes to perform it must offer himself. (5) Two men, representing white-headed eagles, are painted of a dark brown colour; the head, neck, fore arm and hands, and the lower part of the legs, are white; they carry a stick in their hands, and their business is to pursue the antelopes. (6) Two beavers; they wear the robe with the hairy side outwards, have a piece of parchment, resembling a beaver's tail, fastened to their girdle, and are painted brown. (7) Two birds of prey; their shoulders are blue, the breast yellowish and spotted; they have feathers on their heads, and the feet of birds of prey in their hands. (8) Two or four bears, wrapped in bears' skins, with the head and claws, which cover their head and their whole body; they generally walk in a stooping attitude about the dancers, and growl like those animals. (9) Two men represent the dried meat, which is cut in small strips. They wear a cap of white hare skin; their body is painted with zig-zag stripes; round the waist they have a girdle of green boughs, and they dance with the others. (10) Forty or fifty Indians of different ages perform the part of the antelopes; they are painted red on the back, the rest of the body and limbs are white, the nose and mouth black; they carry small sticks, and run about very swiftly. (11) Two men personate the night; they are naked, painted quite black, with white stars; on their backs they have the setting moon, and on their breast the rising sun; they are not allowed to sit, during the whole day, till the sun has set: they then sit down and must not rise till the next morning. (12) One or two wolves; they are painted white, wear a wolf's skin, and pursue the antelopes, which fly before them: if they catch one, the bears come and take it from them and devour it. All these animals imitate the originals to the best of their power. (13) Two prairie wolves; the tops of their heads are painted white, their faces yellowish-brown; they wear dry herbs in their hair, and carry in their hands a stick, painted with reddish-brown stripes, and run in the prairie before the other animals when they leave the village. Almost all these animals are said to have different songs, with words, which the uninitiated do not understand; they sometimes practise these songs for a whole summer, and are often obliged to pay a high price for instruction.

During all these masquerade dances, the penitents have remained three entire days in the medicine lodge, where they have fasted and thirsted, sitting perfectly still and quiet. On the afternoon of that day, the persons of the ten masks also meet in the medicine lodge, and all together then leave this place. The penitents lie down on their bellies, in a circle round the ark, at some distance from it; the masks dance among them and over them, to the sound of the schischikué. Some already begin to suffer the tortures: they give a gun, a blanket, or some other article of value, to an eminent person, to inflict the tortures on them. During this time the Kani-Sachka has been moaning, and leaning on the ark.

The tortures of the penitents now begin. In many of them strips of skin and flesh are cut from the breast, or the arms, and on the back, but in such a manner that they remain fast at both ends. A strap is then passed under them, and the sufferers are thrown over the declivity of the bank, where they remain suspended in the air; others have a strap drawn through the wound, to which the head of a buffalo is fastened, and they are obliged to drag this heavy weight about; others have themselves suspended by the muscles of the back; others have joints of their fingers cut off; others again, are lifted up by the flesh, which is cut across the stomach, or have some heavy body suspended to the muscles, which have been cut and loosened, and other similar tortures. Those who have been tortured on this day return directly to their huts; but those who can bear to fast longer do not submit themselves to the torture till the fourth day.

Fourth day of the Okippe: All those who have endured fasting for four days are now assembled in the medicine lodge. Such as feel themselves faint beg that the dancing may begin early. Accordingly, the masquerade, and the dances performed yesterday, begin at daybreak. They dance on this day sixteen times—eight times in the morning, and eight times in the afternoon. The candidates for the torture are out about two o'clock in the afternoon; and when they have suffered to the utmost of their power, a large circle is formed; two men, who have no part in the festival, take one of the penitents between them, hold him by the hand, and the whole circle moves round with the greatest rapidity. The Kani-Sachka is likewise treated in this manner. The famished and tortured penitents, for the most part, soon fall down, and many faint away, but no regard is paid to this; and they are dragged and pulled about as long as they can possibly bear it; they are then let loose, and remain stretched on the ground as if dead.

The eight buffalo bulls now come foward to execute their last dance. Meantime, Numank-Machana (the first man) stands on one side of the place, and invites the inhabitants to assemble. The men come on foot and on horseback, with their bows and arrows: the arrows are adorned with green leaves at the wooden points; and, when the eight buffaloes have approached, dancing, the first man, and been repulsed by him, they are shot at from all sides, fall, roll on the ground, and then lie still as if dead. The first man then invites the inhabitants to take the flesh of the buffaloes. The latter, whose robes have already fallen off, rise, and retire into the medicine lodge. Then the dancers divide into two parties, extend their arms and legs, strike themselves on the stomach, exclaiming that they feel themselves strong; some, that they will kill enemies; others, that they will slay many buffaloes, &c. They then retire, take food, and rest themselves, and the festival is concluded.

The wounds that have been inflicted on this occasion heal, but they remain visible during the whole life, like thick swollen weals. This is to be observed in a much higher degree among the Minnetarees than among the Mandans; the former seem to submit to much more severe tortures. The buffalo skulls, which these Indians have dragged about with much pain, are preserved in their huts, where they are everywhere to be seen, to be handed down from the father to the children. Many such heads are looked upon by them as medicine; they are kept in the huts, and sometimes the Indians stroke them, and set food before them.

## Corn Dance of the Women

Another medicine feast is celebrated as well among the Mandans as among the Minnetarees. It is a consecration of grain to be sown, and is called the corn dance feast of the women. The old woman who never dies sends, in the spring, the water fowl, swans, geese, and ducks, as symbols of the kinds of grain cultivated by the Indians. The wild goose signifies maize; the swan, the gourd; and the duck, beans. It is the old woman that causes these plants to grow, and, therefore, she sends these birds as her signs and representatives. It is very seldom that eleven wild geese are found together in the spring; but, if it happens, this is a sign that the crop of maize will be remarkably fine. The Indians keep a large quantity of dried flesh in readiness for the time in the spring when the birds arrive, that they may immediately celebrate the corn feast of the women. They hang the meat, before the village, on long stages made of poles, three or four rows, one above another, and this, with various articles of value, is considered as an offering to the old woman. The elderly females, as representatives of the old woman who never dies, assemble on a certain day about the stages, carrying a stick in their hands, to one end of which a head of maize is fastened. Sitting down in a circle, they plant their sticks in the ground before them, and then dance.

While the old women are performing these ceremonies, the younger ones come and put some dry pulverized meat into their mouths, for which each of them receives, in return, a grain of the consecrated maize, which she eats. Three or four grains are put into their dish, and are afterwards carefully mixed with the seed to be sown, in order to make it thrive and yield an abundant crop. The dried flesh on the stages is the perquisite of the aged females, as the representatives of the old woman who never dies. During the ceremony, it is not unusual for some men of the band of dogs to come and pull a large piece of flesh from the poles and carry it off. As members of this band, and being men of distinction, no opposition can be offered.

In autumn, when the birds emigrate to the south, or, as the Indians express it, return to the old woman, they believe that they take with them the presents—especially the dried flesh—that were hung up at the entrance of the village, for the giver and protectress of the crop. They further imagine that the old woman partakes of the flesh. Some poor females among these Indians, who are not able to offer flesh or any valuable gift, take a piece of parchment, in which they wrap the foot of a buffalo, and suspend it to one of the poles as their offering. The birds on their return, go to the old woman, each bringing something from the Indians; but, towards the end, one approaches, and says, "I have very little to give you, for I have received only a very mean gift." To this, the old woman, on receiving the buffalo's foot from the poor women, or widows, says, "This is just what I love; this

poor offering is more dear to me than all the other presents, however costly." Upon this she boils a piece of the foot with some maize, and eats it with much satisfaction.

## Methods of Hunting

The chief occupations of the Indians, besides adorning and painting their persons, looking in the glass, smoking, eating, and sleeping, are the chase and war, and these fill up a great part of their time. The principal beast of chase is the buffalo, or, rather, the buffalo cow. The men generally go hunting in a body, on horseback, in order to be the more secure against a superior force of their enemies. The equipments of their horses are much like those of the Blackfeet, and their saddle resembles the Hungarian; though, now, they sometimes obtain saddles from the Whites, which they line and ornament with red and blue cloth. In riding, they never leave hold of their whip, the handle of which is made of wood, and not of elk's horn, as among the more western nations. They never wear spurs. In the summer time, if the herds of buffaloes are dispersed to great distances in the prairie, the chase, of course, requires more time and exertion; but in winter, when they approach the Missouri, and seek shelter in the woods, a great number are often killed in a short time. On these hunting excursions the Indians often spend eight or ten days; generally they return on foot, while the horses are laden with the spoil. The buffaloes are usually shot with arrows, the hunters riding within ten or twelve paces of them. If it is very cold, and the buffaloes keep at a distance in the prairie (which happened in the winter of 1833–34), they hunt but little, and would rather suffer hunger, or live only on maize and beans, than use any exertion; and when, towards spring, many drowned buffaloes float down the river with the ice, the Indians swim or leap with great dexterity over the flakes of ice, draw the animals to land, and eat the half-putrid flesh, without manifesting any signs of disgust. When a hunter has killed an animal, he generally eats the liver, the kidneys, and the marrow of the large thigh bones, raw. If an Indian has procured some game he usually shares it with others. The entrails and skin always belong to the person who shot the animal.

Dogs are not employed in hunting by the Mandans and Minnetarees. They shoot deer and elks in the forest, antelopes and bighorns in the prairies, the Black Hills, and the neighbouring mountains. They make parks, as they are called, to catch antelopes, but not buffaloes. The Minnetarees make these cabri parks more frequently than the Mandans. They choose a valley, between two hills, which ends in a steep declivity. On the summit of the hills, two converging lines, one or two miles in length, are marked out with brushwood. Below the declivity they erect a kind of fence, fifteen or twenty paces in length, composed of poles, covered and filled up with hay and brushwood. A number of horsemen then drive the cabris between the ends of the lines marked out by the brushwood, which are very distant from each other, and ride rapidly towards them. The terrified animals hasten down the hollow, and at length leap into the enclosure, where they are killed with clubs, or taken alive. There are not many bears in this country; and the Indians are not fond of hunting them, because it is often dangerous, and the flesh, when roasted, is not very good.

The wolf and the fox are sometimes shot with a gun, as well as the white hare, in the winter time, or they are caught in traps. They set for the wolves very strong traps, which are covered with brushwood and buffaloes' skulls, to conceal them. Many such traps are seen everywhere in the prairies, which are surrounded with small stakes, that the animals may not enter them sideways. Beavers are now caught, in great numbers, in iron traps, which they procure from the Whites. Small animals, such as the ermine, are caught with horse-hair springes, set before their burrows. The manner in which birds of prey are caught is said to be very remarkable. The birdcatcher lies down at full length in a narrow pit made on purpose, and exactly large enough to hold him. As soon as he has lain down, the pit is covered with brushwood and hay, pieces of meat are laid upon it, and a crow, or some such bird, fastened to it. The eagle, or other bird of prey, is said to descend, and to sit down, in order to eat, on which the birdcatcher seizes it by the legs. I would not believe this had not men worthy of credit given me their word for it.

MODES OF WARFARE

Next to the chase, war is the chief employment of the Indians, and military glory the highest object of their ambition. It is well known that Indian bravery is very different from that of the Whites; for wilfully to expose themselves to the enemy's fire would, in their eyes, not be bravery, but folly. Cunning and stratagem give them the advantage over the enemy; their strength lies in concealing their march, and surprises at daybreak. He who kills many enemies without sustaining any loss is the best warrior.

When a young man desires to establish his reputation in the field, he fasts for four or seven days, as long as his strength permits him, goes alone to the hills, complains and cries to the lord of life, calls incessantly to the higher powers for their aid, and only goes home, sometimes, in the evening, to sleep. A dream suggests his medicine to him. If the lord of life makes him dream of a piece of cherry-tree wood, or of an animal, it is a good omen. The young men who take the field with him have then confidence in his medicine. If he can perform an exploit his reputation is established. But whatever exploits he may perform, he acquires no respect if he does not make valuable presents; and they say of him, "He has indeed performed many exploits, but yet he is as much to be pitied as those whom he has killed."

When a young man, who has never performed an exploit, is the first to kill an enemy on a warlike expedition, he paints a spiral line around his arm, of whatever colour he pleases, and he may then wear a whole wolf's tail at the ankle or heel of one foot. If he has first killed and touched the enemy, he paints a line running obliquely round the arms and another crossing it in the opposite direction, with three transverse stripes. On killing the second enemy he paints his left leg (that is, the leggin) of a reddish-brown. If he kills the second enemy before another is killed by his comrades, he may wear two entire wolves' tails at his heels. On his third exploit he paints two longitudinal stripes on his arms, and three transverse stripes. This is the exploit that is esteemed the highest; after the third exploit no more marks are made. If he kills an enemy after others of the party have done the same, he may wear on his heel one wolf's tail, the tip of which is cut off. In every numerous war party there are four leaders (partisans), sometimes seven, but only four are reckoned as the real partisans; the others are called bad partisans. All partisans carry on their backs a medicine pipe in a case, which other warriors dare not have. To become a chief (Numakschi) a man must have been a partisan, and then kill an enemy when he is not a partisan.

As soon as they advance to attack the enemy, every one sounds his pipe, and all together utter the war-whoop, a shrill cry, which they render tremulous by repeatedly and suddenly striking the mouth with the hand. Those who fast and dream, in order to perform an exploit, are entitled to wear a wolf's skin. A warrior has a right to wear as many eagles' feathers as he has performed exploits. All Indians, on their military expeditions, erect, in the evening, some sort of fort, in which they are, in some measure, secure against a sudden attack. At such a post the Indians are very vigilant and active; after an engagement they do not bury the dead, but, if they have not time to carry them away, leave them on the spot where they fell. The scalps are often preserved for a long time stretched upon small hoops, and the hair is afterwards used as an ornament to the dress of the men. The skin of the scalp is generally painted red. The Mandans, Minnetarees, and Crows, never torture their prisoners like the Pawnees and the eastern nations. When a prisoner has arrived at the village, and eaten maize, he is considered as one of their own nation, and no person ever thinks of molesting him. Often, however, the women hasten out to meet the prisoners ere they reach the village, and kill them; this is especially an act of revenge for their husbands or sons who may have fallen in the battle.

When the warriors return from their expedition, the scalps are carried on in advance, on high poles: if they have performed any exploits, they paint their faces black; very frequently the whole body is thus disfigured. The women and children go out to meet them, and they enter the village performing the scalp dance. This dance is then repeated four successive nights in the medicine lodge, and is subsequently danced in the open space, in the centre of the village. If the campaign took place in the spring, it is danced, at intervals, till the fall of the leaf in autumn; if in the autumn, it is danced till spring, but should any of the nation be killed in the interim all festivities immediately cease. In the scalp dance the Indians paint themselves in various ways, form a semi-circle, advance, and retreat amid the din of singing, the beating of the drum and schischikué. The wives of those men who have obtained the scalps carry them on long rods.

All the distinguished deeds performed by a war party are placed to the account of the partisan. All the scalps that are taken belong to him, and also the horses that they have captured. He who has killed an enemy is a brave man, and reckons one exploit; but the partisan rises the highest on that account, even though he had not seen any of the enemies who have been slain. When he returns home, the old men and women meet, and sing the scalp song, on which he must make them all presents of value. He gives away all the captured horses, and valuable articles, and is afterwards a poor man, but his reputation is great. Successful partisans afterwards become chiefs, and are highly respected by their nation. The Indian youths go to war when they are only fourteen or fifteen years of age. Sometimes they make excursions on horseback in the winter.

SICKNESS AND DEATH

Disorders are not uncommon among the Indians. The Mandans and Minnetarees often suffer from diseases in the eyes; many are one-eyed, or have a tunica over one eye. In inflammation of the eye they have a custom of scratching the inner eye with the leaf of a kind of grass, resembling a saw, which causes them to bleed very much, and this may often occasion the loss of the eye. Rheumatism, coughs, and the like, are frequent, because they go half naked in the severest cold, and plunge into ice water. Much benefit is often derived from their steam-baths, in a well-closed hut, where a thick steam is produced by pouring water on hot stones. They then immediately go into the cold, roll themselves in the snow, or plunge into a river covered with drifting ice, but do not return to a warm hut, as the Russians do. Many Indians are said to have died on the spot by trying this remedy. Some suffer from gout; but all who survive these violent remedies are stronger and more hardy. Another remedy is trampling on the whole body, especially the stomach, as is practised also among the Brazilians. This operation is performed with such violence, as often to occasion hard swellings in the intestines, or ulcers, especially in the liver. The steam-bath is used as a remedy in all kinds of disorders. Vaccination, the application of which met with no difficulties among several nations on the great lakes, especially the Chippewas, is not yet practised among the Mandans and Minnetarees. Spitting of blood is said to be frequent, but not pulmonary consumption. Gonorrhoea is very common; they affirm that all venereal disorders come to them from the Crows beyond the Rocky Mountains. For such disorders they often seat themselves over a heated pot, but frequently burn themselves. They cut open buboes, lengthwise, with a knife, and then run for a couple of miles as fast as they can. The jaundice is said not to occur among them. It appears that they are not acquainted with emetics, but, if they feel anything wrong in the stomach, they thrust a feather down the throat, and thus produce vomiting.

When a Mandan or Minnetaree dies, they do not let the corpse remain long in the village; but convey it to the distance of 200 paces, and lay it on a narrow stage, about six feet long, resting on four stakes about ten feet high, the body being first laced up in buffalo robes and a blanket. The face, painted red, is turned towards the east. A number of such stages are seen about their villages, and, although they themselves say that this custom is injurious to the health of the villages, they do not renounce it. On many of these stages there are small boxes, containing the bodies of children wrapped in cloth or skins. Ravens are usually seen sitting on these stages, and the Indians dislike that bird, because it feeds on the flesh of their relations. If you ask a Mandan why they do not deposit their dead in the ground, he answers, "The lord of life has, indeed, told us that we came from the ground, and should return to it again; yet we have lately begun to lay the bodies of the dead on stages, because we love them, and would weep at the sight of them."

They believe that every person has several spirits dwelling in him; one of these spirits is black, another brown, and another light-coloured, the latter of which alone returns to the lord of life. They think that after death they go to the south, to several villages which are often visited by the gods; that the brave and most eminent go to the village of the good, but the wicked into a different one; that they there live in the same manner as they do here, carry on occupations, eat the same food, have wives, and enjoy the pleasures of the chase and war. Those who are kind-hearted are supposed to make many presents and do good, find everything in abundance, and their existence there is dependent on their course of life while in the world. Some of the inhabitants of the Mandan villages are said not to believe all these particulars, and suppose that after death they will live in the sun or in a certain star.

They mourn for the dead a whole year; cut off their hair, cover their body and head with white or grey clay, and often, with a knife or sharp flint, make incisions in their arms and legs in parallel lines, in their whole length, so that they are covered with blood. For some days after death the relations make a loud lament and bewailing. Often a relative, or some other friend, covers the dead, as they express it: he brings one or two woollen cloths, of a red, blue, white, or green colour, and, as soon as the body is laid on the stage, mounts upon the scaffolding, and conceals the body beneath the covering. A friend who will do this is, in token of respect, presented, by the family of the deceased, with a horse. If it is known beforehand that a person intends doing this honour to the dead, a horse is at once tied near the stage, and the friend, having performed this last office, unties the animal and leads it away. If a Mandan or Minnetaree falls in battle, and the news of his death reaches the family, who are unable to recover the body, a buffalo skin is rolled up and carried to the village. All those who desire to lament the deceased assemble, and many articles of value are distributed among them. The mourners cut off their hair, wound themselves with knives, and make loud lamentations. Joints of the fingers are not cut off here, as among the Blackfeet, as a token of mourning, but as signs of penance and offering to the lord of life and the first man.

# Index

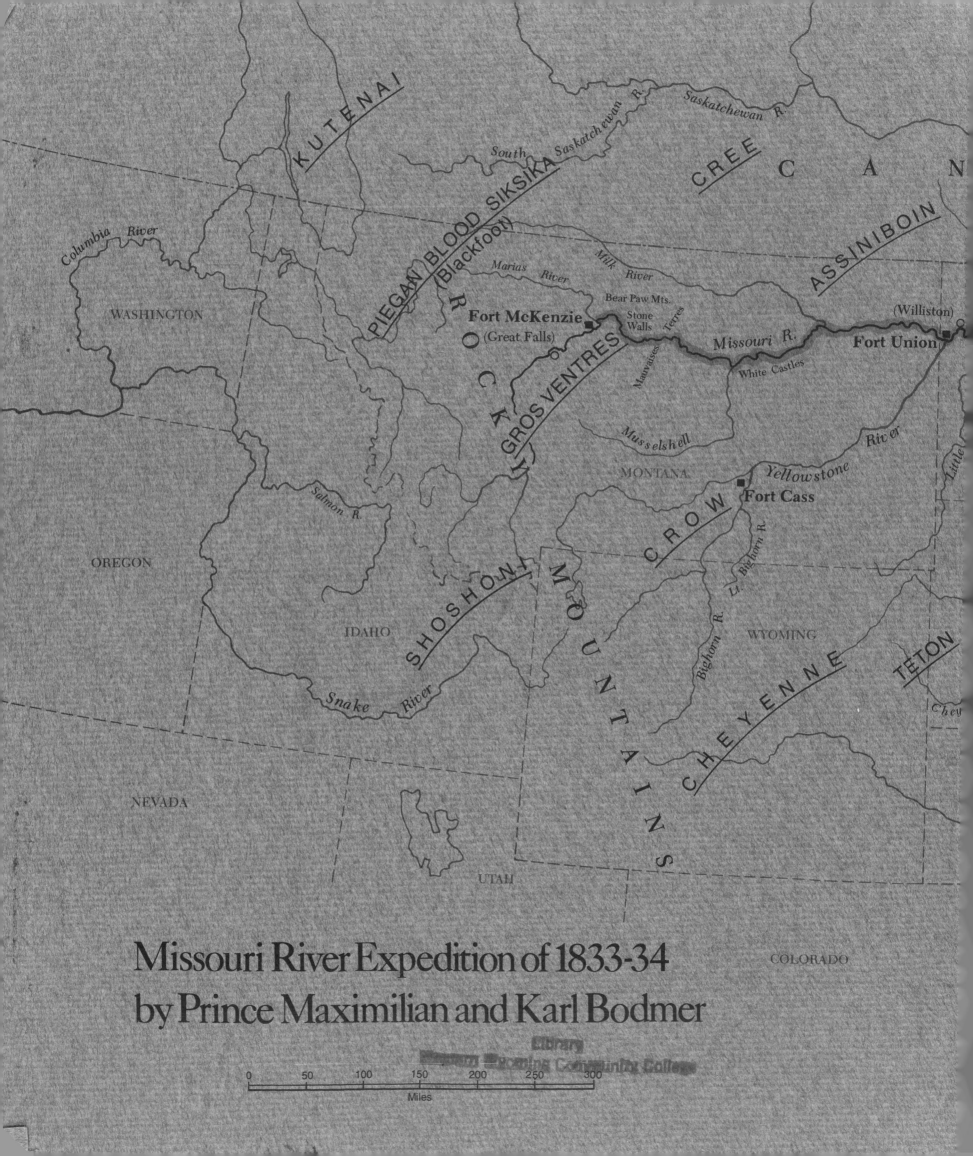

# Missouri River Expedition of 1833-34
# by Prince Maximilian and Karl Bodmer

0    50    100    150    200    250    300

Miles